Redefining
Adaptation Studies

Edited by
Dennis Cutchins
Laurence Raw
James M. Welsh

D1096925

The Scarecrow Press, Inc.
Lanham • Toronto • Plymouth, UK
2010

Published by Scarecrow Press, Inc.
A wholly owned subsidiary of The Rowman & Littlefield Publishing Group, Inc.
4501 Forbes Boulevard, Suite 200, Lanham, Maryland 20706
http://www.scarecrowpress.com

Estover Road, Plymouth PL6 7PY, United Kingdom

British Cataloging in Publication Information Available

Library of Congress Cataloging-in-Publication Data

Redefining adaptation studies / edited by Dennis Cutchins, Laurence Raw,
    James M. Welsh.
        p. cm.
    Includes bibliographical references and index.
    Includes filmography.
    ISBN 978-0-8108-7298-1 (pbk. : alk. paper) — ISBN 978-0-8108-7299-8 (ebook)
    1. Film adaptations—Authorship. 2. Motion picture authorship—Study and
teaching. I. Cutchins, Dennis R. (Dennis Ray), 1963– II. Raw, Laurence.
III. Welsh, James Michael.
PN1997.85.R43 2010
808.2'3071—dc22
                                                                2009043755

∞™ The paper used in this publication meets the minimum requirements
of American National Standard for Information Sciences—Permanence of
Paper for Printed Library Materials, ANSI/NISO Z39.48-1992.

Printed in the United States of America

To John and Margery Raw

—Laurence Raw (Başkent University),
James M. Welsh (Salisbury University, Maryland),
Dennis Cutchins (Brigham Young University, Utah)

CONTENTS

Foreword   vii
  Deborah Cartmell

Introduction: How Should We Teach It? How Could We Teach It?   ix
  James M. Welsh

1   Adapting Wilde for the Performance Classroom:
   "No Small Parts"   1
   Frances Babbage with Robert Neumark Jones and Lauren Williams

2   "It Must All Change Now": Victor Hugo's
   Lucretia Borgia and Adaptation   17
   Richard J. Hand

3   "Never Seek to Tell Thy Love":
   E-Adapting Blake in the Classroom   31
   Richard Berger

4   Adaptation and Creative Writing: *Brokeback Mountain*
   on the London Underground   45
   Mark O'Thomas

5   Pedagogy and Policy in Intermedial Adaptations   55
   Freda Chapple

6   Toward a Pedagogy for Adaptation Studies   71
   Sevgi Şahin and Laurence Raw

7 Writing the Adaptation: Teaching an Upper-Division
College Course for the Screenwriter 85
Diane Lake

8 Whose Life *Is* It, Anyway? Adaptation, Collective Memory,
and (Auto)Biographical Processes 95
Suzanne Diamond

9 The Numbers Game: Quantifying the Audience 111
Alexis Weedon

10 Engaging the Ear: Teaching Radio Drama Adaptations 133
Elke Huwiler

11 The Pleasures of "Theater Film": Stage to Film Adaptation 147
Milan Pribisic

Filmography 161

Bibliography 163

Index 173

About the Editors and Contributors 179

FOREWORD

Deborah Cartmell

Surely, there's not an English teacher anywhere who doesn't use film to illuminate Shakespeare or who doesn't ask students to translate a literary text to a context that is relevant to their own situations. However, this process, utilized by so many educators, is rarely interrogated or explained. This collection does precisely that, offering advice and examples of good practice in the teaching of adaptation.

Redefining Adaptation Studies is a highly welcome intervention in the field of adaptation studies, offering essays from scholars based in Europe and the United States, focusing specifically on issues related to teaching adaptations in various contexts, from high school to postgraduate level. Contributors are drawn from a variety of backgrounds, and the range of contributions extends beyond the literature/film paradigm, exploring more general issues related to adaptation through the practice of adapting texts.

It's hard to understand why there has been so little attention, to date, devoted to the subject of adaptation and pedagogy, given the repeated use of film adaptations in classrooms by teachers to "flesh out" difficult literary texts, as an aid to translation, and as a mode of comparing different performances, to name just a few examples. While there is no doubt that teachers use both film adaptations and creative adaptation practices in their everyday teaching, there has been an almost complete silence concerning the creative use of adaptation beyond the closed doors of the classroom. Adaptation practice and film translations are either dismissed as background, a means to an end rather than having value in their own right, or swept under the carpet in literary and film studies, regarded as an approach that's too frivolous or reductive to be taken seriously. Nonetheless, it's an approach that can be found everywhere.

This book leads the way in acknowledging what can be gained through the teaching of adaptation, filling the gap in a well-trodden but rarely discussed field. The collection ranges from Richard Berger's reflections on teaching a Blake poem through adaptation, to attending to and underlining the importance of the *process* of adaptation, especially when teaching English texts to students from a different language and culture, as discussed by Sevgi Şahin and Laurence Raw. Adaptation and performance are considered in contributions such as Frances Babbage's account of what can be gained in the act of collaboratively rewriting and performing Wilde's *Lady Windermere's Fan*, so that the least important characters are elevated to the most important, indeed the only characters within the play.

The underlying principle of this book is that the term "adaptation" needs to be extended and rethought as a creative process. All the authors in this volume stress that, as all art is based on other art, the best response to a text is another text. The creative adaptations outlined in this volume, accordingly, aim to extend the range of adaptation teaching, producing more and more creative adaptations in the future.

INTRODUCTION

How Should We Teach It?
How Could We Teach It?

James M. Welsh

First we should explain who "we" are, and whom "we" consider our intended audience to include: teachers and lecturers, first and foremost, in high schools, academies, colleges, and universities, at both the undergraduate and postgraduate levels, representing many different disciplines and academic departments. We hope and believe these essays will not only provide a resource book of suggestions as to how "adaptation" might be used in different disciplines but also offer suggestions as to how it might improve the learning experience for teachers and students alike. For example, Laurence Raw had the quaint notion that adaptation might be useful as a means of teaching English as a foreign language and, equally important, as a means of engaging student interest. Then he tried it, with wonderful results, in Ankara, Turkey, where he teaches, then later in Istanbul. This experiment is described by Laurence Raw and Sevgi Şahin in their chapter "Toward a Pedagogy for Adaptation Studies." In other words, a certain idealism informs our purpose, but that idealism may also have helpful practical applications.

Laurence Raw, Dennis Cutchins, and I first knocked our heads together over several issues of adaptation (as we then understood them) in 2007 at the national convention of the Popular Culture and American Culture Associations in Boston. Laurence Raw and I had been arguing mightily over what was really worth discussing several years before that in Towson, Maryland; Carlisle, Pennsylvania; Dallas, Texas (all thanks to the Literature/Film Association); then, more recently, Ankara, Turkey, in 2006; and Istanbul two years later. Originally, we were arguing in very basic terms

about the "adaptation" of literature to film, until Laurence Raw began
to take a broader and much expanded approach. Meanwhile, Laurence
had also drawn other exotic, international academic scholars into this
interpretive dance and debate, such as Richard Hand of the University
of Glamorgan, the founding editor of the *Journal of Adaptation in Film and
Performance,* and two other English academic stars, Imelda Whelehan and
Deborah Cartmell, both of De Montfort University in Leicester, editors
of the Oxford journal *Adaptation.* And as a consequence of these new
journals having been established, manifestos had been uttered; issues
were being navigated, negotiated, mediated, and (my favorite) interrogated; and David Kranz and Nancy Mellerski of Dickinson College
"interrogated" rigorously "The Persistence of Fidelity" in their wonderfully named collection *In/Fidelity: Essays on Film Adaptation* (2008). While
officers of the Literature/Film Association were questioning fidelity
criticism, "logocentrism" was being discredited elsewhere, for example,
to the agony of those old-fashioned sorts who believed that "in the beginning, *was* the Word." But apparently words were "out" and images "in,"
now being the time to interrogate cartoons, videogames, and all manner
of electronic media. My friends were going all avant-garde and berserk,
while I was still bringing up the derriere, though still trying to butt in.

But if logocentrism was "out" of style with one group, it was "in" with
another, willing to think more broadly about translations as adaptations,
since words are literally at the heart of translation. And it doesn't stop
there. Attentive readers will note that radio drama is addressed in one
of the chapters that follow here, so listen up: Elke Huwiler's "Teaching
Radio Drama Adaptations" considers adaptation from a perspective
that may at first seem a little eccentric, but not especially Anglocentric,
for in German, the word for radio drama is *Hörspiel,* involving not only
words but also the interplay of *sounds.* In such ways, then, the writers
in this volume were challenged and encouraged to think differently and
originally, and they, in turn, challenge or *interrogate* the very idea of adaptation. Suzanne Diamond returns to the issue of fidelity in her chapter
"Whose Life *Is* It, Anyway? Adaptation, Collective Memory, and (Auto)
Biographical Processes." Swimming upstream, she asserts that fidelity
studies—"roundly discredited among adaptation theorists—represent
not only a defensible but also a highly *productive* mode of inquiry for
students . . . who are just beginning to think about adaptation, its procedures, and its implications." At the same time, one of our most creative
contributors, screenwriter Diane Lake, who teaches at Emerson College in
Boston, provides a clear and practical description of how a screenwriting
course focused on adaptation might reasonably be organized and taught.
As this screenwriter explains, she has successfully adapted a fairy tale for
Disney, a biography for Miramax, and novels for independent producers;

she also explains why studios produce more adapted films than original ones, stressing that the ability to write adaptive screenplays should be a highly useful skill.

Clearly, as we began this project we all believed that adaptation studies were important, but we did not at first fully understand the scope and potentiality of the field. Nonetheless, we were distressed that the pedagogy of adaptation had not really been fully explored (or "navigated" or "interrogated"), and we thought we could fix that, to a degree. So we put out our antennae in order to scout for suitable new material. We came not in battalions but rather as single spies, infiltrating conferences at Oglethorpe University in Atlanta, at the University of Kansas in Lawrence, in Albuquerque, in Boston, in San Francisco, and in New Orleans. Laurence Raw, who himself went to Wales and Amsterdam, even managed to get an international conference mounted (and funded, thanks to the American Studies Association of Turkey, the Literature/Film Association, and the American Embassy) in Istanbul on the theme "Adapting America, America Adapted." Since we had been effective gleaners, when it came time to tally our riches, we found we had gathered too much material for a single book. The only solution, therefore, was to publish not one but *two* books. One book, entitled *The Pedagogy of Adaptation*, would take an overview of the past and present, whilst also allowing some speculation about the future. The present volume, however, would seek to achieve what its title promised: *Redefining Adaptation Studies*, complete with trendy, postmodern parentheses. For we believed that the whole field of inquiry had been heretofore too narrowly defined and constrained. Our goal, then, was to provide what cable television commentators (who live by clichés) might call truly "cutting-edge" material, to be both edgy and innovative in interesting ways.

First, of course, we had to define the field as it had so far been cultivated. As John Tibbetts notes in his foreword to *The Pedagogy of Adaptation*, "Desperately Seeking Sources," my own chapter in that volume, simply entitled "Adaptability," attempted to "construct a concise and useful history of adaptation studies," and I am grateful to Dr. Tibbetts for having noticed that. Therefore, it was my pleasure in that volume to describe the original pea patch and garden variety approaches we had originally entertained in the journal that Tom Erskine, Gerald R. Barrett, and I cofounded in 1973, *Literature/Film Quarterly*, back during the Dusk of Humanism, before the academic world went all postmodern and 'round the bend and collapsed into cultural rubble. A new audience was emerging, then, heavily influenced by French linguists, French psychologists, and French jargon, extensively used; but we soldiered on in the language we knew best how to use. Since we were the *only* journal in the field, ours was a distinctive (if somewhat old-fashioned) garden, as

I would have described it; I suspect the elitist cinema snobs eventually came to *despise* us for our success—an upstart college in Maryland and not a class-one research institution becoming in this instance the little engine that could—and to dismiss and marginalize us over time, as they sought to establish their own significance, but no matter: by then we had our own functioning organization, the Literature/Film Association (though I hope we were not *too* smug about it), and *Literature/Film Quarterly* had by then a substantial base of library subscribers worldwide, certainly enough to sustain the enterprise and carry it into the new century. The essays collected here have moved far past that antique starting point, however, for this anthology seeks to celebrate the innovative and the edgy. These authors are not so "*desperately* seeking sources"! I might add that some of my best friends might be considered "cinema snobs," in that they were mainly interested in films out of the mainstream. To qualify my phrase earlier, what I meant was *academic* cinema snobs, busy careerists fixated upon the ideologies of the day—what the British archivist, historian, and filmmaker Kevin Brownlow once called a kind of secular priesthood, with its own initiation rites and liturgy. Woe to the Outsiders who had not been properly initiated.

Meanwhile, back here on Earth, the chapters in both of our volumes had generally been tested before live audiences at both national and international conferences. At Boğaziçi University in Istanbul, for example, Tom Leitch of the University of Delaware had suggested that the exercise of adaptive processes be put into practice, and at that very same conference Laurence Raw and his colleagues from Başkent University and Professor Richard Hand from Wales provided just such a demonstration, to the delight and amazement of Professor Leitch. Following that lead, our foremost intent for this book, as expressed by Laurence Raw, was originally described as follows:

> This volume tries to define new horizons for the teaching of adaptation studies, [and for] the use of adaptation in the curricula. Written by specialists in a variety of fields, ranging from film studies, to radio studies, theater and even language studies, the book adopts a pluralistic view of adaptation, showing how its processes vary across different contexts and in different disciplines. What makes this book unique is its claim that adaptation is above all a creative process and not simply a slavish imitation or reproduction of an "original" [source]. Many of the essays show how "adaptation" as a discipline can be used to prompt reflection on cultural, historical and political differences. In brief, this book makes a strong case for treating adaptation studies as a separate discipline.

Well, then, *that* seems a pretty tall order, and it will of course be up to our readers to determine whether or not our mission has been accomplished here. But it was our original intention that this book should break new ground by demonstrating a range of possibilities for adaptation study that far transcend the now dated literature/film paradigm (which has hitherto been the main focus of the discipline). So, bye-bye Bluestone, hello intertextuality and all that may follow in its disruptive wake. This collection of eleven different approaches focuses on the idea of "adaptation" and what it means in different sociopolitical contexts. Above all, it intends to show how cultural and political factors determine the meaning of the term and its potential for developing new strategies of learning. We are therefore hoping to establish new paradigms for old, and in that respect we believe this may be a truly groundbreaking volume, not the last word perhaps but, we believe, the first book to consider certain exciting new directions.

Our acknowledgments go to all those lecturers, students, and others all over the world who have both contributed to and reshaped the views contained in this collection.

ONE

ADAPTING WILDE FOR THE PERFORMANCE CLASSROOM

"No Small Parts"

Frances Babbage

with Robert Neumark Jones and Lauren Williams

This chapter starts from the assumption that adaptation is—certainly, that it can be—both a creative and a critical act. In the introduction to *A Theory of Adaptation*, Linda Hutcheon compares adaptation with the classical concept of imitation, or *mimesis*. In neither process, she insists, is "slavish copying" implied: the purpose of each is rather that of "making the adapted material one's own."[1] Here, then, the notion of creativity is inscribed at the heart of adaptation as a practice, countering the popular prejudice that regards adaptation as essentially derivative and inherently conservative. This necessity for creativity is perhaps most apparent when the adaptation is to a new medium, say, from prose fiction to film or the stage; indeed, the very difference in "language" between source and target medium can be precisely the locus of artistic inspiration, rather than its stumbling block. However, all adaptations that seek to achieve some degree of autonomy must of necessity involve new and distinctive artistic input from their makers.

I have asserted that adaptation is not only creative but also critical. Neil Sinyard argues that the process of adaptation can usefully be compared with that of literary criticism. In his view, "the best" adaptation from literature will offer

> not a pictorialisation of the complete novel, but a critical essay which stresses what it sees as the main theme. Like a critical essay, the adaptation selects some episodes, excludes others, offers preferred alternatives. It focuses on specific areas, expands or contracts detail, and has imaginative flights about

some characters. In the process, like the best criticism, it can throw new light on the original.[2]

Clearly, Sinyard's model has its limitations. To judge an adaptation by its success as "critical essay" implies that the subject of that essay—presumably, the source text—is still at the centre of the investigation; thus, the model moves us away from the conservative preoccupation with "fidelity" but does not allow for adaptations that use their source as a jumping-off point for a radically new work of art. Equally, to valorize an adaptation's critical perspective above all else arguably plays down the importance of the creative challenges posed when a text is adapted into a different medium; the new work produced might be highly original and thought provoking in its deployment of the expressive capabilities of an art form, without adopting an explicitly critical attitude toward the adapted material. Nonetheless, Sinyard's analogy has real value for an understanding of the way adaptations can operate. When writing a critical essay, as he explains, we feel no obligation to tackle the entirety of a text; we are permitted to "read into" it freely, although it might be assumed by a reader that any "imaginative flights" have at least some basis in the source material. One might also argue that the critical essay can attain the level of autonomous artwork—certainly, some achieve iconic status virtually independent of the text that is their ostensible focus.[3]

This combination of creativity and criticism makes setting practical tasks of adaptation a valuable pedagogic method. The project considered in what follows was carried out with MA students in Theatre and Performance Studies at the University of Sheffield in 2007. This master's program is equally weighted between theory and practice—or, more accurately, between seminar-based and studio-based work, since "theory" and "practice" are not readily separable. The students take a core module in Theatre Practice: its remit is very open—allowing different tutors to direct content as they see fit—but it has the premise that the creative practice carried out will represent a form of critical investigation, that is, there will be no "straight" productions of pre-scripted plays, however challenging. The module is also structured so that a staff-initiated project is followed by independent, student-led work; in some sense, then, the first project has to be a model—although not *the* model—that can excite participants and inspire them in subsequent practice.

In 2007, the "cohort" for Theatre Practice consisted, unusually, of just two students. I had worked with Robert Neumark Jones and Lauren Williams previously and to some extent knew their capabilities (which were considerable). We had seven weeks to make the performance, largely by means of workshop sessions held once or sometimes twice a week. With so small a group, I wanted to remain personally involved throughout to prevent them from feeling isolated; however, other demands on my time meant they would need to create or rehearse material independently and ultimately assume ownership of the work produced. I turned to adaptation as a model for this first project. With relatively little time at our disposal, it would be an advantage to have a text to work with rather than create from scratch.

The source text I gave the students was Oscar Wilde's fin-de-siècle social comedy *Lady Windermere's Fan*. The challenge was not based on transposition of medium—the result was to be stage performance—but rather centered on reinventing the play for a cast of two. I had been thinking about Wilde for several reasons. I had supervised a dissertation on films of his plays and retained a strong memory of the wonderful British theater company Ridiculusmus's two-handed take on *The Importance of Being Earnest* (2005).[4] I knew we could not achieve anything quite like the Ridiculusmus show: its success depended on two brilliant, multiskilled comic actors who kept the performance going as if it were an absurdly ambitious juggling act. Instead, I gave Rob and Lauren a definite angle from which we would approach Wilde's text: that of the two servant characters, Parker, the butler, and Rosalie, the maid. I chose *Lady Windermere's Fan* of all Wilde's comedies because there were only two servants who spoke (none were cut); because one was male, one female; and, perhaps paradoxically, because the roles are essentially functional. These are small, frankly dull parts. They are not witty servants, like Lane the butler in *The Importance of Being Earnest*, offering wry commentary on the behavior of his "betters." They serve—that's all. Choosing Parker and Rosalie as the basis for a performance left all the creative and critical work absolutely still to do.

Initially, I had wondered whether I might set the strictest of rules: that the only dialogue we could use would be that spoken by the servants in the play. We began with this idea in mind, seeking to establish what *Lady Windermere's Fan* might look like seen purely through the speeches and actions of these two. Here is Parker's entire "text," extracted from Wilde's play:

Is your ladyship at home this afternoon? Lord Darlington, my lady. Yes, my lady. Lord Darlington, my lady. The men want to know if they are to put the carpets on the terrace for to-night, my lady? The Duchess of Berwick and Lady Agatha Carlisle. Yes, my lord. Yes, my lady. Yes, my lady. Mrs. Cowper-Cowper. Lady Stutfield. Sir James Royston. Mr. Guy Berkeley. Mr. Rufford. Lady Jedburgh and Miss Graham. Mr. Hopper. Lord Augustus Lorton. Mr. and Mrs. Arthur Bowden. Lord and Lady Paisley. Lord Darlington. Mr. Cecil Graham! Mrs. Erlynne! Her ladyship has just gone out. No, madam. Her ladyship has just gone out of the house. Yes, madam—her ladyship told me

she had left a letter for his lordship on the table. Yes, madam. Mrs. Erlynne
has called to return your ladyship's fan which she took away by mistake last
night. Mrs. Erlynne has written a message on the card. Lord Augustus Lorton.
Mrs. Erlynne's carriage has come.[5]

Here is Rosalie's:

Did your ladyship ring for me? His lordship did not come in till five o'clock.
Yes, my lady—at half-past nine. I told him your ladyship was not awake yet.
Something about your ladyship's fan. I didn't quite catch what his lordship
said. Has the fan been lost, my lady? I can't find it, and Parker says it was
not left in any of the rooms. He has looked in all of them and on the terrace
as well.[6]

These texts, divorced from their context, omit the characters' actions
and gestures. For Parker, these constitute numerous entrances and exits,
often carrying something or other on a tray; for Rosalie, no actions are
specified. Despite the texts' brevity, one can still locate the majority of the
drama in and between these lines: key characters are announced; prepa-
rations for the ball are mentioned, as is the mysterious disappearance of
the fan; and the dramatic arrival and ultimate departure of the dangerous
Mrs. Erlynne are both signaled. Thus, although Wilde's plot centers on
the intrigues of the upper classes, those interactions are governed by an
etiquette that is marked, and to an extent "managed," by the servants.
Equally striking, though less surprising, is the monotony of especially
Parker's lines: "yes, madam"; "yes, my lady"; "yes, my lord."

As Lauren explains in her project journal, these two compiled texts
were the stimulus for our first sequence of new theater:

We used the lines to create the characters of servants of the period and created movements based on each line. Using these simple, stylized movements
we experimented by enlarging them, or making them more timid and covert,
and then playing them with a certain attitude, such as scorn, joviality, devi-
ousness, or drunkenness. From these initial experimentations we began to
gauge a sense of characterization for these two parts.[7]

The performance we eventually created concentrated these movements
within a wordless prologue, a repetitive dancelike piece played live with
the opening scene of Fred Paul's 1916 silent film of *Lady Windermere's Fan*
simultaneously projected onto a screen at the back.[8] As opening to the
production, this helped the audience get to grips with Wilde's plot, but
at the same time literally silenced his "main characters" and placed the
servants in the foreground: they did not speak, but their activities—bows
and curtseys, polite coughs, carrying of trays, walking up and down
imaginary stairs—were multiplied and magnified.

Promising as this material felt, it was not enough on its own. Rob comments in his journal,

> We needed actual characters if we were to perform a play based around these two figures—Parker and Rosalie—who were, as it stood, little more than functions to advance the progress of the play. So we set about exploring what type of characters it would be interesting for servants to have. Devious, underhand, running rackets out of the back door, ill-tempered, foul mouthed, sinister, drunkards? All these ideas and more were floated, lots of them stuck. . . . However, we still had a basic problem. Parker had around twelve or so lines. Rosalie had just four, and all in Act IV. Something had to be done and we felt that the story of the play still needed to be told. So we each went away to come up with ways of both exploring our characters and at the same time trying to tell at least a skeletal version of *Lady Windermere's Fan*.

At this stage, as these notes show, we did not have a strong rationale for the way our work was developing: the "critical" dimension of the adaptation was largely absent. In some ways this was inevitable, and to continue without that rationale in view required a leap of faith on my part. I wanted to set a structure for the adaptation at the outset but not provide the content. By choosing the perspective of the servants as the focus, I felt that a critical dimension was implied—most obviously, through consideration of interclass tensions, resentments, and possibilities for resistance—if not directly imposed. The decision to retell each of the play's acts was one that initially made me uneasy, as I was not sure how this would help us stamp our own identity on the source text: our principal motivation was, baldly, to generate some material that we could think of as "ours." The rule agreed was that each "retelling" had to be from the servants' viewpoint, somehow keeping these figures central. Time being short, we were pragmatic and adopted a course I would hesitate to pursue with a larger group or less experienced students: we simply divided the acts between the three of us and agreed to come back with a strategy to approach each one for the next session.

Rob's proposal for Act 1 looked decidedly daunting on paper. Keen to work with the various film versions of Wilde's play that we had watched, he created a staging whereby live actors onstage would seem to "enter" a living room shown on film. The technique allowed us to expose onstage an imaginary servants' quarters—a space not shown in the original—and to juxtapose this visually with the (filmed) action of the "play proper" that takes place in Lord and Lady Windermere's living room. It also enabled us to show how Wilde's text had been understood by adapters in the past: we showed sections of Paul's melodramatic silent film, intersected with moments from the BBC's more "faithful" 1985 version.[9] But the device of juxtaposing live and filmed action also gave us opportunity to imagine new, lightly subversive actions: Parker swigging from a hip flask, or eavesdropping at the point designated as the living room door, for instance, and (more surreally) Rob's idea that Parker might secretly be the author of Lord Darlington's many witty lines, lines he sells to the aristocrat on a regular basis:

> LORD DARLINGTON (*chuckling*): "I can resist everything—except temptation." Hah! Simply marvelous. Lady Windermere is sure to swoon, I can feel it! Well, wish me luck. Today may well be the day. After all, there is the matter of the affair . . .
>
> PARKER: Affair, your lordship?
>
> LORD DARLINGTON: Yes! Lord Windermere and Mrs. Erlynne! Everyone knows about it. (Act I)[10]

Limited elements of original dialogue, here written by Rob, were thus also a means of informing the audience about "official" plot developments. While Rob remained as Parker throughout the act, Lauren played Lord Darlington, the Duchess and Lady Agatha (at the same time), and Lord Windermere, dressed in her maid's costume but wearing a series of added costume indicators: respectively, a top hat; a bonnet, plus a duck head umbrella (thus we relegated Lady Agatha); and a greatcoat. It was a farcical scene, made possible by hours of patient film editing, prior to the performance, and much frantic backstage running around during it.

Act 2—a ball scene—appeared on the surface to be the most difficult: Wilde's original has more than a dozen speaking roles, and the servants play almost no part in it. Lauren came up with an ingenious solution to this difficulty:

> I decided to work with the idea that Rosalie and Parker were clearing up debris after the party, and that to make it more theatrically effective, we would imply it had been a masquerade ball and re-enact the events of the evening using each character's discarded mask to represent that character and we would see the two servants finishing off the champagne and mocking the frivolities of the upper classes. By choosing this method we were able to produce a shortened version of Act 2 which still encapsulated the sense of fun and mockery which Wilde's play reveals.

Inclusion of exchanges from several, relatively minor figures alongside those of the major characters allowed us, as Lauren notes, to "establish a similar sense of the cultural and social context which Wilde had worked to create." This idea that Parker and Rosalie could reenact an edited account of the ball for the audience had a pleasing logic to it that not all our ideas could boast. If the servants were clearing up debris, unobserved, why might they not mimic what they had witnessed and eavesdropped upon, and why not employ the dropped masks, flowers, or champagne glasses as props? Lauren came up with further, witty refinements: each character's mask indicated something of their persona, often in nonrealistic ways, thus the mask for the aging Lord Augustus had wispy eyebrows, while that of Hopper (the wealthy Australian) was adorned with strings of corks. Lauren assumed all female roles, Rob all male ones: the result—a kind of puppet show—worked like Act 1 to offer a subversive take on an upper-class world from an underclass perspective.

My own idea for Act 3 was (I think) less ambitious than the students' proposals. Its focus, in Wilde's play, is a confrontation between Lady Windermere and Mrs. Erlynne in Lord Darlington's rooms, followed by the return of the men and the scandalous revelation of Mrs. Erlynne who steps out from behind a curtain. I decided that Lauren, dressed as Rosalie, would play Lady Windermere and Mrs. Erlynne in swift succession—multi-role-playing seemed inevitable in this production and ultimately became a virtue—and that Rob, dressed as Parker, would represent a kind of composite figure based on all the male characters appearing in this act. The dialogue of the entire act was radically abbreviated. This was the most surreal scene in our production, its strangely disembodied effect heightened by the absence of indicative scenery. "My" act opens like this:

The two performers are spot-lit center stage. At the beginning, LAUREN *faces us, while* ROB *is next to her with his back to the audience.* LAUREN's *lines as* LADY WINDERMERE *are represented in* **bold**.

LAUREN: Why doesn't he come? Why is he not here, to wake some fire within me? I am cold as a loveless thing. Oh! It was mad of me to come here, I must go back—no; I can't go back, my letter—Arthur would not take me back! That fatal letter! No! No, no! I will go back. As for Lord Darlington—What shall I do? Will he let me go away at all? I have heard that men are brutal, horrible . . . Oh!

Lady Windermere! Thank Heaven I am in time. You must go back to your husband's house immediately.

Must?

Yes, you must![11]

Lauren and I worked together to find a way that she could play out this two-handed exchange by herself. The solution we found was the eponymous Lady Windermere's fan. As the rather gauche Lady Windermere, Lauren hid her face partly behind this; as the bolder Mrs. Erlynne, she held it at a distance and addressed it, as if the fan stood in for her coactor. Mrs. Erlynne has just convinced Lady Windermere to return to her home when we hear the return of the men—a mumbling from Rob, whose back is still turned to the audience:

LAUREN: Stop! Voices! Oh! That is my husband's voice! Save me!

Quick—behind this curtain! The first chance you have, slip out, if you ever get a chance!

[*LAUREN as* LADY WINDERMERE *hesitates in panic, then in one swift action drops the fan to the ground and pulls her apron up so it covers her face.* ROB *turns to face the audience, simultaneously representing* LORD DARLINGTON, MR. DUMBY, LORD WINERMERE, LORD AUGUSTUS LORTON, *and* MR. CECIL GRAHAM.]

ROB: Nuisance . . . club . . . cigar . . . ha ha! . . . dear boy . . . thanks . . . I say! . . . Demmed important . . . Mrs. Erlynne . . . The ladies . . . No business of yours . . . Bores me to death . . . Whisky and soda? . . . Wicked woman . . . Demmed amusing . . . Good women . . . Demmed dull . . . A past . . . The future . . . when I was your age— . . . game of cards . . . Cecil . . . Tuppy . . . Lucky fellow! . . . Dreadful cynic . . . I say

[*Sees fan lying on the ground*]

I SAY! . . . *Good* woman? . . . Here in his rooms? . . . By Jove! By Jove! . . . Good God!

[*Seizes the fan*]

Meaning of this?! . . . Darlington! . . . Demand an explanation!

LAUREN: [*lets apron fall*] **Lord Windermere!**

ROB: Mrs. Erlynne![12]

In his journal, Rob describes this third act as the point when the production as a whole "began to take on a more postmodern, metatheatrical feel." He describes Act 3 as "absurdist"; Lauren terms it "schizophrenic," which is especially apt given the acting challenge I set her. The idea I was playing with—not always consciously—when I wrote the act was that of actors practicing parts, perhaps whole scenes, in their rooms at home. I imagined Lauren, although actually cast in the thankless role of Rosalie, pretending to be both the female leads at once, throwing herself into the scene and perhaps sending it up at the same time. Without appropriate scenery, or the costumes for these coveted parts, of course she must improvise with what she has: an apron to substitute for a curtain and her maid's feather duster in place of a fan. Rob, similarly, plays at being every male part: all seem preferable to the one he has been landed with.

The proposals we came back with for Acts 1 to 3, although very different in kind, had one element in common: the notion of the servants—or the actors playing the servants—taking on other parts. It is hardly surprising that this was so, yet it was not always a conscious intention; we might have decided to create a largely original text that was somehow "about" these two servants, a sort of companion play to *Lady Windermere's Fan*. That we did not do this can be explained partly by the pressures of time but also by the real pleasure we took in Wilde's play: we wanted to draw strength from it, not just reject or oppose it. I have explained that in the early stages of working on the piece we struggled to find the driving dynamic or question that we needed to give the work shape and purpose. But after these first "proposals" for the acts had been made, two parallel issues began to emerge: first, what it means to be a servant in life; and second, what it means to be cast as a servant in the theater. We explored those issues in different ways, for instance, by asking (as I have described) what the action of the play might look like through these servants' eyes and what they could do in imagined, further scenes that Wilde did not choose to write. But gradually we became even more fascinated by the *actors'* experience. Is it really true that (as someone allegedly once said) "there are no small parts, only small actors?" Is it not more honest to say that there are some pretty uninspiring roles around (what of the undistinguished "extras" that Ricky Gervais made the basis for his 2005 TV comedy series)? This was a breakthrough in our creative process, the point when we began to recognize the metatheatrical possibilities in developing the attitudes of "Rob" and "Lauren" to the small parts they had been given. It also provided our eventual title: "No Small Parts."

Warming to this new idea, I asked Rob and Lauren each to imagine that they were being interviewed prior to a production of *Lady Windermere's Fan*, the instruction to "talk up" the significance of their small parts in any way they could and disguise their relative insignificance from the interviewer (whose questions we would not hear). The students responded wonderfully with self-aggrandizing monologues that we subsequently filmed and included in the production either side of "our" Act 3. Rob's version of himself was the classic stereotype of the self-absorbed actor, here manifestly deluded about his abilities and opportunities:

> [ROB *lounges in a director's chair. He has a long scarf draped around his neck and is smoking in an affected manner.*] Yes, hello. Well, the play is *Lady Windermere's Fan* by Oscar Wilde of course, and the fan is the main focus of the play— then, of course, there's *my* character. Now, I play the role of the, well, the man who's in control of the whole thing. What do I mean? Well, he's the one responsible for—for who goes in and comes out—the one who—who gets to tell all the BIG news . . . I mean, there's a scene, where he tells Lady Windermere that Mrs. Erlynne has returned the fan, and, as anyone who is familiar with the play will know, that is, of course, *massively* significant.
>
> Lord Windermere? Goodness, no. No, that's not as big a part as you might think. No, my character's name is Parker; Parker, yes; no, not Lord Parker; no, not Duke Parker; just Parker. Look, what are you driving at? The butler? Well,

I guess that's one word for it, yes. But he's really so much more than that. But I shouldn't say much more on the subject; I wouldn't want to spoil the experience for you . . . Favorite speech? Erm, well—the character isn't really given to long speeches. He's more of a terse talker—y'know, the enigmatic type? Look, OK! Look, I didn't want this part, did I? I mean, who the hell wants to be a [*side of mouth*] butler? You ever hear of a butler stealing the show? Precisely! And it doesn't help that the other cast members pretty much ignore us servants, and treat us with this vague, distant contempt. I mean [*scoffs*], the actor playing Lord Darlington actually asked me to fetch him a drink yesterday? And I did it! Jesus, it's even seeping into my subconscious, like I'm *becoming* a butler . . . Well, at least I'm not Rosalie; she only gets four lines! [*Satisfied laugh*] And she *always* makes the tea—even for the stage hands! Speaking of which . . . Lauren! Thank you. [*He gets up from the chair and leaves.*][13]

Unlike Rob, Lauren in her interview refuses ever to admit the limitations of her tiny part. For her, any "littleness" is located rather in the imagination and understanding of her audience:

[*LAUREN sits in a director's chair. She wears an arty black polo neck and mini skirt, and the oversized dark glasses of the supposedly publicity-shy celebrity.*] Well, it was a pleasure to work with such a supportive cast—and a real privilege, as a new actress, to be given such a prestigious character. Wilde is so renowned, and it's an honor really to do any of his parts, let alone one of such . . . caliber. There's such a lot of depth to Rosalie as a character; not only is she Lady Windermere's friend and confidante, but she's also a device, really, which Wilde uses to . . . in many ways . . . orchestrate the entire plot. Her presence can be felt throughout, I think—it resonates through the entire house for the first two acts, with all of the characters and audience aware of this almost omnipotent figure. The final revelation of Rosalie in Act 4 is really the climactic culmination of events, and her seeming obliviousness to what is going on is sheer brilliance by Wilde. Her relentless questioning of the socially superior Lady Windermere, and her bravery in refusing to allow Lord Windermere into his wife's room—telling him she is "not awake yet"—truly reveals how she is, in fact, master manipulator, within the plot. Yes, the lines are few, but the central figure does not necessarily need to speak . . . Often it is what is not said which is most powerful. I mean, Dumbo is known for being Disney's only main character who does not speak, but it doesn't make him any less the protagonist! Yes. I can see why people might think—that. But we must remember that Wilde is a very highbrow writer and his themes and true intent are not always . . . grasped, shall we say, by the . . . erm . . . masses. The critics? Well, I don't like to read reviews. It's what the real people think that counts. [*Fade out.*][14]

Lauren's insistence here on the importance of her role to the plot inspired us in the collective creation of Act 4. In Wilde's play, the opening of this act contains Rosalie's first and only entrance and meager lines. In rehearsal we explored the possibility that the actress might be so keyed up for her long-awaited appearance, so determined to make much of little, that when it came to her big moment everything went terribly wrong. In my research for the project, I had come across a review of one 2006 Oxford Playhouse production that, in commending various actors, praised one who was "only Rosalie but noticeable."[15] The mind boggles rather, given how very little Rosalie has to do—but the reference inspired me to ask Lauren to explore how she might make herself "noticeable" as Rosalie, perhaps distractingly so. She responded with an entrance that simultaneously struck notes of comedy and pathos: her Rosalie, first seen nervously tugging down her apron and doing warm-up stretches in the (deliberately visible) "wings," came on stage with a balletic bound and a too-eager "Did your ladyship ring for me?" followed by a line delivery painfully overburdened with actorish "motivation." Building on the elements of metatheatricality that increasingly were shaping our work, we agreed that at this point I would interrupt the scene from my position in the audience, adopting the role of frustrated director losing patience with her cast: "Lauren, stop! What do you think you're playing at? Is this how you conduct yourself in front of Lady Windermere?" I order her to take the entrance again, and she does, but this time it is still worse, her absurd "interpretation" made still clumsier through her dawning realization that, despite all her efforts, she is somehow getting it wrong. I interrupt again, this time really angry: "No! Lauren! That is not how you should enter a room! Your whole manner is inappropriate! You're not a character, you're a *function*. We should barely notice you!" Increasingly, the moment elides Lauren's status as a (very) minor character with her social status as a servant:

FRANCES: Lauren, do you want this part?

LAUREN: [*Mutters*] Yes.

FRANCES: Do you? *Do* you?

LAUREN: Yes!

FRANCES: Because if you don't, there are plenty of others who would. [*She gets up, starts to walk down the audience aisle toward the stage.*] Have you seen how many girls there are in this place, just queuing up for a chance like this? And any number of them would make a better job of it than you.

LAUREN: [*rebelliously*] The thing is, it's hard doing this role—I mean I know there aren't many lines, but the movement sequence at the beginning is really tiring and repetitive, and the dressing room is cold and poky—

FRANCES: Oh really?

LAUREN: Rob thinks just the same![16]

We decided that, rather than standing by Lauren, Rob—true to the character he portrays in the interview—would protect his own interests. Appealed to for support by his fellow actor, he *"studiously ignores her and makes a kind of shrugging gesture"* by which he signals his allegiance with the authoritative director. Lauren's poor performance brings her disgrace as an actress, and the part—small, but all she had—is ruthlessly taken from her:

> FRANCES: The thing is, Lauren, I thought I saw something in you; I thought you deserved a chance. But now I realize I was wrong. I'm afraid I'm going to have to let you go.
>
> LAUREN: You mean—but—but what shall I do?
>
> FRANCES: That's not my problem anymore. And as I can't in conscience give you a positive reference, you will have to make your own way in the world as best you can. Please, just get your things. [*LAUREN scrabbles around awkwardly, takes off apron and cap, and bundles them up.*] Not those! Those belong here, and they will be kept for the next maid. I meant the various [*with distaste*]—personal items—I've seen lying around in the dressing room. You can pick them up on your way out. [*LAUREN makes an undignified exit, as a last gesture throwing her cap and apron at ROB as she goes. There is an uncomfortable pause.*][17]

Lauren is dismissed without a character, in both senses of the phrase. This moment had an extraordinary impact in performance. The spectators were manifestly taken aback at the first interruption from the auditorium; my association with the project as tutor was known to most of those present, and the irritation with Lauren's work appeared genuine. Of course, the majority realized quickly that the intervention was scripted: at the same time, Lauren's crestfallen face and my merciless exercise of authority drew audible gasps of shock and pity for her plight. Rob, too, receives only a backhanded reward for his obsequiousness: he is informed simply that, until she is replaced, he will have to do her work as well as his own. In this interaction, we drew attention to the power of directors over actors; of the aristocracy over the "lower orders"; and of tutors over their students (however much this last relationship is mitigated by a discourse of collaboration and democratic pedagogy).

The rest of our adapted Act 4 kept very close to Wilde's original script yet still pursued our newfound emphasis on the opportunities available to the actor relegated to low-status parts.[18] Act 4 of *Lady Windermere's Fan* sees the disgraced Mrs. Erlynne make a dramatic reappearance, outraging Lord Windermere who is aware of her identity as his wife's mother and, since he previously discovered her in Lord Darlington's rooms, mistakenly believes her to be guilty of yet another scandalous intrigue. In our adaptation we allowed Lauren—sacked as an actress and, by implication, as a maid—to make her own surprise return to the stage, this time dressed in "leading lady" costume that she has somehow appropriated. As with Wilde's Mrs. Erlynne, it is uncertain whether Lauren, in her new guise, has come back to disrupt or preserve the *status quo*. Shocked by Lauren's audacious reentrance, Rob hisses (in Lord Windermere's own words), "What do you mean by coming back here, after the way you behaved? It is monstrous your intruding yourself like this!" The dialogue between Lauren/Mrs. Erlynne and Rob/Parker/Lord Windermere in our fourth act largely retained the shape of Wilde's original dialogue as well as many of its lines. "You've had your chance," Rob insists, "and you spoiled it!" Lauren/Mrs. Erlynne concurs, "[*with a strange smile*] You are quite right, I spoiled it all." The two actors—and the various characters they personify—embark on a discussion of theater and the choices open to them. Rob claims to believe that playing Parker is just the beginning for him; next time, it will be the slightly larger role of Cecil Graham; and ultimately, he will play Lord Darlington, the part he most covets. Lauren mocks his naive faith in role climbing: "It doesn't work like that! You're stuck when you play a part like this: once a servant, always a servant. I lost my illusions when I got sacked!" She confronts the narrow limits of his vision:

LAUREN: Do you think this little play is the only kind of theatre there is? What about postmodern drama? What about performance art?

ROB: What could you know of such things?

LAUREN: Enough to know that in them, you can play any part—you don't have to be a servant, you can be anything, and even someone like me can reinvent herself! You can recover from your mistakes, in fact sometimes audiences actually *like* you for your mistakes!

ROB: I don't believe in performance like that. I have devoted my life to proper drama—and if I lost my ideals, I should lose everything.

LAUREN: Ideals are dangerous things. You're so dependent on other people to live up to them. Realities are better. They're dirtier, messier—but they're better.[19]

Mirroring Wilde's Mrs. Erlynne, Lauren bids a final farewell and—as herself—leaves to seek her fortune in the world of alternative theater: a theater of adaptation, improvisation, and postmodern deconstruction of which the production just presented has itself been an example. Rob is left alone onstage.

We wrestled until the very last moment of rehearsal to find the "right" ending for our adaptation. We wanted to contrast Rob's decision to stick with his role of servitude with Lauren's choice to abandon hers; at the same time, we desired something more theatrically satisfying with which to conclude than an image of Rob caught in stasis. The best idea we had was, we were aware, something of a theatrical cliché: to close with the actions employed at the production's beginning—Rob repetitively enacting his butler's gestures and movements—with a slow fade to blackout. Happily, the two students can take credit for coming up with and practically creating a far better ending. They elected to reintroduce as conclusion the aesthetic of silent film with which the performance began but this time by means of a *faux* movie of their own making. This, then, is how "No Small Parts" eventually ended:

[Rob *stands alone onstage, "on duty" as Parker. A minute passes. His eyes shift from side to side. He stands on one leg briefly, rubbing his shoe on the back of his trousers. He coughs—and the cough leads him into a version of the choreographed "polite cough" of the opening movement sequence. He tries a couple more actions from this sequence, but gets mixed up whether he is now Parker, Rosalie, or both. He starts to get irritated with himself. He is an actor who has lost his "motivation." . . . Abruptly, as if making a sudden resolution, he runs from the theatre. Immediately, we cut to film footage: on the screen is a projection in the style of a black and white silent film. Rob is seen leaving the main door of the theatre, dressed in his butler's costume. He looks eagerly down the road for* Lauren, *but can't see her. He turns and looks up the road—and this time we see* Lauren, *dressed in her Mrs. Erlynne costume, at the end of the road about to turn the corner. Rob gestures wildly and calls out to her, then runs to catch her up. They meet, talk and laugh: Rob is clearly excited. There is just one intertitle, "spoken" by* Rob:]
    Tell me more about this "Performance Art"!
[*The two link arms and walk off together down the road, conversing with evident enthusiasm. The image closes in from the edges of the screen until it disappears—in the language of early film, an Iris-In—and the final shot appropriates the closing intertitle of Fred Paul's 1916 film:*]
    Lady Windermere's Fan
    The End
    [*Blackout.*][20]

Thus reconciled despite their differences, our conclusion implied that the two actors—or servants, or students—leave, as Lauren's journal has it, "to look for better parts: maybe parts that we have ourselves created."

The collective process of adapting Wilde's play into a new production for a cast of (essentially) two actors was, in our case, a somewhat breathless one. I have explained the pedagogic rationale for employing adaptation as a principle and structure for our work; equally, I have acknowledged that the meaning and value of our adaptation was by no means a known quantity from the project's inception. I feel I was fortunate to have two creative, intelligent, and ambitious students with whom to work, but at the same time I want to suggest that a practical task of adaptation of this kind, carefully presented to a group, immediately poses challenges that inherently invite both critical engagement with the source material and creative contributions from the students themselves. The adaptive process may or may not lead to an active critique of the material that provided the starting point: in our case, the focus was less on Wilde's play and more on deconstructing conservative conceptions of theater and submissive acceptance of institutionalized hierarchies. I close this chapter with three comments, the first from Rob: "'No Small Parts' was a hugely enjoyable process from start to finish. The way our relationship with Wilde's play progressed as we wrote our own, the former unraveling further and further from its origin, but all the time revealing new layers [of meaning], was the most satisfying aspect of the whole thing." Lauren adds,

> *Lady Windermere's Fan* seemed an ideal choice for us as it enabled us to change the focus on characters within a play, yet still allowed us both to tell Wilde's story and create a contemporary work in response. Wilde's narrative and the characters he created are so vivid and entertaining and the language he used so engaging that to select text from the play and create bold characters from snippets of the script was a thoroughly enjoyable task. I think that the piece we were able to make encapsulated a sense of fun not unlike that which Wilde shows in his plays.

Finally, I quote Wilde himself. In *The Importance of Being Earnest*, the dandy Algernon remarks of his own piano playing, "I don't play accurately—anyone can play accurately—but I play with wonderful expression."[21] Our adaptation of *Lady Windermere's Fan* was, certainly, Wild(e)ly inaccurate, but the work produced did, ultimately, find authentic expression of its own.

NOTES

1. Linda Hutcheon, *A Theory of Adaptation* (London: Routledge, 2006), 20.
2. Neil Sinyard, *Filming Literature: The Art of Screen Adaptation* (London: Croom Helm, 1986), 117.
3. An example might be Jacques Lacan's essay on Edgar Allan Poe's "The Purloined Letter," first published in 1956, which is at least as much a critique of Freudian psychoanalysis and proposal of (what has become known as) Lacanian psychoanalysis as it is a reading of Poe's tale. Jacques Lacan, "Seminar on 'The Purloined Letter,'" trans. Jeffrey Mehlman, *Yale French Studies* 48 (1973): 39–72 (originally published in Lacan's *Écrits*).
4. Ridiculusmus, "The Importance of Being Earnest," www.ridiculusmus.com/performance/current-show (accessed 19 January 2009).
5. Speeches extracted from Oscar Wilde's *Lady Windermere's Fan* (Harmondsworth: Penguin, 1995), passim.
6. Wilde, *Lady Windermere's Fan*, passim.
7. The students were each asked to keep a journal detailing the creative process (February to April 2007), and I quote extensively from these in what follows. Since

the journals are the students' own unpublished, sometimes handwritten records, it is not possible to give full references and page numbers; however, I always make it clear from which student's work I am quoting.

8. *Lady Windermere's Fan* [1916], Dir. Fred Paul, Perf. Milton Rosmer, Netta Westcott, Nigel Playfair (VHS, London: British Film Institute).

9. *Lady Windermere's Fan* [1985], Dir. Tony Smith, Perf. Helena Little, Tim Woodward, Stephanie Turner (DVD B000062XE1: BBC Video, 2002). We wanted to include elements from *A Good Woman* (2005) also but simply ran out of time. *A Good Woman* [2005], Dir. Mike Barker, Perf. Helen Hunt, Scarlet Johansson, Stephen Campbell Moore (DVD B0003UAFC: Lionsgate Video, 2006).

10. Frances Babbage, Robert Neumark Jones, Lauren Williams, and Oscar Wilde, "No Small Parts" (unpublished play script, 2007, passim).

11. Babbage et al., "No Small Parts."

12. Babbage et al., "No Small Parts."

13. Babbage et al., "No Small Parts."

14. Babbage et al., "No Small Parts."

15. David Tudor, review of Oxford Theatre Guild's *Lady Windermere's Fan* for *Rogues and Vagabonds*, 12 April 2006, www.oxfordtheatreguild.com/ (accessed 19 January 2009).

16. Babbage et al., "No Small Parts."

17. Babbage et al., "No Small Parts."

18. This emphasis on actors' ambitions was comically expanded upon in the program for the show. On the reverse side of the usual sheet of credits were photos of Lauren and Rob accompanied by *faux* British Equity CVs detailing their achievements to date. Lauren offers role-playing ages from "17 to 65" and features sword swallowing and glass blowing amongst her accomplishments; Rob has an impressive range of "specialist" accents—"Australian, Trinidadian and Edwardian"—but is let down somewhat by three acting courses, all of which are listed "(unfinished)."

19. Babbage et al., "No Small Parts."

20. Babbage et al., "No Small Parts."

21. Oscar Wilde, *The Importance of Being Earnest*, in *The Plays of Oscar Wilde* (London, Wordsworth, 2002), 363.

Two

"It Must All Change Now"

Victor Hugo's *Lucretia Borgia* and Adaptation

Richard J. Hand

Dedicated to the memory of Claude Schumacher

When teaching approaches to adaptation to students of both critical analysis and scriptwriting within a theater studies curriculum in the United Kingdom, I have found it beneficial to suggest that they locate what I call the Five Creative Strategies of Adaptation:

- Omission
- Addition
- Marginalization
- Expansion
- Alteration

In the strategy of "Omission," narrative or textual material is removed when a source text is dramatized. In "Addition," narrative or textual material not in the source text is introduced in the adaptation. In "Marginalization," thematic issues are given less prominence in the dramatization. In "Expansion," thematic issues suggested in the source text are given more prominence in the dramatization. In "Alteration," themes, textual style, narrative events, and details are modified. Identifying these strategies has proved important in my own academic research on adaptation, but it also offers a constructive point of entry into the teaching of adaptation.[1] For students of critical analysis, locating the use of the five strategies can be useful in analyzing a source text and its dramatization (for the stage but also for the screen, radio, or other media): In the creation of a new work for a different medium what has disappeared or been added?

What has been changed, made more of, or lessened? These are simple questions but can prove an excellent groundwork from which to embark on more profound levels of critical and theoretical analysis. When such manipulations have been located, what do they tell us about the source text and its adaptation? When we understand "what" has happened and "how" it has been implemented, can we begin to speculate "why" it has been done? For students of scriptwriting within the syllabus, assessing the same creative strategies can be invaluable to equip the creative writer with an awareness of options and skills or to permit objective self-assessment. Locating the Five Creative Strategies of Adaptation can also be valuable in comprehending the large-scale projects undertaken by a drama department. To this end, this essay offers a case study: the touring production of Victor Hugo's *Lucretia Borgia* mounted by the drama department at the University of Glamorgan for the 2007 International Victor Hugo Festival.

Arguably, Victor Hugo (1802–1885) remains the preeminent figure of not merely French Romanticism but also the French literary establishment as a whole: he has become quite possibly the "Shakespeare of France." The legacy of the Hugo text, at least outside of France, abides with the prose fiction. Hugo's novels *Notre-Dame de Paris* (*The Hunchback of Notre Dame*, 1831) and *Les Misérables* (1862) have steadily become favorites for adaptation into performance media. Hugo's romantic historical novel named after Paris's most emblematic cathedral has appealed to filmmakers from as early as 1905 with Alice Guy and Victorin-Hippolyte Jasset's *Esmeralda*.[2] Moreover, it is fascinating that, as well as being a Disney animated feature film—*The Hunchback of Notre Dame* (Gary Trousdale and Kirk Wise, 1996)—the story's remarkable creation Quasimodo has become an icon of popular horror culture, most notably through the performances of Lon Chaney in the 1923 Universal Pictures version, and Charles Laughton in William Dieterle's 1939 production for RKO.[3] If anything, *Les Misérables* is even more popular as a source for dramatization with countless film, television, and radio adaptations as well as being the source of the most successful stage musical in history in Claude-Michel Schönberg and Alain Boublil's 1980 version.

The richness of *The Hunchback of Notre Dame* and *Les Misérables* for adaptation has eclipsed Hugo's other achievements, at least in Anglophone culture. In addition to being a novelist, Hugo was a poet, essayist, and political figure of major importance. He was also an extremely significant playwright. It is perhaps somewhat ironic that, despite his importance as a dramatist, he has become much more celebrated as an "adaptive source" and not simply in the era of film: indeed, even one of Hugo's most significant and controversial plays, *Le roi s'amuse* (1832)—banned after just one performance—is certainly most famous in the guise of Giuseppe Verdi's 1851 operatic adaptation: *Rigoletto*. Even Hugo himself was engaged in adaptation when he wrote the libretto for Louise Bertin's *La Esmerelda* (1836), an opera version of *Notre-Dame de Paris*.

It was partly in the spirit of redressing the neglect of Hugo's drama that Claude Schumacher edited *Victor Hugo: Four Plays* (2004) for which I translated *Lucrèce Borgia* (1833)—with the anglicized title *Lucretia Borgia*—and *Ruy Blas* (1838).[4] In establishing the translation brief, Schumacher made it clear that he wanted something between the *literal* and the *performable*. This is one reason he requested a prose translation of *Ruy Blas*, not the rhyming Alexandrine couplets of the original: adhering to the original lyrical patterning of the original would have maintained, as it were, the *rhythm and pulse* of the original but not the closeness of semantic *meaning*. Although the scripts would not be cut or radically restructured, the editor wanted plays that could be efficaciously spoken and enacted by English-language performers and presented to a twenty-first-century audience. From a personal perspective, the Hugo translations were to be an example of individual research and scholarship. Nevertheless, because I am an academic working within an active drama department, there was never a shortage of performance students willing to assist and participate in the development of the scripts; and they played an important role in sampling and testing the journey from page to stage, fine tuning the plays for the purposes of the living voice of the actor and the living ear of the spectator. The assistance the students gave to further the transition from translation to adaptation at this stage, however, was strictly extracurricular. Eventually—and significantly after the publication of the 2004 volume—the Hugo translations would form an integral and formal component of a major pedagogical venture within the degree's syllabus.

After the publication of the 2004 plays, the Victor Hugo Society approached me, asking if there was a professional theater company that might mount the world premiere of one of my translations at the Gatehouse Theatre for the London leg of the 2007 International Victor Hugo Festival. Although the process of linguistic translation is itself a journey of adaptation of the interlingual variety, the staging of a theatrical production is always about adaptation: the cross-media journey from page to stage, the interpretation and reinvention of text into a process in time and space, and text ciphers becoming flesh and blood people. Given the large ensemble casts demanded by both plays—*Ruy Blas* has well over twenty speaking parts and *Lucretia Borgia* is only marginally smaller—most theater companies other than the most heavily subsidized would only be able to stage a production with major edits, or the "doubling" of numerous roles. Such a large-scale theatrical enterprise is an ideal project, however, for a university drama department such as ours at the University of Glamorgan, which holds performance practice as central to its pedagogical ethos and vocational aspirations. The challenge of a large ensemble touring production participating in an international festival had the potential to be extremely rewarding for the staff in terms of teaching, research, scholarship, and professional practice; while for the students (who range in age from eighteen to those more mature in years and have, in some cases, little or no theatrical experience outside of coursework to full British Equity membership), the prospect was immensely exciting.

The script the Victor Hugo Society commissioned for full production at the festival was *Lucretia Borgia*, "Hugo's most successful play in terms of theatrical achievement, popularity . . . and financial gain."[5] This three-act play is a highly dramatic, audaciously violent, and erotic reimagining of one of the most (in)famous figures of the Italian Renaissance: the ultimate *femme fatale*. The play is a thrilling melodrama, with a profound and genuinely epic treatment of themes such as maternal love and generational conflict, and it explores an iconic figure's failed attempts at self-redemption before embarking on a ruthless reassertion of her diabolical reputation. Hugo's play has a sweeping narrative; it is full of twists, turns, and dramatic irony; it features a large cast of distinctive characters; and it is a historical epic of intrigue and revenge that leads, unremittingly, to a devastating climax: the combination of these aspects make *Lucretia Borgia* an irresistible challenge for theatrical production. However, it is also, for precisely the same reasons that make it so enticing, an extremely difficult play to produce on the contemporary stage. Following Claude Schumacher's principles as editor of the 2004 Hugo plays, the decision was taken not to edit or tamper with the original's structure, and yet it was clear that *Lucretia Borgia* would offer a rich canvas for *adaptation*, sometimes out of choice, sometimes out of necessity.

My experience as translator and subsequently director would reveal and draw upon different adaptive processes. The journey of interlingual adaptation (linguistic translation), textual adaptation (revision of the text for performance purposes), and intermedial adaptation (page to stage) was further compounded by the fact that the production had a major and focal role in underpinning the teaching activities of the faculty. More precisely, some twenty-seven students were directly involved in the physical tour to London: eighteen performers, three technical crew, two stage managers, two assistant directors, and two production assistants. However, many others were involved in different components of the production. One group of students specializing in theater history conducted research for the program notes and collected visual material for illustrative purposes. A group of filmmaking students created four films based on aspects of the *Lucretia Borgia* narrative in the style of early cinema, to be screened within the performance using students specializing in screen acting. Whole teams worked on prop design, manufacture, and testing. Ultimately, it involved literally dozens of students across all levels of the undergraduate program (in the roles of actors, assistant directors, stage managers, technicians, costume and stage designers, prop manufacture, publicity designers, and disseminators), the majority of whom opted to use their contribution to the production as a key component of their coursework assessment. For all involved, "adaptation" was a guiding principle in the realization of the production from concept to opening night. For colleagues, too, the *Lucretia Borgia* project offered the chance to consolidate their teaching (as well as their interests in research, scholarship, and professional practice) toward a tangible and ultimately public project with a strict deadline. For all involved, their work met the ultimate test in a public forum: most obviously the actors but also the "unseen" participants whose contribution was equally important in enhancing and facilitating the production.

Lucretia Borgia is ostensibly a work of historical re-creation "set in Venice and Ferrara during the sixteenth century,"[6] and yet it is almost entirely Hugo's fantasy, an adaptation of history that goes beyond poetic license in extrapolating the myth of the Borgia family, while dramatizing the life and death of Lucretia. In reality, Lucrezia Borgia (1480–1519) was a member of an extremely powerful dynasty headed by her father Rodrigo Borgia (Pope Alexander VI), and her brothers included Cesare Borgia and Juan Borgia. Often seen as the epitome of Machiavellian ambition and action, the Borgias were notorious in their own time as is evident in contemporary accounts of their political intrigue as well as the orgies, obscene masques, and other debaucheries alleged to have been orchestrated by Rodrigo, Cesare, and Lucrezia.[7] The notoriety has continued ever since, although it is immensely difficult to separate reality from the legend of "the impetuous Borgia blood that combined brutality and splendour and was free from morals."[8] Certainly, the myth offers rich material for adapters in addition to Hugo: Gaetano Donizetti adapts Hugo's play into his opera *Lucrezia Borgia* (1833), while films such as *Lucrèce Borgia* (Christian-Jaque, 1953) and the BBC miniseries *The Borgias* (Brian Farnham, 1981) capitalize on the dynasty's infamy as well as its vibrant historical context.[9] Although impossible to prove, there were contemporary rumors of incest within the Borgia family, which Hugo extrapolates into Juan Borgia being the father of his sister's child. Hugo builds his tragedy around the relationship between Lucretia and Gennaro and the fact that, although the mother knows her own son, the heroic Gennaro has been raised an orphan and only knows to despise the notorious woman who looms like "a terrible phantom haunting the whole of Italy."[10] In Hugo's play, Lucretia is mother to only one child, whereas

in reality Lucrezia Borgia had numerous children. In her lifetime, however, rumors abounded around the paternity of her son Giovanni Borgia,
with her father the Pope or brother Cesare named as the child's parent.
Evidently, Hugo draws on this legend surrounding Giovanni in creating
Gennaro. In reality, Lucrezia died following complications after giving birth, but Hugo prefers the shocking finale of Gennaro stabbing his
mother to death before succumbing to the Borgia poison.

Lucretia Borgia is a radical adaptation of historical "truth" on Hugo's
part, a "factionalization" for the sake of genre in order to create a blood
tragedy as well as a religious and political satire of the Catholic Church
and contemporary France in allegorical form, abounding with the values
and rhetoric of French Romanticism. Nevertheless, Hugo clearly enjoys
the (literal) texture of historical detail as some of the stage directions
reveal: "A hall in the ducal palace of Ferrara. Tapestries of Hungarian
leather decorated with golden arabesques adorn the walls. Magnificent
furniture in the style of late-fifteenth-century Italy, including a ducal
throne covered in red velvet with the Este coat of arms embroidered on
it."[11] With stage descriptions like this, Hugo can be seen as creating his
"ideal" production. Hugo himself had the opportunity to see his ideal
play become reality by taking an active role as the play headed toward
its premiere, painting some of the decor himself and standing "with stop-
watch in hand, timing the scene changes."[12] Rather than feeling obliged
to re-create this ideal/historical staging, we decided to develop a new
concept for the production. This was also a logistical necessity in some
respects: because the production was commissioned as a touring production, we needed a stage design that would be robust as well as easily de-
mountable and transportable. The final stage design used modular blocks
of various sizes painted to resemble cream-colored marble: the blocks
could be easily moved to create thrones, tables, or palaces. Although
capturing a sense of opulence and power, our lighting design ensured
that the marble blocks frequently resembled the cracked ruins of antiq-
uity symbolizing the Ozymandias-like hubris of the past dynasties Hugo
reanimates. However, the deliberately adaptable design dictated that we
could invest more in costume and prop design as a way of establishing
specific locale and context.

In developing the production concept that would underpin the script,
I considered both the trajectory of the central character and the context.
Lucretia is acutely aware of her own reputation and capitalizes on it as
much as she is haunted by it. This is evident in a scene early in the play
when Lucretia, in disguise, talks to her most steadfast assistant:

> GUBETTA: I have one more piece of advice to give you: whatever you do, do
> not remove your mask, you most certainly will be recognised.

LUCRETIA: So what? If people do not know who I am, I have nothing to fear; if they do recognise me it is they who should tremble in fear.

GUBETTA: We are in Venice, madam. You have many enemies here, enemies on the loose. Certainly the Republic of Venice would protect you from any attempts on Your Highness's life, but they cannot protect you from insults.

LUCRETIA: Ah, indeed, you're right . . . my name evokes horror.

GUBETTA: Besides, it isn't just Venetians here. There are Romans, Neapolitans, Romagnols, Lombardians: Italians from all over Italy.

LUCRETIA: And the whole of Italy despises me! You're right! But it must all change now. I was not born to do evil, I feel that now more than ever. My family has made me what I am.[13]

The sense of Lucretia scrutinizing her own iconic status in a mood of sinister narcissism brought to mind a cinematic parallel: Norma Desmond (Gloria Swanson) watching her old movies in *Sunset Boulevard* (Billy Wilder, 1950).[14] Knowing that we would use elements of screened film within the play—with a different ensemble of performers interpreting the story of *Lucretia Borgia* for the camera—the parallel became even more compelling. In terms of context, the tumultuous epoch Hugo animates brought to mind another point of filmic reference: *Lucretia Borgia* is set in the Renaissance Italian world so admired by Harry Lime (Orson Welles) in *The Third Man* (Carol Reed, 1949): "In Italy for 30 years under the Borgias they had warfare, terror, murder, and bloodshed, but they produced Michelangelo, Leonardo da Vinci, and the Renaissance. In Switzerland they had brotherly love—they had five hundred years of democracy and peace, and what did that produce? The cuckoo clock."[15] In the production we would set the play in the Italian states of the 1920s: the era of the rise of Fascism combined with an exciting Modernism; the shift from pre–First World War certainties into a cataclysmic mood of uncertainty; and the shift in the performance aesthetics of film from screen melodrama to Expressionism. The production was governed by a "Ritz" style of black tie and ball gowns, with recurrent elemental colors of blood red, rich gold, and cold blue. The final, nightmarish scenes of the play transformed into an Expressionistic aesthetic (the "other" 1920s). The overall effect was an adaptive "time tunnel": the reanimation of sixteenth-century Venice and Ferrara through 1830s French Romanticism set in the 1920s for a twenty-first-century audience.

Having the opportunity to direct a play I had translated myself made it tempting to revise the script and reconsider earlier decisions I had made. However, as the play was commissioned by the Victor Hugo Society for the British leg of the International Victor Hugo Festival, the primacy of the Hugo text as translated in the 2004 edition was expected and respected. That said, setting the production in the twentieth century would mean rewriting sentences that were highly specific historically. For example, at the beginning of the play, a notorious story surrounding the Borgias is recounted:

JEPPO: Very well. It was in the year of Our Lord, fourteen hundred and ninety . . .

GUBETTA: (*in the corner*) Fourteen ninety-seven.

JEPPO: Quite so! Fourteen ninety-seven. In the early hours of a Thursday morning . . .

GUBETTA: No. *Wednesday.*[16]

In the production this became the following:

JEPPO: Very well. It was twenty-two years ago . . .

GUBETTA: (*in the corner*) Twenty-three.

JEPPO: Quite so! Twenty-three years ago. In the early hours of a Thursday morning . . .

GUBETTA: No. *Wednesday.*

Such textual adaptations were necessary to avoid the potentially jarring spectacle of characters attired in dinner suits and bowties or flapper dresses and bead necklaces talking about being in the sixteenth century. In contrast, the names of the various noble dynasties featured or mentioned remained unaltered: d'Este, Tudor, Orsini, Liveretto, and, of course, Borgia. To an extent, the names still have a currency and for the performers were imbued with lyricism for the voice.

Perhaps the most profound narrative adaptations were compelled by gender. Despite the gender of the eponymous antiheroine, the play is otherwise dominated by male characters. Like most university drama departments in the United Kingdom, the University of Glamorgan has more female students than male. The dominance of male roles in the Western dramatic tradition can often make it difficult to approach classical text drama with a gender balance. However, *Lucretia Borgia* offered a relatively easy adaptive solution: it is a play of warring factions and vendettas with Lucretia constantly scheming with her henchmen and allies while being schemed against by equally ruthless adversaries and dissemblers. For the sake of the production—and for the sake of the teaching cohort—a guiding principle was established: *Lucretia would only trust a woman.* This meant that one of the chief characters in the play, Lucretia's deadly right-hand man Gubetta became her right-hand woman; her spy and assassin Astolfo became the similarly merciless Astolfa; the "Black

Pages . . . dressed in gold brocade" in attendance at the Negroni Palace were replaced by Lucretia's loyal women;[17] and the monks of Saint Sixtus, who devotedly help Lucretia dispatch and dispose of her victims, became nuns, Lucretia's lethal holy mothers. Changing the gender of characters in this way inevitably had an impact on language and compelled a revision of the script. For example, in this scene, two of Gennaro's friends discuss Belverana (who is, as the audience knows, Gubetta in disguise):

> JEPPO: My word, if it isn't the Count of Belverana! Let's all go together this evening and have the time of our lives!
>
> (*To* GUBETTA) How good to see you, sir!
>
> GUBETTA: God bless you, my dear friend!
>
> MAFFIO: (*quietly to* JEPPO) I'm afraid I am rather apprehensive, Jeppo. And if you have ever trusted me, trust me now: we must not dine with the Princess this evening. The Negroni Palace adjoins the ducal palace. Besides, I am a little uneasy seeing our Spanish "friend" here.
>
> JEPPO: (*quietly*) Don't be ridiculous, Maffio. Princess Negroni is a charming lady. I told you I love her! As for Belverana, he's a fine fellow. I made some inquiries into him and his family. My father and his fought at the siege of Granada in 1480-something.
>
> MAFFIO: That does not prove that this really is the son of your father's friend.[18]

This became the following, revealing both gender and time reference changes:

> JEPPO: My word, if it isn't the Lady Belverana! Let's all go together this evening and have the time of our lives!
>
> (*To* GUBETTA) How good to see you, madam!
>
> GUBETTA: God bless you, my dear friend!
>
> MAFFIO: (*quietly to* JEPPO) I'm afraid I am rather apprehensive, Jeppo. And if you have ever trusted me, trust me now: we must not dine with the Princess this evening. The Negroni Palace adjoins the ducal palace. Besides, I am a little uneasy seeing our Spanish "friend" here.
>
> JEPPO: (*quietly*) Don't be ridiculous, Maffio. Princess Negroni is a charming lady. I told you I love her! As for Belverana, she's a fine lady. I made some inquiries into her and her family. My father and hers fought at the siege of Granada . . .
>
> MAFFIO: That does not prove that this really is the daughter of your father's friend.

As is evident from the above, the changes were easy to accomplish.

At the end of the play, the tragic journey is sealed in blood with Lucretia and her son killing each other. It seems that Hugo desired that as she dies Lucrèce should utter her shocking revelation "Je suis ta mère"—"I am your mother!"—"avec joie"—"with joy"—but to Hugo's chagrin "his actress, Mlle George, could not bring herself to be anything but 'tragic' at the climax of the play."[19] The startling enunciation that Hugo desired—an ecstasy as her son "penetrates" her with a dagger—proved less problematic in a contemporary context, especially in a version that enhanced the significance of gender and sexuality. Similarly, the party scene at Princess Negroni's palace that marks the beginning of the final act was adapted into a more sexually dynamic "orgy" in keeping with Borgia mythology,[20] in which Negroni's debutantes became ostensible courtesans before revealing their true identities as the nuns of Saint Sixtus.

Hugo's play functions with the melodramatic devices of its historical context, some of which are very alien to the contemporary performer and audience. For example, the play belongs to a theater of convention, whereby characters wear half-masks but fail to recognize each other, almost fainting with shock when faces are revealed. For the twenty-first-century student of performance, typically schooled in postmelodramatic realism, such moments are terminally risible or at best "cheesy." *Lucretia Borgia* obliged the actors to adapt themselves and their habitual practice, embracing the shifts of melodrama with conviction and energy and avoiding the conscious irony and knowingness of pantomime. In all cases, the actors succeeded in this adaptation of performance practice and found the process to be an extremely valuable one in increasing their repertoire of acting methodologies. The melodramatic world of *Lucretia Borgia* is particularly evident in the last moments of the play when Gennaro's closest friend Maffio Orsini staggers onto the stage, dying from poisoned wine, and screams "Gennaro, I'm dying; avenge me!" before he falls down dead.[21] Such a sequence risked being humorous if not completely ludicrous, but through rehearsal the actor playing Maffio and those witnessing his demise came to approach the scene with heightened conviction. All involved stared with wide eyes like figures from an Expressionist film as Maffio physically contorted his body, sweat pouring down his face, his eyes darkened and his cheeks pallid with stage makeup. The result was that the scene no longer risked being "silly" but became a compelling, nightmarish sequence.

Likewise, the performer playing the villainous Gubetta had to develop a unique relationship with the audience, taking the spectators into her confidence not unlike Shakespeare's King Richard III. In this speech Gubetta talks about Lucretia:

GUBETTA: What the devil is she up to? And who exactly is this Gennaro? I do not know all the secrets of my lady, of course not, but this piques my curiosity. In faith, she has not confided in me on this matter and so she must not expect me to assist her on this occasion. Let her set up a little intrigue with Gennaro if she can. But how strange it is to see her love a man in such a chivalrous manner. She is the daughter of Roderigo Borgia and Vanozza, the blood of the Pope and the blood of a courtesan mingle in her veins. But now Donna Lucretia has discovered Platonic love! Nothing will surprise me now—I wouldn't even be surprised if someone told me that the Pope believes in God![22]

This monologue is a challenge for a contemporary performer unfamiliar with historical melodrama: it has an expository function that spells out the workings of psychology in an artificial way; and it features some examples of archaic words, phrasing, and concepts. It would be easy for the actor—and even the audience—to be subsumed by the speech. It was decided that the key to performing the scene was the final line in the extract. The line may be making a historical observation on the notorious reputation of Pope Alexander VI and a satirical jibe at the Catholic Church, but most importantly it is, of course, a joke. Our Gubetta therefore approached the speech almost as though it was stand-up comedy: she took the audience into her confidence, made eye contact with individuals, and smiled at them, as she unraveled her account while heading toward the utterance of a punch line that always secured a laugh.

As *Lucretia Borgia* was a curriculum project requiring student assessment and evaluation, how did we make sense of the overall process? If we return to the approach outlined at the beginning of this essay, the Five Creative Strategies of Adaptation proved an instrumental way to understand the adaptive journey that was *Lucretia Borgia*. All participants understood that *Lucrèce Borgia* was a 1830s French play translated into English in 2004: in basic terms, an example of linguistic "Alteration." More pertinent for the participants was the three-stage journey from the 2004 edition through working script to stage production. As we have seen, because the production was commissioned by the Victor Hugo Society, the application of creative strategies on the published translation were kept to a minimum, although there were significant alterations in terms of gender (some male characters became female with a domino effect on respective pronouns within the dialogue), while setting the play in the 1920s required changes in costume (Alfonso d'Este's "splendid formal attire" became a tuxedo)[23] and precise historical references ("1497" became a less specific "Twenty-three years ago.")

The most complex journey was the final phase, the page to stage adaptation of the working script into live performance. Although Lucretia says of her own character and notorious past "it must all change now,"[24] ultimately the infamous noblewoman is unable to amend her character and actions any more than she can evade the inexorable tragedy in which

Hugo has trapped her. Ironically, although Hugo himself may have monitored the running of the play to the second and have instructed "experienced actors in the minute nuances of diction,"[25] the essence of live theatrical production remains flux and movement: all does "change" even though the story remains the same. No two live performances can ever be the same. Every live event has unique moments and determinants. In the case of *Lucretia Borgia*, various factors made this clear: using an understudy in a performance changed the "sound" and interrelationships between relevant characters; the audience can behave in erratic ways in their reactions (laughter, surprise, or approbation); and even stage properties such as stage blood emitted from a trick knife can often be unpredictable in use, landing variously on actor, floor, or spectator.

In her classic study of *Metafictional Characters in Modern Drama*, June Schlueter writes on the fictive character within drama and how the medium of live theater gives the character an even more complex identity:

> When a fictive character exists in drama, its identity is even more complex. In addition to being an imaginative creation of both author and reader, it also becomes a physical presence functioning before a live audience, which brings to the interpretation not simply the private response of the . . . reader, but a collective, communal response as well. Not only does the fictive character take on representational tangibility in drama, but the individual doing the acting also becomes part of the creative process, presenting and interpreting from yet a third creative mentality. Hence, in terms of components and variables, the dramatic character is the most complex of fictive creations.[26]

A fictional construct within a script is forced into the complexity of practical drama. On one level, Lucretia Borgia became a flesh and blood woman. Not only did textual constructions like Lucretia Borgia "come alive" in the actor's body but also through the creation and use of props such as the notorious poison-infused Syracuse wine that was poured and consumed (even if it was in actuality safely potable blackcurrant juice). The complexity of a stage production gives the fictional world a "representational tangibility" mediated by the creative input of the performers. In this regard, the stage *Lucretia Borgia* was dominated by "Addition" and "Expansion." Additions included the deployment of various channels of live performance: nondiegetic music composed by music colleague Georg Boenn added a musical soundtrack to certain scenes and transitions between scenes that established moods of celebration, portent, or intrigue; the silent films back projected in the production created a degree of commentary on individual psychology and a counterpoint to, or reinforcement of, the live-action tragic narrative. Expansion is, however, the most potent creative strategy in this case study of adaptive practice. The script-bound constructs of *Lucretia Borgia* became three-dimensional characters with idiosyncratic mannerisms, voices, and articulation. Similarly, Hugo simply describes everyone at the party at Princess Negroni's palace as "eating and drinking, roaring with laughter":[27] this was expanded into a long, atmospheric scene of music, carousal, and seduction before a single word was uttered.

For all involved, locating the points of adaptive transition suggested by the Five Creative Strategies of Adaptation was a useful way to unravel the complex processes that occurred in the *Lucretia Borgia* journey and proved instrumental in the students' learning processes. The difficult text and conventions of *Lucretia Borgia* were made accessible and meaningful for all participants through the identification of adaptive processes: for the student designer, composer and/or performer adaptation provided a conduit to understanding. The decision to translate then produce a work of drama functioned like the rings in a felled tree or, more aptly, ripples in a pond: a core text has a catalytic function, extending and encompassing, changing and evolving, and growing in strength as it does so.

NOTES

1. Richard J. Hand, *The Theatre of Joseph Conrad: Reconstructed Fictions* (London: Palgrave, 2005), 17–18.
2. *Esmeralda* [1905], Dir. Alice Guy, Victorin-Hippolyte Jasset, Perf. Denise Becker, Henry Vorins (Societé des Établissements L. Gaumont, 1905).
3. *The Hunchback of Notre Dame* [1996], Dir. Gary Trousdale, Kirk Wise, Voices Jason Alexander, Tom Hulce (DVD B00005NYXO: Buena Vista Home Entertainment, 2001); *The Hunchback of Notre Dame* [1923], Dir. Wallace Worsley, Perf. Lon Chaney, Patsy Ruth Miller (DVD B000TEUS16: Image Entertainment, Ultimate Edition, 2007); *The Hunchback of Notre Dame* [1939], Dir. William Dieterle, Perf. Charles Laughton, Cedric Hardwicke (DVD B000B8V9FE: Warner Home Video, Warner Classics Mega Collection, 2005).
4. Victor Hugo, *Victor Hugo: Four Plays*, ed. Claude Schumacher (London: Methuen, 2004), 211–398.
5. Hugo, *Victor Hugo: Four Plays*, xxxi.
6. Hugo, *Victor Hugo: Four Plays*, 212.
7. See Burgo Partridge, *A History of Orgies* (London: Anthony Blond, 1958), 106–8.
8. Maria Bellonci, *Lucrezia Borgia* (London: Phoenix, 2000), 34.
9. *Lucrèce Borgia* [1953], Dir. Christian-Jaque, Perf. Martine Carol, Pedro Armendáriz (DVD B000NTPB9S: LCJ, 2007); *The Borgias* [1981], Dir. Brian Farnham, Perf. Oliver Cotton, Adolfo Celi, Louis Selwyn (BBC Television, 1981).
10. Hugo, *Victor Hugo: Four Plays*, 239.
11. Hugo, *Victor Hugo: Four Plays*, 243.
12. Graham Robb, *Victor Hugo* (London: Picador, 1997), 180.
13. Hugo, *Victor Hugo: Four Plays*, 219.

14. *Sunset Boulevard* [1950], Dir. Billy Wilder, Perf. Gloria Swanson, William Holden, Erich von Stroheim (DVD B001EXE2ZG: Paramount Video, Sunset Boulevard Centennial Collection, 2008).

15. *The Third Man* [1949], Dir. Carol Reed, Perf. Joseph Cotten, Orson Welles, Trevor Howard (DVD B000NOK0GM: Criterion Collection, Two-Disc ed., 2007).

16. Hugo, *Victor Hugo: Four Plays*, 214.

17. Hugo, *Victor Hugo: Four Plays*, 269.

18. Hugo, *Victor Hugo: Four Plays*, 237.

19. Victor Hugo, *Oeuvres Complètes: Théâtre I* (Paris: Robert Laffont, 1985), 1426; Hugo, *Victor Hugo: Four Plays*, xxxiv.

20. Hugo, *Victor Hugo: Four Plays*, 271.

21. Hugo, *Victor Hugo: Four Plays*, 285.

22. Hugo, *Victor Hugo: Four Plays*, 233–24.

23. Hugo, *Victor Hugo: Four Plays*, 243.

24. Hugo, *Victor Hugo: Four Plays*, 219.

25. Robb, *Victor Hugo*, 180.

26. June Schlueter, *Metafictional Characters in Modern Drama* (New York: Columbia University Press, 1979), 7.

27. Hugo, *Victor Hugo: Four Plays*, 269.

THREE

"NEVER SEEK TO TELL THY LOVE"

E-Adapting Blake in the Classroom

Richard Berger

Never seek to tell thy love
Love that never told can be;
For the gentle wind does move
Silently, invisibly.

I told my love, I told my love,
I told her all my heart,
Trembling, cold, in ghastly fears—
Ah, she doth depart.

Soon as she was gone from me
A traveller came by
Silently, invisible—
He took her with a sigh.

—William Blake.[1]

Adaptation studies as a discipline has opened up texts to critical examination, based on relationships of exchange between source and target texts. Despite a significant canon of methodologies, the fidelity approach still seems the dominant discourse when appraising adaptations. Some theorists have sanctioned more medium-specific approaches, such as Brian McFarlane and Sarah Cardwell.[2] Others, such as Linda Hutcheon and Julie Sanders argue that adaptations should be experienced *as adaptations*, therefore in direct comparison with their source texts.[3] On the Web, new forms of fanfic (where contributors adapt and appropriate aspects of popular film and television shows) are proving very popular, particularly with younger audiences and in some cases have led to amateur films being produced with relatively high production values. Some authors such as J. K. Rowling encourage this engagement with their work. All of this provides a rich wealth of material for the teacher wishing to explore this new terrain of adaptation studies, and beyond, with their students. Emerging forms of digital media have also provided new tools in enabling our students to be more independent.

This chapter is based on a case study where second-year Interactive Media Production, Scriptwriting for Film and Television, and Television Production undergraduates at Bournemouth University in the United Kingdom were asked to adapt William Blake's poem "Never Seek to Tell Thy Love" as a means of exploring medium-specific and comparative theories of adaptation. Almost all of the students concerned have studied English Literature and Language to Advanced Level (A-Level); this is a mandatory condition of entry for the Scriptwriting program. The students are generally aged between nineteen and twenty-four years, and have already studied narrative structures and theories of authorship in their first year. The adaptation course then is offered as a discrete elective in the second year and is generally taken by around sixty students who are divided into four seminar groups of fifteen each. The students will have already had an introduction to the theories of adaptation in their first year and so are well aware that most adaptation studies discourses focus on the relationship between literature and film. As Peter Reynolds writes, "The student is encouraged to recognise that meanings in novels are fluid and unstable, made and not given, and that their study may involve exploring parallel texts (such as paintings, film and television) without a dominant hierarchy that assumes literature as origin."[4] Even now, there is little work on other forms of adaptation, such as comic books and video games. Our course encourages students to apply adaptation theory to other media and explore these "parallel" texts as they occur elsewhere.

In my teaching, all the students are expected to keep a blog, where they reflect on their own learning and their own learning journeys. So, the blog effectively becomes a narrative in itself. However, with a lot of e-learning, or blended learning, there is a temptation to deterministically build in such activities just for the sake of it. In my teaching of adaptation theory, I use the blogs as a space where students carry out a number of tasks loosely defined by me, which act as the framework for the whole course of study. The trick here is not to be too prescriptive but at the same time to ground the student's own journey in clear debates about adaptation and to act as an arbiter of quality, as there are still clear learning outcomes for the students to meet so they can obtain the credits they need. The material generated in these exercises is incorporated into my own teaching, and the material is used to generate the content for subsequent sessions. This builds over a period until the students are providing 100 percent of the content for their own teaching.

In her book *Technology, Literacy and Learning* (2006) Carey Jewitt argues that e-learning can reinforce "traditional" relationships in the classroom.[5] In this instance, instead of writing theoretical papers, the students used their creative and production skills to interrogate theoretical ideas and to understand that adaptation can be seen as a form of *reception*. This focus on the process of adaptation—and the subsequent reflection on that process—becomes quite a sophisticated pedagogic tool with many possible applications. The array of different ideas and proposals generated in this exercise allows the students themselves to challenge ideas of supreme source texts and supreme authors on their own terms and drawing from their own experiences. As we shall see, such judgments originate from both the culture they have been exposed to and their previous and concurrent studies. When writing about such reader response criticism, Elizabeth Freund notes that "literary texts in general . . . constitute a reaction to contemporary situations, bringing attention to problems that are conditioned though not resolved by contemporary norms."[6]

As we shall see, the students' own adaptations are certainly significant texts in themselves, as they both respond to the "source" material of Blake's poem "Never Seek to Tell Thy Love" as well as important events in their own lives. Here I will argue that encouraging students to produce their own adaptations deepens their understanding of a subject and the theoretical matrix it occupies. For the adaptation scholar such student-centered texts can constitute a rich array of reader responses to set texts.

Most student-generated material seeks to "close the loop" between teaching and learning and forge a greater dialogue between theory and practice. In a sense the students end up writing their own lectures, over time, but through being directed—initially by me but, as the weeks develop, by each other—to some key readings and texts. Good teaching then is about discovery on the student's part, not in the "reveal" of the teaching. While Timothy Corrigan notes that, "in most discussions of adaptation, a key term is fidelity,"[7] Joy Gould Boyum correctly surmises that "adaptations themselves reflect very different notions of 'fidelity.'"[8] Robert Stam goes further by asking whether "strict fidelity is even possible."[9] These are the key ideas I want the students to unpack and critique, and one way of doing this is to problematize the whole notion of a "source" text. By doing this, I hope the students will themselves get close to Hutcheon's more plural definition of adaptation: "Like classical imitation, adaptation also is not slavish copying; it is a process of making the adapted material one's own."[10]

The students I teach are predominantly production students. They spend most of their time in creative activity. There is often a perception

among them that they always have to produce "original work" and that
adapting and repurposing existing material is somehow inferior to starting from scratch. So, there is a wider purpose here, through teaching adaptation studies, to get the students to challenge notions of "originality"
and privileged texts. This reflection on the process of adaptation can be
used to frame debates and discussions relevant elsewhere in the students'
studies. If used effectively as a pedagogic tool, this method can forge links
between hitherto perceived discreet units of study making for a much
more cohesive (and logical) educative experience.

THE INTERPRETATION

The first part of the task, which ran for two weeks, involved the students
writing in their blogs about what they thought the main themes expressed
in Blake's poem ("Never Seek to Tell Thy Love") were. This phenomeno-
logical approach allowed the students to problematize the whole notion
of a fixed "source" text, and this material was used in the formal teaching
sessions that ran alongside this task. The responses to Blake's poem were
very varied, as expected. The main reason for selecting such a poem was
initially for its polysemic potential:

> JOSH: While the male in the poem has confessed all his "heart," the female
> presence in the poem returns the gesture instead with an obvious display of
> "ghastly fears" suggesting that her feelings are quite contrary.

> TEX: A cautionary tale of love and loss with potentially supernatural under-
> tones.

> DAN: Maybe the person we should be paying attention to is the girl, who has
> suffered these incessant advances from a man that she feels nothing more
> than apathetic towards?

> CHARLOTTE: [Blake] is talking about how love is too great to be described and
> explained to someone.

> JENNIFER: Consequences of not taking risks . . . both want to take it further,
> but neither can pluck up the courage.

> CHARLI: A love that doesn't seem honest or right.

> ALAN: [Blake] is advising that people should never force love onto someone,
> or tell a person you love them just for sake of telling them; it must be said at
> the right time to ensure that person will feel the same.

Some of these responses to the poem privilege the author, which can
be seen as a consequence of the students' own education and experience; they live in the world of the "auteur," based on their experience

of the "authors" they studied in high school to the names of the film directors that emblazon the posters they have on their bedroom walls. There is a sense perhaps in the student that authorship is something of a received truth, but it's a truth that adaptation studies can challenge very effectively. In the adjacent online discussion forums that further supplemented the classroom discussions, students debated Michel Foucault's notion of "author function" and Roland Barthes's "death of the author/ birth of the reader" position, as well as more general ideas of "auteurism." The general consensus seemed to be that "originality" depended on a secure authorial voice.

Some of the students took a far more cynical view of the poem's themes and meanings:

> KATIE: [An] eerie presence within the poem . . . images of stalkers and pedophiles spring to mind!

And of course, there were more humorous ones:

> GEORGE: And then he takes her with a sigh—I think we all know what than means!
>
> COLIN: Don't tell someone you love about your weird perversions.
>
> KEVIN: He's very frustrated!

Some students read the poem as not being one single narrative, with one authorial voice, but rather as three different stories:

> MATEUSZ: Three mini-stories, each separate yet all . . . from a[n] overarching narrative.
>
> VYKKII: A slightly different part of the story in each verse.
>
> DEAN: First verse: paean to the ethereal and ephemeral qualities of love; second verse: warning of the ethereal and ephemeral qualities of love; third verse: lament for the ethereal and ephemeral qualities of love/time heals all wounds.

So here, the students are not only questioning the subject matter of the poem but also its structure, which must have a profound impact on any adaptation or reception of such an adaptation. It becomes clear in this stage of the course that the students' previous and concurrent learning has an impact—in this case their high school studies and the narrative and authorship theories they had engaged with in their first-year undergraduate work. While this is encouraging, it does perhaps highlight the often narrow focus of high school education.

So, this task serves to open up a text in a way perhaps not experienced by the students to date. Much A-Level teaching in the United Kingdom is "teaching by rote" and is fairly dictatorial and unimaginative. Students are encouraged to commit facts about the texts to memory, while writing essays in a particularly defined way. In this task, by opening up texts and locating the learning as an experiential process, the student gains confidence and begins to see the creativity inherent in application of theory to texts. The knowledge a student has gained previously or elsewhere can be revisited, recontextualized, and reapplied. Consequently, for the purposes of exploring the very idea of source texts, or originality, some students used adjunct material in their interpretations, drawing on Blake's own life and other works:

> FLAURA: Blake believed in the concept of "free love" and many of his other poems (e.g., *The Sick Rose*) reiterate this.

> EMMA: Blake . . . was well known for a few common themes: the innocence of children, the belief in free love, using nature to convey his ideas, and the firm belief we should not restrict our minds and creativity.

It was these last comments that provoked the most debate, as students began to question the fixity of source material in any adaptation, and again the notion of authorship. This allowed the students to explore Julie Sanders's view that "encouraged interplay between appropriations and their sources begins to emerge, then, as a fundamental, even vital, aspect of the reading or spectating experience, one productive of new meanings, applications and resonance."[11]

The students were beginning to understand the idea of multisourced texts, and most agreed at the end of this element of the activity that "a text could be adapted by fundamentally changing the original."[12] This served to prepare the students for the next task, which was to create their own adaptations of the poem.

THE ADAPTATIONS

The next task, which again ran for two weeks, was one where the students had to pitch their ideas for an adaptation based on Blake's poem. The brief was as follows:

> The BBC is celebrating seminal British poets and is commissioning work based on, or adapted from, key poems. Your poem is William Blake's "Never Seek to Tell Thy Love." Your task is to write a treatment (400 words maximum) for either a television program for BBC Two; a film for BBC Films/ BBC One; a documentary for BBC Four [the specialist culture channel] or a piece of interactive media/art for BBCi [BBC Interactive]. The best work will

be challenging, but at the same time will be grounded in *your* own interpretation of Blake's poem.

As expected, the students' adaptations were very varied. This serves to further highlight that no one adaptation is the same as another, as well as problematizing notions of definition and textual supremacy. Hutcheon notes that "an emphasis on process allows us to expand the traditional focus of adaptation studies on medium specificity and individual comparative case-studies in order to consider as well relations among the modes of engagement: that is, it permits us to think about how adaptations allow people to tell, show, or interact with stories."[13] In this activity I wanted to highlight the dialogue between an interpretation of a text and its subsequent adaptation, and I wanted the students to reflect on that *process*, as Hutcheon suggests, supported by Wolfgang Iser's view that the "reading process is a dynamic *interaction* [original italics] between text and reader."[14]

The following are the summaries of the treatments I took from the blogs and used in the teaching sessions. Interestingly, there were some attempts at fidelity versions:

JAMES: A short animation which illustrates Blake's poem in voiceover.

ROSANNA: An animation which uses the metaphor of the wind to illustrate the poem's love triangle.

KEVIN: A period piece set in the sixteenth century about a competition to win a lady's affections.

Some students went for a "period adaptation," and others overtly referenced other texts and adaptations in their interpretations, again drawing from their own educative and cultural experiences:

LUKE: A supernatural demonic serial killer is pursed through the underworld by . . . himself . . .—like *Jacob's Ladder/Underworld*.

DAN: Ellena Blake is hurtled into a parallel universe in the aftermath of 9/11. Can she prevent the 100 year war? A bit like *The Sarah Connor Chronicles*.[15]

FLAURA: Loosely based on real-life events, and the murder of Milly Dowler—a bit like *Boy A*.[16]

There were also some versions that depended on some element of interaction to "complete" the adaptation:

BEN: You are Death, and you have to piece together a dying woman's memories, and ultimately judge her. In the style of *Myst*.[17]

Other referents, or sources, came largely from other visual media, rather than from literature, and many students drew upon Guerric DeBona's view that, "as a general rule, those writing about film adaptation tend to think of the 'precursor' text in purely literary terms, not recognizing that every move is conditioned by a large set of influences from other media."[18]

Again, furthering the problematizing of source texts, some students drew upon references that sat outside the scope of the poem, often in the factual arena of current affairs:

> RICHARD: A Marine in Afghanistan sends a video message to his mother, the night before he is killed on patrol.
>
> DEAN: A young filmmaker receives an anonymous email which is a script based on Blake's poem, but set in Ceauşescu's Romania.

This last treatment generated some discussion in the online forums where some students seemed to automatically adopt a fidelity position by pointing out that there was no e-mail in Ceauşescu's reign (1965–1989). So, it seemed that license could be taken with the text, as Cartmell suggests,[19] but when using specific historical instances, the adaptation had to be faithful to the temporal and spatial context, if not the poem itself.

Some of the work critiqued theory, with one version explicitly exploring Roland Barthes's "readerly" and "writerly" texts:[20]

> PATRICK: An interactive version of the poem where people can upload their own interpretations, and adaptations, and can view/comment on each others. The public then become "authors."

Several students were of the view that new media had changed adaptation, and that was what they wanted to explore in their versions, a position that chimes with Stam's view that "the digital media have further undermined the notion of original and copy by making virtually everything 'copyable,' so that the language of 'originality' gives way to a language of cut 'n' mix and sampling."[21] So, there were several ideas for "dating" and relationship websites based on the poem and a raft of video game treatments that all had a romantic bittersweet narrative at their core.

REFLECTION

During the final two weeks, the students were asked to reflect on their own adaptations and the adaptations of their peers. Again, these comments were used as the primary content for the supporting lectures and seminars. The students had to draw upon adaptation theory to explore and critique their own work. The students were quick to start categorizing the work into different "types" of adaptation.

As well as the obvious fidelity versions (or attempts at ideas of "faithfulness" to a defined source), a popular tool was Geoffrey Wagner's (1975) three categories, with many students deciding that some of the adaptations were clearly offering a "commentary" on Blake's poem, as Sanders notes: "Adaptation is frequently involved in offering commentary on a source-text."[22] One such commentary was as Swpnil's idea of making a documentary where the philosopher Slavoj Žižek deconstructs each line of the poem, based on the 2005 documentary *Žižek!*[23] Colin's "complicated love-triangle, where one of the characters dies, another becomes an alcoholic and the other gets arrested for indecent assault" was thought to be an "analogous" adaptation by the other participants, again drawing on Wagner's rubric. Other analogous adaptations included this from Katie: "Existential narcissistic drama, where a man suffering from a multiple personality disorder falls in love over the web. But it's with his other personality. He kills himself." So, over the two weeks, in the blogs, and in the online discussion forums, some almost natural categories started to emerge, based on the adaptation theories the student had been reading. As well as the fidelity, commentary, and analogous adaptations, there were also "intertextual," "heteroglossic," and "participatory" adaptations. Some interesting arguments developed online and in the formal teaching sessions as to what constituted a heteroglossic or intertextual adaptation and whether or not they were the same thing. Also, some students claimed that their adaptations were "readerly" with others stating that all adaptations must be "readerly" in some way—therefore, all texts must be "readerly," and thus fidelity comparative positions are dishonest.

Many students wrote about the way in which their adaptation had altered the poem, citing Cardwell's view that adaptations can "rewire, review, reactivate and reconfigure" their source material.[24] One student even went as far as to state, "I predict that [this adaptation] has so much quality to it that I feel it threatens the poem and could become 'canon'" (William). This rather provocative view began a discussion that focused on the impact an adaptation could potentially have on the reputation of the adapted work, or source text, and its author(s). One student posted that she had not read Tom Wolfe's *The Bonfire of the Vanities* because she had found Brian De Palma's 1990 film adaptation so disappointing.[25] Others felt that adaptation served to enhance an author's status, with many commenting that the reason for Jane Austen's continuing popularity was entirely due to the Austen adaptation "industry."

A NEW FORM OF ADAPTATION STUDIES?

After six weeks of preparation and reflection, the students were set a two-thousand-word essay—the traditional method for assessment on undergraduate courses. However, in encountering the list of essay questions, the students realized they had already completed the research for their essay. I had set the questions myself, but I took my cue from the online discussions and often posed the same questions the students were asking themselves and each other. Most of them found they had already answered pretty much all the essay questions—often in great detail—in the blogs. This was especially true of an essay question that asked if an adaptation could damage or enhance an author's reputation or status, as this was a popular thread. This was a deliberate design of the course as often the essay is seen as the end or "exit point" by both teachers and students. Here it is much more part of the dialogue of learning, and the essay questions were designed to respond to students, not the other way around, which is often the case.

This reinforces the more traditional aspects of teaching and makes student participation and response central to the understanding of the subject. The students naturally dig deep into the literature to find support for their *own* creative work, rather than to find support for writing an essay. This I would argue is a far more meaningful way of teaching and one that facilitates a far deeper understanding of a topic. This teaching, then, grounded adaptation studies in a more relevant context for today's students and ultimately led to a more fruitful, enjoyable, and critically productive experience than other forms of more directed study. As Iser suggests, "The reader's enjoyment begins when he himself becomes productive."[26]

However, beyond pedagogy, I would also suggest that these methods have something to offer adaptation studies and scholarship too. Here, then, adaptation is situated as a form of reception. These tasks can be read as reader responses to Blake's poem. As Freund discusses, there has been the perception that the "text" is in a privileged position, surround by the "universe," the "artist," and the "audience." She argues that any focus on the reader can look as if it is decentering the authority of the text.[27] I would suggest that this is no bad thing, and the approach outlined in this chapter perhaps offers a more plural way of understanding the relationship between different media and the texts that are the result of that relationship; therefore, this position does not privilege one text, or one media, over another.

Through these adaptations, we can see how Blake's poem can be received and interpreted by different audiences, as for Claude Lévi-Strauss: "The function of repetition is to render the structure of the myth apparent."[28] Also, by its very nature, this exercise imbues a text—in this case

"Never Seek to Tell Thy Love"—with what Walter Benjamin calls an "afterlife": "An adaptation is not vampiric: it does not draw the life-blood from its source and leave it dying or dead, nor is it paler than the adapted work. It may, on the contrary, keep that prior work alive, giving it an afterlife it would never have had otherwise."[29]

Over the six-week course, the students applied a range of methodologies in critically examining their own and each other's work. Questions were posed throughout the period, asking the students if their treatments should be compared to other adaptations (as argues Cardwell);[30] if their adaptations are dependent on a prior knowledge of the source material (Hutcheon[31] and Sanders[32]); if these adaptations highlighted mutual dependencies between media (Corrigan[33]); or if their interpretations stood as autonomous works of art. More significantly, the students discovered that adaptation can be seen as a response to a text where the reader becomes the writer. It also shows that there are no preferred readings of any text. Just as reading any fan fiction (fanfic) on the Web can tell us much about the reception of film and television programs, allowing students to create their own adaptations can tell teachers how texts are received and interpreted. Adaptation furthers our understanding of a text, and a focus on process serves to illuminate this. Encouraging the students to reflect and document that process furthers this understanding and allows them to learn much about adaptation, literature, television, and new media as "fundamental to the practice, and indeed, to the enjoyment of literature."[34] I would suggest here that the enjoyment of all texts depends on this dynamic dialogue between texts and the continual process of repetition and repurposing, a process artificially replicated over a six-week period by second-year media undergraduates.

Finally, as a pedagogic tool, this method can be extended into other subject areas: reconstituting literary and other texts for a new application and then reflecting on that process is a very effective way of teaching. Online exercises foster team building and expose participants to the type of dialogue and debate that some never experience, especially if they are apprehensive of more "traditional" forms of classroom interaction. Using the students' own examples and experiences as part of formal teaching also builds confidence on the part of the students, and over time the students will learn far more from each other than from the teacher. So, here the teacher acts as a guide and facilitator, and no more.

The combination of e-learning and experiential learning, coupled with the framing device of more traditional classroom-based practices can foster a host of transferable skills that students will take with them through their educational lives into their working lives, but on a personal note, I also hope they will retain a disdain for the perceived supremacy of one text, form, or media over another.

EPILOGUE

When I told my students I was "adapting" their adaptations for this chapter, they were amused to say the least and immediately pointed me toward Sarah Cardwell's work again: "It would be more accurate to view adaptation as the gradual development of a 'meta-text.' This view recognizes that a later adaptation may draw upon any earlier adaptations, as well as upon the primary source text."[35] The following year, some students continued their dialogue with texts by attempting to produce adaptations of their own. One student, Chris, made a Flash animation adaptation of the Stephen King novel *The Running Man*. His reason for doing so was that he found the 1987 filmed version, directed by Paul Michael Glaser, disappointing. In his accompanying reflective analysis, Chris stated that his animation was more of a "commentary" on the 1987 adaptation than a straight attempt at fidelity to the original novel.

With thanks to second-year students on the 2006–2007 and 2006–2008 Adaptation course at the Media School, Bournemouth University, UK. Special thanks also to Chris Leinster and Chris Wensley.

NOTES

1. William Blake, *Selected Poems* (London: Wordsworth, 2000).

2. Brian McFarlane, *Novel to Film: An Introduction to the Theory of Adaptation* (Oxford, UK: Clarendon Press, 1996); Sarah Cardwell, *Adaptation Revisited: Television and the Classic Novel* (Manchester, N.Y.: Manchester University Press, 2002).

3. Linda Hutcheon, *A Theory of Adaptation* (London: Routledge, 2006); Julie Sanders, *Adaptation and Appropriation* (London: Routledge, 2006).

4. Peter Reynolds, *Novel Images: Literature in Performance* (London: Routledge, 1993), 2–3.

5. Carey Jewitt, *Technology, Literacy and Learning: A Multimodal Approach* (London: Routledge, 2006), 158.

6. Elizabeth Freund, *Return of the Reader: Reader Response Criticism* (London: Methuen, 1987), 146.

7. Timothy Corrigan, *Film and Literature: An Introduction and Reader* (Boston: Prentice Hall, 1999), 20.

8. Joy Gould Boyum, *Double Exposure: Fiction into Film* (New York: Plume Books, 1985), 68.

9. Robert Stam, *Literature through Film: Realism, Magic and the Art of Adaptation* (Malden, Mass.: Blackwell, 2005), 3.

10. Hutcheon, *A Theory of Adaptation*, 20.

11. Sanders, *Adaptation and Appropriation*, 32.

12. Deborah Cartmell, "Screen to Text," in *Adaptations: From Text to Screen, Screen to Text*, ed. Deborah Cartmell and Imelda Whelehan, 143–45 (London: Routledge, 1999), 145.

13. Hutcheon, *A Theory of Adaptation*, 22.

14. Wolfgang Iser, *The Act of Reading: A Theory of Aesthetic Response* (Baltimore: Johns Hopkins University Press, 1978), 107.

15. *Terminator: The Sarah Connor Chronicles* [2008–2009], Dir. Various, Perf. Lena Headey, Thomas Dekker, Summer Glau (DVD B000T9OP7G: Warner Home Video, the Complete First Season, 2008).

16. *Boy A* [2007], Dir. John Crowley, Perf. Andrew Garfield, Alfie Owen (DVD B001CDFY6Y: Miriam Collection, 2008).

17. A series of adventure games beginning in 1993.

18. Guerric DeBona, "Dickens, the Depression and MGM's *David Copperfield*," in *Film Adaptation*, ed. James Naremore, 106–28 (London: Athlone Press, 2000), 114.

19. Cartmell, "Screen to Text," 145.

20. Roland Barthes, *S/Z*, trans. Richard Miller (Oxford, UK: Blackwell, 1974), 4.

21. Robert Stam, "Introduction: The Theory and Practice of Adaptation," in *Literature and Film: A Guide to the Theory and Practice of Film Adaptation*, ed. Robert Stam and Alessandra Raengo (Malden, Mass.: Blackwell, 2005), 12.

22. Sanders, *Adaptation and Appropriation*, 18.

23. *Žižek!* [2005], Dir. Astra Taylor, Perf. Slavoj Žižek (DVD B000FII32Y: Zeitgeist Films, 2006).

24. Cardwell, *Adaptation Revisited*, 205.

25. *Bonfire of the Vanities* [1990], Dir. Brian De Palma, Perf. Tom Hanks, Bruce Willis, Melanie Griffith (DVD B00004VYLV: Warner Home Video, 2000).

26. Iser, *The Act of Reading*, 108.

27. Freund, *Return of the Reader*, 5.

28. Claude Lévi-Strauss, *Structural Anthropology*, trans. Claire Jacobson and Brooke Grundfest Schoepf (Harmondsworth, UK: Penguin, 1972), 229.

29. Walter Benjamin, *Illuminations*, trans. Harry Zohn (London: Pimlico, 1999), 67.

30. Cardwell, *Adaptation Revisited*, 25.

31. Hutcheon, *A Theory of Adaptation*, 6.

32. Sanders, *Adaptation and Appropriation*, 26.

33. Corrigan, *Film and Literature*, 1.

34. Sanders, *Adaptation and Appropriation*, 1.

35. Cardwell, *Adaptation Revisited*, 25.

FOUR

ADAPTATION AND CREATIVE WRITING

Brokeback Mountain on the London Underground

Mark O'Thomas

Adaptation has much in common with creative writing. Both processes, like their kindred sister translation, necessitate a reviewing and appraising of past events, and past texts, through an engagement with those events and texts in a manner which Gillian Bolton has called *reflective practice*, where critical reflection through the process of creative writing allows us to enter "a process of laying open to question our own and others' daily actions."[1] If we want students of adaptation studies to gain knowledge of the field, then it might be more pedagogically appropriate to begin to think about adopting a traditional art school approach—to teaching the theory *through* the practice—a kind of practice-based research methodology that has become popular on a range of arts-based disciplines in master's and doctoral programs in the United Kingdom. Jon Cook has written about the emergence of practice-based research methodologies with particular reference to creative writing, where he alludes to the irony that creativity has historically been seen in opposition to rather than a product of method.[2] For Cook, the answer to tensions between creativity and method or other juxtapositions such as "craft" and "technique," lies in the essential force of rewriting in literature. Writing, then, is a means of discovery—a journey of recollection and revelation—which, like adaptation itself, is at the same time always open to new interpretations and meanings.

If there is a strong case for creative writing to have a methodological presence in the teaching of adaptation studies, then there is an equal case to be made for adaptation to be taught in creative writing. Adaptation, in its exploration of concepts such as originality, its challenge to authorial intention and authenticity, and its problematizing of a privileging based on anteriority, provides a blueprint for writers to try out new projects offering possibilities of structure and content, and theme and style, that can be selected or rejected at whim. The supposed dualistic binary of creativity striving against the immutable forces of constraint conflates into possibility, offering students of writing props if and only when they might be needed. And of course quite simply, now that we have arrived out of a postmodern age in all its deconstructive, postfeminist, poststructuralist pluralities, it is almost a self-evident act of candor to declare that *all* creative writing is essentially adaptation.

Adaptation constitutes a whole course of study within the wider framework of the Creative Writing master's degree at the University of East London, an interdisciplinary program for poets, playwrights, screenwriters, and fiction writers. Indeed, the nature of the program being so wide, crossing genres and forms, makes the study of adaptation even further appropriate as it not only allows scope to develop a particular discipline but also necessitates an attention on an other. Students who embark on the adaptation course (a compulsory module for all creative writing students) begin their first session with two activities that they then pursue throughout the whole semester: an individual adaptation of their own choice and a collective adaptation to which everyone in the group will contribute. Writing can be a lonely, solitary activity, and a central purpose of creative writing programs is to throw some light on the dark corners of despondence when writers write but have no sense of what to do or what to say next. Critical feedback from others, guided by a staff of resident professional writers, is crucial for students to progress, and the collective adaptation exercise offers a unique opportunity for students to hone skills in adaptation by actively reflecting on their work and that of others in an ongoing way. As the weeks go by and further insights are gained through the study of canonical adaptations as well as key adaptation theorists, so too the work develops hermeneutically, constantly evolving.

One of the less-studied couplings in an area that has been dominated by the novel's transformation into film is that of the cinematic adaptations of short stories. Short stories in many ways upset the traditional notion that a film adaptation must always be somehow a poorer relation to its literary source, since any feature-length film version of a short story will always need to extemporize, improvise, and generally provide greater depth to the (shorter) story. The Taiwanese film director Ang Lee has shown considerable skill in tackling this particular hybrid of adaptation, and his two adaptations *Brokeback Mountain* (2005) and *Lust, Caution* (2007) as well as their literary sources are all standard texts on the East London Creative

Writing MA program, where the former was chosen last year (2008) as the group's collective adaptation.

Setting the task of a group adaptation is by necessity a prescriptive activity. At the outset, parameters need to be clarified and established in order for learning to be successful. An absence of drawing such lines in the sand would make a group adaptation a difficult exercise, wherein competing needs and agenda might collide in a structureless vacuum. From the beginning of the activity, the 2008 cohort of students was told what the adaptation would be—*Brokeback Mountain*—and what form it would initially take. These parameters—which might also be thought of as constraints—allow for immense freedom and play, and in many senses echo the many constraints placed on writers working in the "adaptation industry" itself.

Studying adaptation *through* adaptation, and in this case *Brokeback Mountain*, immediately problematizes one of its core precepts—the original/copy binary. For most students, *Brokeback Mountain* is synonymous with Lee's film of the same name rather than Annie Proulx's short story, whose first outing appeared on the pages of the *New Yorker* in 1997. When addressing the question of how to adapt it once again, we have to go back to the *what*: are we adapting the film text or the short story text, or both? While adaptation as a creative writing exercise appears to offer structure, theme, and content when needed, it also reveals how flimsy and ephemeral texts are—there are no "standard wholes" to use Dudley Andrew's phrase in a world where every text is inextricably linked with another.[3] In the event, Proulx's short story, Lee's film, and Larry McMurtry and Diana Ossana's screenplay all served as textual sources for the group's adaptation, as well as the contextual essays by the writer and screenwriters reflecting on the adaptation process.[4] The problematical nature of "authorship" and its dubious status immediately became apparent for the students, who could not decide initially (even in the case of the film text) whether it was Ang Lee's text, McMurtry and Ossana's, Proulx's, or our own as readers of these texts. In this way, the urgent need to declare the source(s) dead in order give birth to the group adaptation validated both Roland Barthes's assertion of the reader, and Michel Foucault's questioning of what exactly it is that constitutes "authorship."[5]

Brokeback Mountain, story and film, deals with the relationship between two men, Ennis Del Mar and Jack Twist, whose intimate friendship spans decades and sees them each try to come to terms with living heterosexual lives, despite their repressed desire to be together. The story is set in Middle America in 1963, and while clearly much of its content relates to the two decades that take it to its end, its themes of closeted bisexuality and societal prejudice resonate with life in the twenty-first century. In looking at the issue of (re-)adapting this story, the issue of time and place was central. Students discussed a variety of options, but working on the premise that "what you know is what you should write," they decided to set the adaptation in London over a period of time that would start from now and project itself into the future. Instead of two young American guys looking for work in 1963, then, the students worked on creating an Ennis Del Mar and a Jack Twist (the story's two main characters) who were of school leaving age.

Group writing is a complex exercise, and so it was important for me as the tutor of the class to impose a structural framework in order to facilitate the task, something I did by using the technological solution of electronic mail. I created two e-mail addresses—one for Jack Twist and one for Ennis Del Mar—and gave the students in the class the log-ins and passwords for both of these addresses. The idea was that we would create an e-mail exchange between our two characters, which would be completely anonymous—no one in the group would know who was writing as one of the characters, nor who was replying. In this way, the writing would grow organically, and although everyone knew what the ultimate arc of the story would be, there was huge scope to improvise within that structure. The adaptation grew slowly at first, as students were hesitant about committing their words to something that would inevitably impact the whole. Once e-mails were sent, they were not allowed to be changed (at this stage); this encouraged an immediacy of response. E-mail exchanges and mobile phone text messages operate their own kind of language that can seem insignificant, flippant, and ultimately disposable. Working in this form encouraged students to take on aspects of this form but also, as writers and adapters, to objectify their words and see them within a wider framework, outside of the everyday and the commonplace.

Like the short story, the students' adaptation began with the Del Mar/ Twist relationship already an established fact; the e-mailed texts were constructed as confessionals:

From: "jack twist"
To: "Ennis Del Mar"
Subject: Re: Underground
Date: Tue, 1 Oct 2008 03:42:40 -0500

Dear Ennis,

Today, there was a security alert on the Underground. I was trapped on a train for over an hour, stuck in a tunnel. I ain't ever felt so scared in all my days. My heart was pounding. I wanted to sit down but it was choca full. I closed my eyes and kept counting: by the time I get to 100 the train will start to move. Like magic. Only the magic ain't working. Do you ever feel stuck like that?

JT

From: "Ennis Del Mar"
To: "jack twist"
Subject: Re: Underground
Date: Sun, 12 Oct 2008 15:01:01 -0500

hola jack, I'm glad u emailed coz i wasn't sure if u would after last time. i thought about what u said, about splitting and stuff but i don't know. we can meet on friday. over where we normally go? The underground story sounds like shit. i hate it anyway, you know now with all them terrorists stories. i don't know, feeling stuck . . . maybe that's just what all of it is about. and nothing else happens. i mean i don't know but like u says magic ain't working. maybe coz when u get born and u ain't lucky that's just the way it is. maybe we should run away to Spain and work in a bar and eat fish and stuff. i mean by the sea? friday, right? email me. E.

Spain, in this adaptation becomes synonymous with the mountain of the original story and film—both a place and a moment in the lives of the two characters, when for a short while they could really be who they wanted to be. As such, it becomes a motif in the text and a common reference point that alludes to the eternally elusive—*what might have been but was never meant to be*—that continues to express for many young men and women the prevailing gay experience of life.

From: "jack twist"
To: "Ennis Del Mar"
Subject: Re:
Date: Thu, 20 Nov 2008 04:37:00 -0500

COME ON DELMAR . . . I need to see ya! Its been 7 months now since Spain. How's the tattoo? Mine's been weeping pus for a while maybe the razor wasn't clean, Man it hurt but I like it. Bin asked loads about it but I ain't saying nuffin. I started that new job up central, working with homeless guys. Boy some of them have it well rough out there but they are FREE . . . I ENVY THAT. Hey if they wanna take a dump guess wot they do: they line their trouser wiv newspaper, squat down and shit . . . then take the paper out n stick it in a street bin . . . clever eh! HEY MAN I NEED TO SEE YA BIG TIME, SOON, TODAY, NOW . . . What the fuck ya bin doing anyway? I can't live on texts n emails . . .

JACK

To: "jack twist" (jacktwist@london.com)
CC:
Subject: Re: easy
Date: Thu, 20 Feb 2010 11:21:53 -0500

Jack

I can't always get online now I'm living at her's . . . plus with looking
for work still. My Tats cool . . . my girlfriends pissed about it wonders
what it means n why I disappeared that week! Listen, she's pregnant!
Thats somefin I've always wanted: A KID!

nuffin changes between us tho, u know what I SAID IN SPAIN—IT
HOLDS!

I guess living rough has its good point. FREEDOM as u say! The night
sky your ceiling eh n shitting in newspapers . . . your anonymous tho,
no-one looks at u, they see right thru ya and no one gives a fuck who
you fuck either! I ain't gay I just happen to —— you. Make what u want
of the —— but it's all good. I woke up the ova night with a big grin
on my face, can't remember details but it was you n me in that hotel
squashed up in that bath, n water was just pouring out on the floor but
we were just shrieking and mucking around like we did. Thank god for
dreams, now there's freedom there too . . . just wish I could program
my brain to play it every night, like it was real . . . I even had a boner
to die for . . . SOON JT but can't say when . . . BE SAFE, DREAM . . .
I'll be there.

EDM

As the relationship develops over its inevitable course, the original trajectory is paralleled with events affecting the twenty-first-century coupling.
However, the joy of this kind of collaborative but anonymous writing
exercise is the ability of students to surprise each other (and themselves),
enabling the writing to take unexpected turns. One such turn took place
when this entry appeared in the e-mail chain:

From: "Ennis Del Mar"
To: jacktwist@london.com
Subject: Hello Jack
Date: Sat, 29 Nov 2010 15:01:12 -0500

Jack I'm Ennis' GIRLFRIEND . . . I just want you to FUCK OFF n DIE
. . . He ain't a PERVERT like you . . . he's just confused and he don't
need this shit! I've read your messages and can see ITS ALL YOU . . .
BEGGING HIM FOR SEX!! He's straight ya know . . . NOT GAY! He's

told you that in his email (I ain't no faggot) so just leave us the fuck alone. He don't know I'm sending this cos the idiot forgot to log off and I've SEEN IT ALL. I ain't telling him that I know either cos of the baby BUT IF YOU HAVE ANY CARE FOR HIM AND HIS FUTURE (his family would KILL him if they found out, one of his brothers has DONE TIME for assault on a gay man in Hoxton two years ago . . . the man is permanently scarred and blind in one eye) This ain't no joke so I BEG YOU PLEASE . . . find some one else, there's plenty out there nowadays but not MY ENNIS.

While playing outside the "rules" of the formal duologue structure that was set up in the beginning, this entry reveals a radical ability to seize the adaptive form and improvise with it, privileging the reader who now begins to see the story not from two but three sides. The ability of an adaptation to take on its own life, then, apart from its original source, even in what is a rather contrived creative writing exercise, is something that students experienced firsthand where their learning was guided and supported by their peers rather than imposed from above. The final entry in the e-mail exchange projects itself eight years in the future from its original starting point in 2008, and shows much of the anguish and injustice invoked by both the story and film originals:

From: "Ennis Del Mar"
To: jacktwist@london.com
Subject: Hope ya get email up there!
Date: 15th Mar 2016 11:21:53 -0500

Jack Twisted fucking Delmar . . .

When you died that summer I wanted to kill someone . . . I did find a face that I thought could be the one . . . down by the river and I just let rip . . . then I legged it after, and as I ran I felt sweet . . . "THIS IS FOR YOU JACK," kept going round and round in my brain . . . I went to the heath a few days after and saw all them flowers for you and ugly police tape and I couldn't leave, I sat there all day remembering, drinking . . . shit it was weird cos THAT WAS ONE OF THE WORST and BEST DAYS . . .

Jack . . . .WHY? why did they do this to YOU? I can't believe that you were on the heath that night . . . you know wot goes on there for fuck's sake! If you'd a just come down like I said you fucking be ALIVE man . . . CRUISING?!! ya didn't need to go so far . . . they really fucked ya up didn't they, your teeth n they were GREAT teeth knocked out, your head caved in BY A ROCK . . . JACK WHY? I left something there for

ya . . . did ya get it? Its buried a little but if ya dig down you'll find
two pebbles from that beach in spain . . . yeah I always kept em in my
pocket man one black n shiny the other speckled and rough: like you n
me . . . hey maybe now were HITCHED like ya wanted . . . Hope you at
peace man!! I MADE A CHOICE THAT DAY . . . I ain't ever gonna lose
my self again . . . so I'm up here in Glasgow, volunteering working wiv
alcoholics, got a room and Samson stays at weekends . . . it's sweet and
MAN DO I DREAM at night like I used now I'm off that liquid cosh shit
n NO ONE CAN TAKE THAT FROM ME . . . see ya tonight, JACK, don't
forget the beer and I won't forget my PACK of cards . . . Laters man x

Ennis Twisted fucking Delmar

Annie Proulx has written about the experience of "getting movied," in an
unusually positive way for a fiction writer whose work is adapted onto
film. Proulx is both excited and invigorated by the process where, rather
than diminishing her short story, the screenwriters managed to augment
it, "adding new flesh to its long bones, filling out the personalities, introducing a little humor and new characters who moved the story along its
close-set rails."[6] Indeed, this is perhaps not so surprising in that Ang Lee's
film sits so close to the original, far more in fact than even his Chinese-
language adaptation of the Eileen Chang short story *Lust, Caution*.[7] Ang
Lee's adaptation of *Brokeback Mountain* is one that seeks to clarify and
embellish the original; it is in many senses an *ideal* adaptation in the ideal
envisioned by many readers of novels who seek out adaptation as the
cinematic realization of their reading. The students' adaptation, however,
began to problematize these seemingly benign issues, which are generally
labeled under the rubric of *fidelity* in adaptation studies, since the starting
point for their adaptation was that the story would be set elsewhere in
time and space from its original(s). The notion that fidelity (which usually means *anteriority*)[8] is a primary goal and measure of an adaptation
became a point of debate, whose solution resided in the firsthand experience of engaging in the process of adaptation rather than focusing on the
habitual comparing and contrasting of sources and targets—the common
methodological practice of both translation and adaptation studies.

   The novel's transformation into film remains the dominant area of
study in the discipline of adaptation studies, which possesses the potential to be much wider in its scope than this comparatively narrow focus,[9]
responding to new media forms offered by new technologies such as
video games. The students' adaptation—a kind of creative online e-mail
game—exploited this technology in new and exciting ways, enabling
them to reflect on a much broader sense of adaptation beyond the novel/
film binary as well as a practical interrogation of the question of what
actually constitutes an adaptation in the first place. But further still, the

online text created by the students lived on and got adapted further as a piece of theater performed by two acting students. This further adaptation involved a certain amount of rewriting of the collective material, as well as its dramatization onto the stage through paratextual additions such as stage directions and sound and lighting effects. *Medium specificity*, then, became a term that was not only studied in relation to adaptation theory that has heralded it as its primary directive but also contextualized in an ever-evolving adaptation framed by and for the students themselves.[10]

Writing inevitably means rewriting, redrafting, looking again at the words, and reforming them with new insights. The final draft of both the students' online adaptation and its eventual staged version went through several rewrites as they became honed into their new incarnations. This is what makes the practice of writing as a method for learning essentially reflective in nature, and one that makes it a way of teaching adaptation theory that is immediate, relevant, and creative.[11]

NOTES

1. Gillian Bolton, *Reflective Practice: Writing and Professional Development* (London: Paul Chapman, 2001), 33.

2. Jon Cook, "Creative Writing as a Research Method," in *Research Methods for English Studies*, ed. Gabriele Griffin, 179–97 (Edinburgh: Edinburgh University Press, 2005), 195.

3. Dudley Andrew, *Concepts in Film Theory* (Oxford: Oxford University Press, 1984), 97.

4. See Annie Proulx, Larry McMurtry, and Diana Ossana (eds.), *Brokeback Mountain: Story to Screenplay* (New York: Scribner's, 2005), passim.

5. Roland Barthes, "The Death of the Author," trans. Stephen Heath, in *Image, Music, Text* (New York: Hill and Wang, 1977), 142–48; Michel Foucault, "What Is an Author?" in *Reading Architectural History: An Annotated Anthology*, ed. Dana Arnold (London: Routledge, 2002), 71–81.

6. Annie Proulx, "Getting Movied," in *Brokeback Mountain: Story to Screenplay*, ed. Annie Proulx, Larry McMurtry, and Diana Ossana, 129–38 (New York: Scribners, 2005), 134.

7. Eileen Chang, *Lust, Caution* (London: Penguin, 2007).

8. Thomas Leitch, "Twelve Fallacies in Contemporary Adaptation Theory," *Criticism* 45, no. 2 (2005): 162.

9. Linda Hutcheon, *A Theory of Adaptation* (London: Routledge, 2006), 118.

10. See George Bluestone, *Novels into Film* (Berkeley: University of California Press, 1957).

11. The MA students' adaptation of *Brokeback Mountain* can be accessed online at www.uel.ac.uk/writing/projects/underground.htm.

FIVE

PEDAGOGY AND POLICY IN INTERMEDIAL ADAPTATIONS

Freda Chapple

> The subject who knows, the objects to be known and the modalities of knowledge must be regarded as so many effects of [the] fundamental implications of power-knowledge and their historical transformations. In short it is not the activity of the subject of knowledge that produces a corpus of knowledge, useful or resistant to power, but power-knowledge, the processes and struggles that traverse it, and of which it is made up that determines the forms and possible domains of knowledge.[1]

My approach to the pedagogies of adaptation in the arts and humanities is informed by the field of intermediality where the learning processes are centered on the student's critical and creative exploration about and within mediality in the arts and humanities. My understanding of the field of adaptation studies is that the core of its work is an exploration of the processes of change that happen as one or more cultural artifacts move across medial and disciplinary boundaries to inhabit the space of another; and in that process, previously discrete boundaries become porous as the new artifact inhabits the space in-between media, disciplines, and art forms—traditional and contemporary. The effect of the production of new cultural artifacts through the processes of adaptation from one medium—whether that medium be literature, film, television, theater, or digital media—is to produce an intertextual, polyphonic, intermedial weave that is created by artist of many kinds, whether they be authors, playwrights, film directors, musicians, actors, or technicians, and completed for "a moment in time" by us as we receive and respond to that creation. We are part of the process. Any work of art, whether it is in the written, spoken, musical, or image medium, requires the perception of the minds and bodies of the receiver to produce a meaning that matters to them in response to the artist's intermedial weave. Although I have been enlightened, enlivened, and interested in recent debates about adaptation, I have also been slightly puzzled, simply because I have always seen adaptation as an intermedial exchange that is not a linear movement—for me it is an intermedial network structure that operates like the structure of digital media in an interactive way to create new perceptions—and because it crosses disciplinary and medial boundaries, so it adds to knowledge creation. Adaptation in the arts, for me, is an intermedial form that needs the medium of the bodies and minds of receivers to complete it: it is a poststructural, postmodern chain linking together interdisciplinary, intertextual, intercultural, and intermedial fields of knowledge. This belief guides my pedagogical approach—not just to texts that have been formally adapted and therefore announce their presence as *adaptations* but also to all forms operative in the arts.

Because "teaching and learning styles strongly influence the curriculum and in practice they cannot be divorced from it,"[2] an examination of the *pedagogies of adaptation* needs to be related to the changing content and form of the curriculum (what should be taught to learners and how it is organized); the changing curriculum pedagogies (how the content of the curriculum is delivered, taught and communicated); and the curriculum assessment (what aspects of the learning are formally tested and measured and how it is done).[3] Therefore, the chapter draws on my personal experience of designing and teaching an undergraduate program of higher education in the United Kingdom that examines the relationship between literature, theater, film, and digital media and the student responses to their study, which is revealed via extracts from a recently completed questionnaire. Under discussion are the pedagogies of the BA (Honors) English Studies and Performing Arts (ESPA) at the University of Sheffield; its recently renamed younger version, the BA (Honors) Literature and Creative Media (LCM); and associated certificates in Creative Writing and Music and Creative Media. The degrees and related certificates aim to provide an academic enquiry into the relationship of English literature to the performing arts of theater, music, art, photography, and film; analyze the relationship of literature to the performing arts within a historical and cultural context; examine the process of creative activities related to the disciplines of English literature and the performing arts: reading, writing, performing, listening, and looking; set the examination of the processes within the context of the contemporary academic theoretical framework; examine how the processes of reading, writing, performing, listening, and looking might be changing with the growth of the new technologies; and provide the opportunity for employment or future study within English literature and the performing arts. Here, I suggest, is a skills and knowledge field pertinent to scholars of adaptation studies, which could also be described as a contemporary curriculum for English studies. At the center of this discussion is the students' analysis of the intermedial elements of adaptation and their own practice of creative writing and performance skills in theater, music, and digital media.

The theoretical framework of the chapter is provided by the insights of Foucault, which seems to be appropriate, given that the curriculum as a whole is a political as well as a cultural product in higher education. How we teach (as well as what we teach) is a political as well as an institutional matter, and this affects academics: we, too, are part of the process. Therefore the chapter concludes with a short reflection on the intermedial position of lecturers who teach in higher education institutions in the United Kingdom, which continue, by and large, to promote discrete forms of disciplinary study.

As far as I am aware, adaptation studies has not yet become recognized as an undergraduate degree; however, at the modular level, courses such as Literature into Film, for example, are found readily in the postgraduate and undergraduate curriculum: "Modules on higher education programmes, which examine the transition of literature into film, are fairly common these days, and any student engaged in such work is implicitly, if not explicitly studying adaptation, thinking critically about what it means to adapt or appropriate."[4] Thinking critically about the affect of the adaptation or appropriation of one medium to another positions us *in-between* media and thereby enables us to inhabit a philosophical terrain that lies, I believe, at the heart of adaptation in the humanities. However, this process is often subverted by the ways in which modules are positioned within an institutional curriculum, something that reflects external influences as well as individual academic staff research interests:

Change in the knowledge fields—and in the curriculum—took three main forms. First, *the structure of the knowledge field might itself be taking a new shape.* . . . However, the established disciplines, too, have dynamic structure that is expressing itself in the curriculum. . . . The humanities find a dynamic internal to knowledge as such: history, for example, has become more sociological in character. Secondly, new topics emerge *within* knowledge fields. Women's history has emerged with history; media technology has entered electronic engineering . . . what is striking, particularly in the science-based and technological fields, is how temporary some of the movements might be: . . . what was felt worthy of study today may be felt not to yield profitable skills and knowledge tomorrow. Thirdly, *new techniques and new forms of realisation emerge within knowledge fields.* Computers are to be found in the developing epistemological structure of all of the knowledge fields we looked at, but not yet central outside of the science and technological domains.[5]

From this, we may take the idea that adaptation is part of a constantly changing curriculum and/or field of knowledge, where the humanities are seen to have dynamic internal movements. Such changes are part and parcel of the dynamic process of knowledge building, which is, as Ronald Barnett and his colleagues suggest, constantly evolving and adapting. Therefore, as a next step, I would like to suggest a conceptualization of *the pedagogies of adaptation* as an intermedial, interactive structure of relationships that operate in-between subject areas, disciplines, faculties, and fields of knowledge in the arts and humanities; which connect interactively with the social sciences, science, and engineering; and which can be considered within the structures of British government educational policy and practice.

This model places the student and the teacher in an intermedial, interactive position as they engage with material that crosses and merges medial, textual, and institutional boundaries. Placing students at the center of a creative and critical exploration of adaptation of literature, theater, film, music, and digital media enables them to adapt their views of the

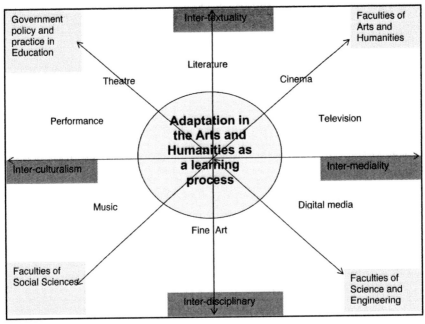

Diagram 5.1

political, social, and educational frameworks they inhabit and to create opportunities to find their own voices in response. Adaptation becomes, in this process, an active change in the learner's perspective:

> I think that the degree enabled me to orientate myself in society; being able to study, through texts, the political forces at work has given me an understanding of how those forces impact on the individual (i.e., myself). In addition, I guess that inevitably you compare your own life with those who make literature and the arts and the characters within literature and the arts. This enables you to appreciate the sacrifices people make and the effort they put in to their lives and compare them to your own. This opens up new avenues and pathways for your own life and you can weigh up the effort and commitments required and decide whether it is right for you.[6]

PEDAGOGIES OF INTERMEDIAL ADAPTATION— LEVEL 1: SKILLS MODULES

Building Block 1: Words, Sounds, and Images Module

In the first section of the *words, sounds, and images* core module of the degree, students are introduced to the language of literature through

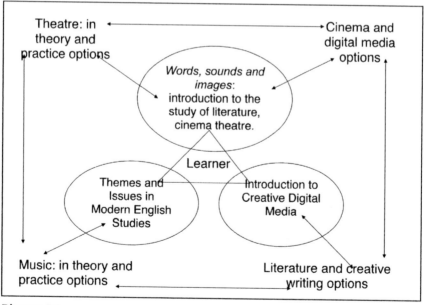

Diagram 5.2

language awareness games, followed by an introduction to Saussure and the sign system through the close analysis of selected extract material. The extract material of poems and prose provided for analysis are very short and do not have any author information available to the students, so they learn how to recognize the impact of sounds, rhythms, and images embedded in the texts through basic phonetic interpretation and the twin concepts of denotation and connotation. The language of the literature section culminates in close textual analysis of narrative perspectives—notably the omniscient narrator, the first-person narrator, and the internally inscribed narrator. The second section of the same module focuses on the language of film, where students learn to replace the author with the camera lens and interpret the *mise-en-scène* through the shot; the relationship of the shot to editing; and the relationship Saussure to the cinematic image. The semantics of connotation and denotation are again explored but this time in relation to the visual medium of film; similarly, the narrative techniques of film are compared to literature, so that through seminar discussion students learn the similarities and differences in narrative structure between the two media.

Section 3 of the module explores the language of theater from page to stage, via seminars on the field, tenor, mode, and function of theater, which is followed by a theater visit to explore the live dimension of the medium, settings, set, and lighting concepts, reading the actor's body and thinking about the audience's response. By the time section 4 begins, students are aware of the similarities and differences *between* the media, so they are introduced to concepts that transcend different media: genre, pragmatics, intertextuality, and polyphony.

Assessment of the module is conducted by means of four short assignments of close analysis of topics discussed in class: the first requires students to analyze a poem and a piece of prose fiction; the second is a choice of two film extracts; in the third assessment they analyze one play text extract and one performance analysis; and the fourth assessment allows for a choice of two different media. The students responded enthusiastically to this part of the program: "I wasn't aware that we were undertaking adaptation studies or that this was a new area of research. However, I believe that the close analysis, semiotics and critical theory studies that we undertook in the areas of music, literature, film, and new media enabled us to think and write critically about most areas of the arts including adaptations."

The modules on words, sounds, and images from level 1, Hollywood cinema, and literature and the World Wide Web from level 2 in particular are relevant to the field of adaptation studies as adaptation involves the transfer of signs from one medium to another. The level 1 module introduces the skill of close reading to fully understand the signs and signifiers and how we attach meaning to them.[7]

The ideas of intertextuality and polyphony in section 4 are particularly helpful when a text has been adapted more than once, and the viewer can hear and see traces of the "original" text behind the current representation, as Linda Hutcheon suggests: "For the reader, spectator, or listener, adaptation *as adaptation* is unavoidably a kind of intertextuality if the receiver is acquainted with the adapted text. It is an ongoing dialogical process, as Mikhail Bakhtin would have said, in which we compare the work we already know with the one we are experiencing."[8]

Building Block 2: Themes and Issues in Modern English Studies

This module explores the relationship of contemporary literature in English to the issues of ideology, gender, class, and race. Using examples selected from a range of genre and media, including prose fiction, drama, poetry, and/or film, students investigate how the formal features of a text can constrain, reveal, or challenge ideological positions, while being introduced to basic concepts and methods of contemporary theoretical analysis. The selected texts enable students to consider the different ways in which literary and film media represent or respond to the historical and cultural contexts in which they were produced. What is perhaps most intriguing about this module is the method of assessment, which is based on two assignments focusing on intermedial strategies of group research and performance work: (1) a formative assessment culminating in an oral presentation prepared and delivered in small groups—equivalent to 1,500 words and of ten to fifteen minutes duration (40 percent)—in which the students select, research, and discuss one of the course texts to show how elements of form relate to themes of gender, ideology, race, or class; and (2) a summative assessment of an essay of 2,500 words (60 percent).

Building Block 3: Introduction to Creative Media

Here students are introduced to the creative use of computer technology, so they can explore and gain experience in using programs that enable the sequencing and sampling of sounds and images. The audiovisual project can take a variety of forms, including a sound track to an existing video clip, still images, a student's own video clip, abstract sonic art in the form of "acousmatic" or "electroacoustic" music, or spoken word material—all of which can be used to produce a complete audiovisual multimedia project. Assessment is by (1) a multimedia project (50 percent) and (2) a critical commentary (two thousand words; 50 percent).

Developed by one of my colleagues, this module is designed to enable students to learn how to manipulate new media programs and to explore the creative possibilities in the new media. Through their own creative practice, the students learn what exactly happens when the basic elements of sound and image are exchanged and adapted to operate within the medium of another—and how their manipulation of elements in two or more "original" artifacts produces another cultural artifact.

In these three core modules, which are expanded in greater depth by a range of choices in theater, creative writing, music, or literature options, the students are constantly assessing the adaptation process of medial exchange and intermedial relationships. There is no hierarchy in their study, for creative writing is valued as much as literature, and learning through the processes of performance in music and theater is central to the ethos of the degree.

LEVEL 2: KNOWLEDGE MODULES

There are two progression lines that run from level 2 to level 3: (1) critical theory and (2) digital media and education.

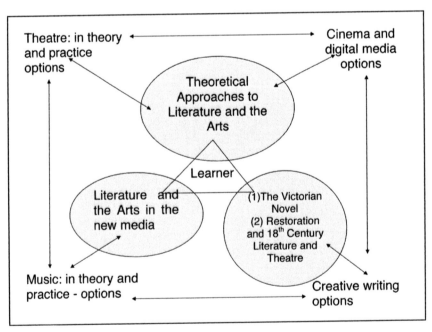

Diagram 5.3

Critical Theory Progression Route

Theoretical models carry philosophical content and ask important questions about how we understand our humanity in relation to the "real" world. We may live, as the song says, in a material world, but in the arts *the idea* of who we are is represented in another form and medium; and so when an artist adapts a representation of humanity in art, they adapt our ideas of who we are, and where we are, in relation to power, place, and space. Hence, "theory" is an important element in the pedagogies of adaptation. At level 2 in Theoretical Approaches to Literature and the Arts students examine how we read, write, and tell stories (Saussure, the Russian Formalists, Bakhtin, and Barthes); the relationship of literature and the arts to class structures, the economic base, and revolutionary views on society; and the history of political power and intellectual thought (Marxism, Marxist-Feminism, Cultural Materialism, Williams, Eagleton, and Foucault). From there we move on to discuss the human psyche, sexuality, and gender (Freud, Lacan, Kristeva, Cixous, and Irigaray) and the interrelationships between theory and practice in literature and the arts. The module operates closely with the Victorian Novel module and some texts do overlap; this is quite deliberate. The investigation is continued at level 3, in Reflections on Critical Theory in Literature and the Arts. Here the ideas of poststructuralism and thoughts of Derrida and Foucault underpin the investigation into the arts and history (New Historicism and Cultural Materialism); revising and rewriting the empire (postcolonialism); power, play text, and performance (postdramatic theory and theater); and literature and sexuality (gay, lesbian, and queer theory)—all of which I imagine are very familiar to authors writing about adaptations. The module concludes with a debate as to whether theoretical approaches to the arts are a useful tool or whether "the moment" of these critical approaches has passed.

In my recent questionnaire to the graduates, I asked whether they had been advantaged or disadvantaged by their study of the relationship between the art forms and media in the context of critical theories:

> Looking through the lenses of different theorists brings out many different levels in the art forms which help in the understanding of how these art forms developed in the first place and what they say about us and how we know our place in the world.
> Learning how to look at a piece of art, an opera, a piece of literature from different perspectives and at different angles has been enlightening. I had never thought much about the politics behind art until this course.

Despite my constant griping you never look at things the same after
exposure to critical theory.

This course helped me to look beyond my traditionalist upbringing. I
suddenly found a voice to express my frustration with the world and
the way it works.

The New Media and Education Route

Literature and the Arts in the New Media examines works in literature
and the arts available on the World Wide Web and assesses whether or
not Web technology is changing creative and interpretive practices. The
students do close analysis of poetry on the Web, where the sounds and
the images inherent in words are heard and seen alongside the words;
sometimes, they are even animated. The students become familiar with
the concepts of hyperfiction and hypermedia, and acquire the ability at a
click of a mouse to move into the virtual reality of hyperspace. Students
are also introduced to philosophical issues raised through the integration of literature and the arts with new technologies and create their own
multimedia projects. It is in their study of the history of ideas, specifically
Walter Benjamin's seminal essay "The Work of Art in the Age of Mechanical Reproduction," that their understanding becomes clearer. Thus, adaptation becomes what it is to be human, in an age where we experience
the world through multiple images of a represented reality. This, too, is
adaptation—of our consciousness:

> Adaptation retells the stories from another medium and possibly another
> age, transferring the signs and reinterpreting them for the modern age so
> that we can rediscover who we are and find our place in the world. In the
> postmodern age where it appears to be increasingly difficult to find reality,
> adaptation of previous media helps to affirm that human beings are the same
> whatever age they live in, that underneath the technology all the basic stories
> are the same.[9]

LEVEL 3: REFLECTION AND RESEARCH

However, it is perhaps the module Postmodernism, Policy and Practice in
Contemporary Culture that engages most with the notions of adaptation.
In this final core module the learning outcomes are defined as follows:
students will be able to

- locate and critically discuss the ideas of postmodernism in contemporary culture;

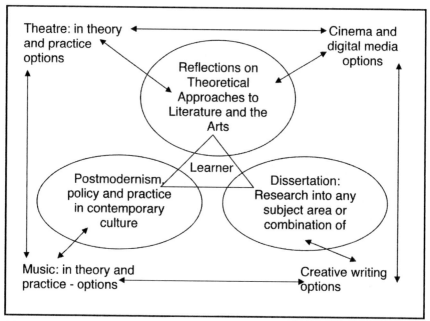

Diagram 5.4

- discuss critically British government policy and practice in the post-modern age;
- discuss the impact of government cultural policy and practice on the representation of society in the postmodern age; and
- articulate how the postmodern elements in higher education relate to employment.

The course examines contemporary literature, the arts, and new media through the lens of postmodernism—a term often used to describe a society that may be in the process of becoming fragmented and unsure of its roots in the age of the new media. It is taught through four connecting themes:

- Modernism/postmodernism: The students learn to identify key features of early and late twentieth-century representations of society in literature and the arts, and ask how they relate to each other—if they do—and how their artistic practice might engage with the cultural and national politics of their historical moment in time.
- Policy and practice in the arts: Selected literature and theater performances are used to explore postmodern concerns about history and

multicultural expression, and raise the question as to whether it is possible to relate them to social and cultural change in society as a whole.

- Is multiculturalism a product of government policy and practice in the arts and education? If so, then what is its effect on theater, literature, art, music, and festivals and how do we engage with it?
- Arts funding in Great Britain: Who decides who tells the stories about us and how?
- Interdisciplinarity/intermediality/education: Under this section students examine the structure of the degree program, or other modules, taken within the Institute for Lifelong Learning. They question whether the trend in academic study toward a breakdown of traditional academic disciplines is a positive or negative factor. There are also discussions about the "unspoken" or "presented" Institute for Lifelong Learning syllabi, in relation to the types of employment for which higher education level work has previously prepared students, prompting questions about whether interdisciplinary degrees are more or less relevant than "traditional" degrees in a multicultural society.
- The new media: fragmentation or integration? No discussion of twenty-first-century cultures can ignore the presence of the "new technologies" in the world of work that is the arts. So students reflect on whether knowledge about and skills in the new technologies prepare students for work in an arts-orientated employment (or any other employment).

Using the concepts of postmodernism as a tool for reflection, the course analyzes a variety of literature, performing arts, media, critics, and theorists. It has to be said that this is the most fun module to teach, while the questionnaire revealed that this is the module that has had the biggest effect on the students' lives after their university education has concluded:

Postmodernism has proved—most unexpectedly—to be one of the most useful spheres of knowledge. I use the presentation skills on a regular basis and Postmodernism as a theory is invaluable in my interpretation work in contemporary art—so useful to stimulate thought and discussion in my clients.

Postmodernism struck a chord with me at university and I enjoy art that has elements of the postmodern. In teaching drama postmodernism opens up a lot of possibilities for adapting texts into performance and adapting new media to work alongside performance. For example, I have been teaching a module on Lilliput and using elements of the text to explore and present conflict and resolution in performance. In the school play (John Godber's *Teechers*) they used video projection to present some aspects of the character's lives.

I think that the course has changed some of the ways in which I think, it has certainly given me the confidence to realise that my views are as valuable as the next person. Equally, I have more patience with other people's views. I think the biggest way in which I have changed is not making up my mind quickly about people's situations, belief's and taboo subjects. I now realise I wasn't as open-minded before as what I thought I was. This said my own strong beliefs about what is right and wrong have not changed but are now strengthened with a better thought out and researched argument, what has changed is that I can now tolerate that other people may not agree.

The benefits of this kind of module are manifold and can be illustrated by the photo. This shows a workshop presentation of a work in progress: "Give me your blessing for I go into a foreign land," with original music by Elena Langer, which was devised and directed by opera director Tim Hopkins and presented in February 2009 at the Clore Studio in the Royal Opera House, Covent Garden, London. Here the individual elements of dance, song, film, and music are separated from a contextual frame, and musicians, dancers, singers, technicians, and technology appear to operate as individual elements, but they are held together by the perceiver of the performance, who makes their own interpretation of the multiple narratives presented. The network structure of digital technology underpins the performance even though many of its elements predate the

Photo by Patricia Pinsker, reproduced by permission of the photographer.

digital age, and in a striking performance the intermedial form of opera
is adapted from the proscenium arch to the workshop to engage in multi-
and intermedial reflection. Crucially, Tim Hopkins, as well as being an
established opera director, is also a holder of an Arts and Humanities Research Fellowship, funded by the British government, and researches into
the uses of technology in opera at the Centre for Research in Opera and
Music at the University of Sussex. The workshop performance was developed as part of the Royal Opera House's OperaGenesis program, which is
their contemporary opera development program that is supported by the
Genesis Foundation—a British-based charity created to support emerging
artists and help build new audiences and projects in the fields of opera
and theater. As such, it forms part of the British government policy in the
"Creative Industries," which began with the *Report of the National Committee of Inquiry into Higher Education* chaired by Sir Ron Dearing (1997), who
set the agenda in which higher education, theater, and new media were to
play a central role.[10] The impact of the Dearing report led to the *National
Policy for Theatre* (2000) and the "Creative Industries Framework," which
began the process of bringing together professional theater and academic
study; the *Higher Education Act* (2004); the *Leitch Review of Skills* (2006); the
Widening Participation Act (2006); and the *Arts, Enterprise and Excellence:
Strategy for Higher Education* (2006).[11] Central to the Dearing report was
a vision of an inclusive learning society, with widening participation to
higher education and lifelong learning skills embedded in the new curriculum where the chosen tool to achieve both was digital technology.

It is in this final module of the degree that pedagogy most clearly meets
the political power that controls the curriculum, pedagogy, and assessment of higher education and of cultural expression in the arts. As artists,
teachers, and researchers in the United Kingdom, we are all part of a national policy that links the Department for Education and Skills and the
Department for Culture, Media and Sport.

It is interesting to notice how connected the various elements of educational and cultural policy are in the United Kingdom and, I suggest, at the
European level since the Bologna Agreement (1998), when the education
ministers of Germany, France, Italy, and the United Kingdom signed the
Sorbonne Declaration concerning the harmonization of European higher
education degree systems. As members of academic institutions, who are,
of course, funded by the government and who all have policy and strategy documents to implement the educational policy of the nation, we, as
members of academic staff of the institutions, are part of the process. It is
part of our professional practice to participate in the quality assurance of
our teaching and in the periodic research assessment exercises that determine the teaching and research funding for all the institutions of higher

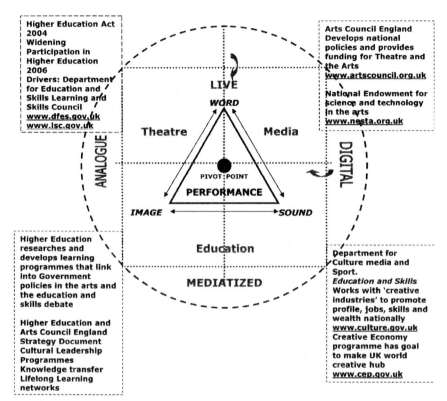

Diagram 5.5. Adaptation of the model of Intermediality in Theatre and Performance to show the relationship of the Departments of State; the agencies who distribute funds to arts organizations; the Acts of Parliament who fund both higher education and the arts; and the research councils. (From Freda Chapple and Chiel Kattenbelt, "Key Issues in Intermediality in Theatre and Performance," in *Intermediality in Theatre and Performance*, ed. Freda Chapple and Chiel Kattenbelt, 11–25 [Amsterdam: Rodopi, 2006], 24.)

education. Like the structure of Web technology itself, the deep structures and pathways that link each element are not necessarily visible, but once we are aware of the structure, it may be that we adapt our selves accordingly. If this argument holds good, then we can now think of adaptation studies not as being "in the margins" and only involving one or two disciplines but rather, I suggest, as an underlying structure that has the power to become integrated into all elements of the curriculum, pedagogy, and assessment in higher education. It will be interesting to see if this ever happens—or, just maybe, it is already operative via the new pedagogies of digital technology, but we have not yet noticed it.

NOTES

1. Sara Mills, *Michel Foucault* (London: Routledge, 2002), 27–28.
2. Quoted in Ronald Barnett, Gareth Parry, and Kelly Coate, "Conceptualising Curriculum Change," *Teaching in Higher Education* 6, no. 4 (2001): 435–49.
3. Steve Bartlett, Diana M. Burton, and Nick Peim, *Introduction to Education Studies* (London: Sage, 2001), 73.
4. Julie Sanders, *Adaptation and Appropriation* (New York: Routledge, 2006), 19–20.
5. Barnett, Parry, and Coate, "Conceptualising Curriculum Change," 445–47.
6. Extracted from research project into BA English Studies and the Performing Arts (Combined Studies) on student learning and progression after graduation (2009).
7. Extracted from research project into BA English Studies and the Performing Arts (Combined Studies) on student learning and progression after graduation (2009).
8. Linda Hutcheon, *A Theory of Adaptation* (London: Routledge, 2006), 21.
9. Extracted from research project into BA English Studies and the Performing Arts (Combined Studies) on student learning and progression after graduation (2009).
10. Ron Dearing (chair), *Higher Education in the Learning Society: Report of the National Committee of Inquiry into Higher Education* (London: HMSO, 1997).
11. *Art Council England National Policy for Theatre in England*, 2000, www.artscouncil.org.uk/publication_archive/arts-council-of-englands-national-policy-for-theatre-in-england/ (accessed 12 October 2009; *The Higher Education Act* (London: HMSO, 2004); *The Widening Participation Act* (London: HMSO, 2006); *The Leitch Review of Skills*, "Prosperity for All in the Global Economy—World Class Skills Final Report" (London: HMSO, 2006); *Arts, Enterprise and Excellence: Strategy for Higher Education*, 2007, Arts Council England, www.artscouncil.org.uk/publication_archive/arts-enterprise-and-excellence-strategy-for-higher-education/ (accessed 12 October 2009).

Six

Toward a Pedagogy for Adaptation Studies

Sevgi Şahin and Laurence Raw

In an expanding series of essays and lectures, as well as in his recent book *Film Adaptation and Its Discontents* (2007), Thomas Leitch calls for a major reorientation in the way literature should be taught. Based on his experience teaching in the English Department at the University of Delaware, he advocates a move away from

> passive literacy—being uncritical consumers of the texts they [the students] face—to active literacy—being able not only to follow texts word by word and point by point but to engage them critically and productively. Meeting our students as readers of whatever level of accomplishment, we seek to transform them into writers capable of rewriting whatever they read instead of simply listening to it and obeying it—or, at a slightly higher level of sophistication, of asking whether they agree or disagree with it.

Courses in adaptation studies, he believes, might be the ideal means of fulfilling this requirement:

> Their double focus on reading and writing leads to a natural emphasis on the necessary element of rewriting in both writing and critical reading. By treating every text as a text to be rewritten, they empower students with a sense of themselves as rewriters rather than consumers of texts. Instead of taking sides in the debate between literacy and inquiry, the mastery of a field versus the ability to add to that field, they focus on the radical interconnections between the two by taking the ability to rewrite a text as the criterion of mastery.[1]

71

Leitch's theory of "active literacy" might be developed in different ways. Using L. S. Vygotsky's notion of the Zone of Personal Development (ZPD), we might rethink the process of adapting a text as one which "impels or awakens a whole series of functions [in the student] that are in a stage of maturation lying in the zone of personal development."[2] These functions include reflection, analysis, and critical thinking. Vygotsky conceives education in terms of concepts—the scientific on the one hand and the everyday or spontaneous on the other. Scientific concepts (which might be grouped under the "theoretical framework" of a discipline) are characterized by a high level of generality, and their relationship to objects is mediated through the students' consciousness. To formulate their own ideas of adaptation, students should be introduced to its basic scientific concepts (for example, the idea of "fidelity," or "the original text" and "the adapted text") and subsequently reinterpret them in their own way, using their spontaneous concepts (as Vygotsky might term them). In this way, scientific concepts are rendered concrete and meaningful. However, this process can only be accomplished if the teacher refrains from pedagogical input. Vygotsky remarks that "the teacher who attempts to use this approach achieves nothing but a mindless learning of words, an empty verbalism that stimulates or imitates the presence of concepts. . . . Under these conditions, the child learns not the concept but the word, and the word is taken over by the child through memory rather than thought."[3] The notion of "empty verbalism" might be a harsh one (many teachers who lecture often communicate great ideas), but Vygotsky's ideas suggest that many students are taught to memorize theoretical formulae while being unable to experiment with them for themselves. Good teaching must be student centered, allowing students to make their own decisions and promoting an atmosphere of cooperation and collaboration.[4]

Leitch's notion of "active literacy" might also be usefully developed with reference to the work of the pedagogical theorist Henry A. Giroux. In *Critical Pedagogy: The State and Cultural Struggle*, Giroux argues for the creation of "a pedagogy . . . that allows teachers to understand how subjectivities are produced within those social forms in which people move but which are often only partially understood."[5] By creating an adaptation of a text (whether classic or otherwise) for themselves, they can learn how their subjectivities are inscribed within specific forms of social, moral, and political behavior. The act of textual rewriting can help them understand how experiences are constructed and reconstructed in different contexts. This type of activity might be described as "learning for empowerment [that] both confirm[s] and critically engage[s] the knowledge and experience through which students authorize their own voices and social identities."[6] Leitch's view of active literacy could also form the basis of a pedagogy that promotes reflection on why a text has been adapted in a certain way, either by the students themselves or by professional writers and filmmakers. This type of learning moves away from fact-based instruction and creates instead what Paolo Friere describes as a "problem posing" environment that affirms students and lecturers alike as "beings who transcend themselves."[7]

This chapter will reflect on how the ideas of Leitch, Vygotsky, and Giroux could be incorporated into the pedagogy of adaptation studies, by means of a case study involving our own teaching experiences. We begin by reviewing existing approaches to adaptation in university departments of foreign language and literature, where attention focuses largely on what is gained and lost when a classic text is re-created in a different medium. Students are not required to draw on their everyday experiences (or, in Vygotsky's formulation, their spontaneous concepts) in the process of evaluation. Rather, they are encouraged to judge an adaptation on the grounds of appropriateness; whether it successfully captures the qualities of the "original." We suggest that there are culture-specific reasons for favoring this approach (especially in departments of foreign literature) that have a lot to do with the belief—shared by many older academics—that they should commit themselves to the Turkish Republic's long-standing policies of westernization. Some departments have tried to challenge this model by adopting what might be described as an inter- or cross-cultural approach, in which students draw on their own experience to interpret an adaptation. This certainly has its advantages, but it still presupposes that the (Western) text is the most important object of study. In the next section of this chapter, which describes in detail our experiences of teaching adaptation studies in a department of English Language Teaching (ELT) at Başkent University, Ankara, Turkey, and subsequently presenting our findings at a conference in Istanbul, we show how greater attention needs to be given to the *process* of adaptation, enabling students to reshape classic texts to their own local culture, using whatever language—English or Turkish—they prefer. By this means they can understand how the act of adaptation offers a research-based space for experiment and creativity, promoting active literacy as well as creating an atmosphere suitable for Giroux's learning for empowerment.

To understand existing attitudes toward adaptation in the Turkish Republic, especially in humanities or foreign-language departments, it is necessary to go back to the early 1920s, when Mustafa Kemal Atatürk introduced a wide-ranging program of language reform. In 1928 the Roman alphabet was adopted in place of the Arabic script, and throughout the 1940s, thousands of words of Persian and Arabic origin were replaced by newly created terms borrowed from Turkic dialects or technical terms derived from ancient and modern Western languages. The Ministry of

Education published a series of Western classics in translation, using up-to-date Turkish; these were designed to reduce the Ottoman influence over the national culture and thereby encourage the people to support Atatürk's republic and its aims. In 1941 the ministry established a Translation Bureau, with the participation of leading critics, writers, and lecturers, who were responsible for the production of unabridged translations from original sources.[8] A year later the ministry collaborated with the British Council in a scheme to render "selected English classics" into Turkish; by 1945, the first of these—*Coriolanus*—had appeared.[9]

Although translation norms at that time were very much dependent both on individual translators and their (imagined readerships), the Ministry of Education encouraged a policy of staying close to the source text in order to provide examples of what they perceived as the best of Western culture—to create a canon of so-called great works that contained (in true Arnoldian fashion) the best that has been thought and said in the world. This would not only help to educate the people but also demonstrate the success of Atatürk's language reforms, proving that great literature could be successfully rendered into Turkish for the widest possible audience.[10]

But translation, like adaptation, is not only a linguistic process; it involves more formal operations. It is a mode, as well as a specific act, whereby fundamental structures are reproduced and/or reinvented in different contexts. To ensure that translators acquired the kind of cultural literacy that would guarantee their future careers, several newly established departments of foreign languages—known in the 1940s and 1950s as philology departments—were created and with government support created an impressive output of research and publication, together with new curricula based on Western models. In the Department of English at Ankara University, the origins of the undergraduate program could be traced back to Oxford University, combining basic literature courses (Shakespeare, the Romantics, the eighteenth- and nineteenth-century novel) with courses in grammar, philology, Latin, and Greek.[11] In the subsequent decades, there has been a gradual drift toward specialization: English philology departments have morphed into language and literature departments with the dominant pedagogical focus on English literature. Meanwhile, ELT is carried out in a variety of contexts—language schools, secondary schools, university preparatory schools, and departments of education. Meanwhile, translation studies has become a discipline in its own right; there are at least two departments in state universities, while several private institutions offer electives in the discipline. The development of translation studies, and how it differs from adaptation studies in the Turkish context, is a fascinating topic but does not concern us here. Instead, we will explain how adaptation studies has become part of university curricula and what students and teachers have come to expect from it in recent years. Gönül Pultar and Ayşe Lahur Kırtunç observe that, at the state-funded Ege University, Izmir, the Department of American Literature used courses in semiotics and films to promote "awareness [amongst students] that they could adapt the same skills [acquired] in deconstructing and analyzing academic cultural products for texts that were not part of their curriculum. This meant a significant improvement in the critical thinking abilities of the students."[12] In this model, adaptation studies is approached from a cultural studies perspective: students view films (or other types of adaptation) as products of a particular moment in American history and engage with the social, political, and historical issues raised by them. The objective here is not to reinforce the status of the literary canon but rather to show how the meaning of classic texts can change over time.[13] If students can understand this, then they will enhance their "critical thinking abilities." The same approach also underlies some of the adaptation studies–related courses introduced into foreign literature and language departments in private institutions: in the late 1990s at Bilkent University, Ankara, a two-semester basic English course offered a variety of courses ranging from the Holocaust in film to media adaptations.[14] At Sabancı University, Istanbul, the Faculty of Arts and Sciences curriculum incorporates courses in cultural studies (incorporating a substantial adaptation element)—for example, Advertising and Culture, History Goes to the Movies, Introduction to Film and Media Studies—all of which are available to all students with a primary or secondary interest in the humanities.[15]

But we are not sure that such courses develop *active* engagement with an adapted text. The Department of Cultural Studies at Sabancı University claims that, by means of their "critical pedagogical practice" of comparing locally produced texts to those produced in other countries (especially the West), students will be able to both analyze and participate in "contemporary cultural dynamics in Turkey and the world at large."[16] This goes some way toward fulfilling Giroux's vision of "learning for empowerment" by promoting inter- or crosscultural comparison. For example, students can analyze texts closely as a means of investigating their own received opinions about the foreign culture, which are often of a partial and prejudiced nature.[17] However, this approach still has its neocolonialist elements; it does not permit students to *value* their own experience but simply to *draw* upon it as a way of interpreting a Western text (whose significance as an object of study remains unchallenged). The lecturer's role in this critical pedagogical practice remains unclear; what strategies should they use to analyze the "contemporary cultural dynamics in Turkey and the world at large?"

The solution, it seems to us, lies in creating a pedagogy for studying adaptation in Turkish higher education institutions that admits the fact that there have been profound changes in the way lecturers and students participate in learning over the last fifteen years or so. Partly, this can be attributed to the rise of student-centered approaches (especially in departments of ELT) and the consequential decline of the lecture mode, as well as the creation of more innovative curricula—not only in Turkey but also elsewhere. The remainder of this chapter will concentrate on our joint efforts to achieve this in our own department of ELT, focusing in particular on how poetry might be taught to both trainee teachers of English and the students they will eventually work with in schools.

Before describing in detail our efforts to create an alternative pedagogy for adaptation studies, we will briefly describe our current academic situation. In 2007, Laurence Raw transferred from the Department of American Culture and Literature at Başkent University, Ankara (which practices a model of "critical pedagogical practice" similar to that of Sabancı University), into the Department of English Language Teaching (ELT) within the same institution. Sevgi Şahin graduated from the same department in 2008 and now works as a research assistant there. What we describe here is a collaborative process involving Laurence as the teacher, together with the students (including Sevgi) taking courses in literary study.

In our ELT department, undergraduates undergo a course of professional training, combining theoretical work with a survey of popular language teaching techniques. A course such as Approaches to English Language Teaching introduces them to presentation strategies as well as to understanding the significance of nonverbal communication in the classroom. In the final two years of their curriculum, students work part-time in high schools with practicing teachers, at first acting as observers and subsequently teaching classes on their own (to a maximum of twenty hours per semester). Students work with learners of English from a variety of age groups ranging from seven to seventeen.

The four-year undergraduate curriculum also contains six literature-based courses (out of a total of thirty-five), comprising a two-term foundation course (Introduction to English Literature), plus four courses in Analysis and Teaching focusing on the short story, the novel, poetry, and drama. Hitherto, these courses had been taught as survey courses, giving students an introduction to classic British and American literary texts in an attempt to expand their knowledge of foreign cultures. Most of the teaching to date has been through lectures, in the belief that this is the quickest and most effective means to transmit information. With the approval of our department chair (who wanted to improve the students' linguistic skills as well as their teaching techniques), Laurence moved away from the lecture format and collaborated with the students to create alternative syllabus designs designed to focus on various adaptive processes—novels, poems, films, and sound recordings. The inspiration for this came from Vygotsky's model of collaborative learning, in which the teacher becomes a participant in classroom activity as well as an information provider. This approach to syllabus design also exploited the students' existing skills; by their third year, they have become accustomed to adapting materials for their ELT lesson plans, using textbooks and other available resources (newspaper cuttings, website material, etc.). Laurence's second major objective was to develop ways of increasing the students' self-confidence through negotiation. With this in mind, the first week of the course was devoted to defining its aims and objectives, focusing in particular on how the material adapted in class might best benefit everyone in terms of improving their teaching technique. In the end, we came up with the idea that, while the choice of texts for the course was very much the students' responsibility, they would seek to adapt them according to their own (and their learners') culture-specific social, cultural, and academic requirements. Rather than simply comparing cultures (as in the Sabancı University model), we acknowledged the fact that texts are consumed differently in different contexts. The metaphor here is deliberate: we were not focusing on *content*—what is adapted—but rather on *process*—how an adaptation takes place. To the best of our knowledge this kind of creative pedagogy had not been attempted before in an ELT literature course in the Turkish Republic: the prospect was not only fascinating (especially at Başkent University, where a large proportion of the students originate not from the three principal metropolises—Ankara, Istanbul, and Izmir—but rather from smaller provincial cities or rural villages) but also daunting. All of us had to draw upon our own experience (acquired through teaching and learning other courses as well as preparing materials for use in schools) of selecting, adapting, and presenting materials and subsequently justifying our decisions.

In the course Poetry: Analysis and Teaching, students chose their own texts and tried to create new and innovative ways of adapting them in class, using role plays, prediction and writing activities, or comparative tasks. The reasons for this were not hard to discern; hitherto, they had only learned poetry by rote or through the lecture mode as a content-based activity. Consequently, they wanted to develop more active modes of teaching and learning that would not only promote closer textual reading but also increase awareness of the sound, as well as the sense, of words used in the poetic text. This was an important aspect of learning English: once the students (and learners) understood how words sounded, their pronunciation skills would automatically improve. Among the most popular texts were poems specifically intended for children—such as Lewis Carroll's "Beautiful Soup" or Roger McGough's "The Leader"—as well as short lyrics such as Emily Dickinson's "A Bird Came Down the Walk." Basing their activity on the popular Turkish television program *Yemekteyiz* (itself an adaptation of the British lifestyle program *Come Dine with Me*), one group adapted the Carroll poem into an allegory of greed, with the speaker portrayed as a harassed mother trying to satisfy her children's insatiable desire for "beautiful soup." In the end, the children had had enough, but the mother decided to teach them a lesson by giving them so much soup that they were eventually sick. The last stanza ("Beau-ootiful Soo-oop! / Beau-ootiful Soo-oop! / Soo-oop of the e-e-evening, / Beauti-ful, beauti-FUL SOUP!") was delivered in a gleeful tone, as the mother watched her children suffering. This adaptation parodied *Yemekteyiz*—a program where five contestants cook dinner for one another on successive days—in which most contestants take a dislike to one another's food, even before they have sampled it. The overt references to this ratings-topping television program automatically rendered this adaptation a success in class. McGough's poem "The Leader"—chosen by a mixed group of students (three girls and one boy)—was designed to expose prevailing gender stereotypes in Turkish high schools, where the boys are expected to be dominant, even if they have no idea what to do. This is partly due to family background (patriarchy is still very strong, especially outside the main urban areas) as well as cultural conditioning within most high schools, whose curricula actively promote a division between "masculine" subjects (e.g., maths and science) and "feminine" subjects (e.g., English and foreign languages). With this in mind, McGough's poem, especially when delivered by a male foreign-language learner, becomes a lament for his lost masculinity:

> I wanna be the leader
> I wanna be the leader
> Can I be the leader?
> Can I? I can?
> Promise? Promise?
> Yippee I'm the leader
> I'm the leader
>
> OK what shall we do?[18]

Sevgi worked with Emily Dickinson's "A Bird Came Down the Walk" in the belief that the poem's basic premise (the speaker observing a bird's movements) could be easily appreciated by learners of any age. She also believed that the rhyme scheme could help to improve pronunciation skills and thereby increase the confidence of both learners and teachers in using the foreign language. This suggests that poetry, written in the target language, has a psychologically effective influence on learners in the field of ELT. The traditional lecture-based way of teaching poetry in the classroom requires close analysis of structure, language, metaphor, and so on; but in many classrooms, such tasks only demotivate students as they try to make sense of what might seem an intractable text. Sevgi tried to overcome this by developing dramatic activities that are essential to create involvement and to achieve a better understanding and response from the learners.

A Bird Came Down the Walk

A bird came down the walk:
He did not know I saw;
He bit an angle-worm in halves
And ate the fellow, raw.

And then he drank a dew
From a convenient grass,
And then hopped sidewise to the wall
To let a beetle pass.

He glanced with rapid eyes
That hurried all abroad,—
They looked like frightened *beads*, I thought;
He stirred his velvet head

Like one in danger; cautious,
I offered him a crumb,
And he unrolled his feathers
And rowed him softer home

Then oars divide the ocean,
Too silver for a seam,
Or butterflies, off banks of noon,
Leap, splashless, as they swim.[19]

Sevgi's lesson plan was divided into three parts. At the very beginning of the class, a warmer activity focused on the title "A Bird Came Down the Walk" and what it might mean to students (and their learners). The responses were culturally significant: the memory of watching a bird eating a worm evoked memories of childhood, family, and social stability. In many communities in Turkey, the family constitutes the basic unit of society; when students graduate, they are often expected to return home and prepare for marriage and parenthood. In the second activity, Sevgi read the poem out: any unknown vocabulary was explained on the board by means of visual equipment and materials. She then read the poem out once again, but this time one of her fellow students acted out each line with the help of props such as a cardboard beak and a feather boa extending across the shoulders and arms to approximate wings. The basic actions—eating a worm, having a drink of dew, letting a beetle pass by, and accepting food from a human being—were acted out. All other unknown vocabulary was illustrated by means of realia or handmade materials (an oar, leaping butterflies, etc.). Having witnessed the role play, the other students in the class were asked to divide into groups and discuss the poem's meaning. Again the theme of childhood, home, and family became an important topic: why did the bird's eyes look like "frightened beads," for example? Was it because he was alone, without the security of anyone to look after him? And what did the metaphor of "rowed him softer home / Then oars divide the ocean" actually mean? There were several possible explanations, many of them focusing on the bird's and the butterfly's size. They were so small that they made no impression on the sea or the ocean. However, they were all living creatures; it was just that human beings did not recognize them as such. Once again, this stimulated memories of the students' childhood, and many of them remained oblivious to the world around them—especially those living in the large concrete apartment blocks that disfigure many of Turkey's urban landscapes. In the final activity, Sevgi asked the students to write a short story based on the poem but choosing other animals instead of birds. So the poem could be rewritten as "A Cat Came Down the Walk," "A Dog Came Down the Walk," or even "A Human Being Came Down the Walk." This activity proved particularly interesting; some of the students' work was deliberately comic—suggesting, perhaps, a certain reluctance to engage with Dickinson's themes—with a dog taking a bone or a biscuit, suggesting (perhaps) that the poem might be about an animal's feeding rituals. Others took the poem as a romantic idealization of a bird by a speaker longing to possess its freedom, yet painfully aware that she could not. Dickinson remained a human being, unable to fly. Once again this evoked painful associations: many students likened themselves to caged birds, unable to realize their dreams of freedom in a family environment where their destiny had already been mapped out. This perhaps helps to explain why ELT is such a popular subject for study amongst young women; once they graduate, they are expected to return home, teach English in local schools, and raise a family.

When Sevgi presented this activity as an example of classroom practice at a conference in October 2008, one American participant likewise identified the poem as a nostalgic evocation of childhood. The bird was reimagined as a symbol of lost youth flying over an endless ocean, while the butterflies "off banks of noon" evoked a springlike world of perpetual sunshine ("noon" in this sense, being recharacterized as a symbol of the best part of the day). Dickinson's poem appealed so deeply to his inner soul that he could not bear even to read it out to his fellow conference participants, even though Sevgi encouraged him to do so.

What are the conclusions that might be drawn from such activities for the future of ELT and adaptation studies, both in Turkey and elsewhere? We have already commented on the ways in which students were empowered as a result of cooperation and collaboration in group activities. This experience helped them to become more confident participants in the activities presented in class (by talking personally about their own lives), which rendered them more confident teachers when they presented the same activities to young learners during their school experience. From the lecturer's point of view, such activities could only flourish with the minimum of extra input; rather than telling students whether their interpretations were "right" or "wrong," Laurence asked them to develop their ideas. By doing so, the students learned to "consume" the poems, in other words, adapt them according to their own cultural values. As this chapter has suggested, this process taught everyone a lot about their backgrounds and aspirations (or lack of them, in some cases). This is perhaps the best form of "learning for empowerment" (to invoke Giroux's phrase): students and teachers adapt a text and by doing so learn about themselves and their capabilities.

Once the course Poetry: Analysis and Teaching had been rethought in this way, it provided an alternative to the norms experienced in many ELT courses taught in English at the university level, which according to one researcher tend to be "overwhelmingly prescriptive," denying the students the opportunity to learn "through explanatory talk and discussion."[20] The same applies to courses taught in Turkish both within ELT and other teacher training departments.[21] From a language teaching perspective, our course emphasized the fact that "language is not a neutral medium that passes freely and easily into the private property of the speaker's intentions; it is populated—overpopulated—with the intentions of others. Expropriating it, forcing it to submit to one's own intentions and accents, is a difficult and complicated process."[22]

By taking into account their own cultural backgrounds, our students dealt successfully with the potential "sense of dislocation and bewilderment" that might arise when a text from a foreign culture is introduced into the foreign-language teaching classroom.[23] Once that problem had been dealt with, then everyone forged the kind of active literacy that Thomas Leitch believes is fundamental to the future of adaptation studies. In many ways, the inspiration behind these activities recalls Gideon Toury's idea, as expressed in his seminal work *Descriptive Translation Studies and Beyond*: "The locus of study is never the text as an entity in itself [but rather] the options at the translators' [or adapters'] disposal, the choices made by them and the constraints under which these choices were affected. . . . In order for such results to gain significance, *a lot of contextualizing would have to be done, which is really what target-centeredness is all about*" (emphasis added).[24]

Could this model be reproduced in other educational contexts within Turkey or elsewhere? In ELT departments, the answer is certainly yes. Teacher training encompasses various methods of assessment, ranging from portfolios of essays, lesson plans, and peer evaluation of performance in the classroom. By focusing on how and why texts are adapted, using the theoretical models of Vygotsky, Giroux, and Friere (as proposed in the beginning of this chapter), we can identify the student's needs more closely and perhaps reformulate the curriculum to accommodate them. At present, this looks like a remote prospect; most ELT curricula in Turkey are determined by the Ministry of Education, which appears indifferent to regional and cultural differences. However, we can still reorient individual courses (such as the Poetry: Analysis and Teaching course). Other contributions to this book illustrate how active literacy might be acquired through other methods, using online as well as direct teaching methods. In other contexts—especially in more traditional English departments—greater time might be devoted to considering how and why a text is adapted, drawing more on Leitch's notions of critical reading. The fact that adaptation studies can accommodate both approaches is proof of its interdisciplinary potential.

Nonetheless, we do believe that this account of our teaching experiences attests to the value of a Vygotsky-inspired approach to collaborative learning, in which students and teachers alike engage in a process of discovering not only how texts can be reshaped but also more about the contexts in which they live and work. By "doing" adaptation studies—writing, creating, and discussing—we forged a mutual bond, while simultaneously learning to understand one another better.

NOTES

1. Thomas Leitch, "How to Teach Film Adaptations, and Why," unpublished paper given at the 33rd American Studies Association of Turkey Conference, Istanbul, 8–10 October 2008, 14–16. Cf. Thomas Leitch, "Adaptation Studies at a Crossroads," *Adaptation* 1, no. 1 (2008): 76.

2. L. S. Vygotsky, *The Collected Works of L.S. Vygotsky Vol. 1: Problems of General Psychology* (New York: Plenium, 1987), 252.

3. Vygotsky, *The Collected Works*, 170.

4. Vygotsky, *The Collected Works*, 68–69, 216.

5. Henry A. Giroux, "Schooling as a Form of Cultural Politics: Towards a Pedagogy of and for Difference," in *Critical Pedagogy: The State and Cultural Struggle*, ed. Henry A. Giroux and Peter McLaren, 142–67 (Albany: State University of New York Press, 1989), 145.

6. Giroux, "Schooling as a Form of Cultural Politics," 149.

7. Donaldo Macedo, "Preface," in *Politics of Liberation: Paths from Friere*, ed. Peter McLaren and Colin Lankshear, iv–xxii (London: Routledge, 1994), xviii.

8. See Şehnaz Tahir Gürçağlar, *The Politics and Poetics of Translation in Turkey 1923–1960* (Amsterdam: Editions Rodopi, 2008), 116–17.

9. See Laurence Raw, "Translating Theatre Texts: *As You Like It*," *Shakespeare Worldwide* 14/15 (1995): 92–93.

10. Özlem Berk, *Translation and Westernisation in Turkey: From the 1840s to the 1980s* (Istanbul: Ege Yayınları, 2004), 167–68.

11. Laurence Raw, "Reconstructing 'Englishness,'" presented to the 6th University of Warwick/British Council Conference on British Cultural Studies, September 1999, www.britishcouncil.org/studies/england/raw.htm (accessed 4 January 2000).

12. Gönül Pultar and Ayşe Lahur Kırtunç, "Cultural Studies in Turkey: Education and Practice," *Review of Education, Pedagogy and Cultural Studies* 26, nos. 2/3 (2004): 132.

13. Laurence Raw has adopted a similar approach in two recent books: *Adapting Henry James to the Screen: Gender, Fiction and Film* (Lanham, Md.: Scarecrow Press, 2006) and *Adapting Nathaniel Hawthorne to the Screen: Forging New Worlds* (Lanham, Md.: Scarecrow Press, 2008).

14. Daren Hodson, letter to Laurence Raw, 10 April 2000.

15. Sabancı University, Faculty of Arts and Social Sciences, 2008 course list, http://suis.sabanciuniv.edu/HbbmInst/SU_DEGREE.p_list_courses?P_TERM= 999999&P_AREA=FC_FASS&P_PROGRAM=&P_FAC=S&P_LANG=EN&P _LEVEL=UG (accessed 28 October 2008).

16. Sabancı University, Department of Cultural Studies, "Welcome," www .sabanciuniv.edu/ssbf/cult/eng (accessed 28 October 2008).

17. Laurence Raw, "Perspectives on British Studies in Turkish Universities," in *British Studies: Intercultural Perspectives*, ed. Alan Mountford and Nick Wadham-Smith, 21–35 (Harlow, UK: Pearson Education, 2000), 26.

18. Roger McGough, "The Leader,"www.poemhunter.com/poem/the-leader/ (accessed 5 November 2009).

19. Emily Dickinson, "A Bird Came Down the Walk." http://quotations.about .com/cs/poemlyrics/a/Bird_Came_Down.htm (accessed 6 November 2009).

20. Zuhal Akünal, "English Medium Education in Turkey: A Myth or an Achievable Goal? An Evaluation of Content-Based Second Language Education at Middle East Technical University," unpublished PhD diss., University of Kent, 1993, 257.

21. Many graduates of teacher training departments other than ELT have drawn on their experiences as a basis for research into teaching standards. See, for example, Gülşen Bağıoğlu, "Genel, Mesleki, ve Teknik Eğitim Fakültelerindeki Öğretmenlik Uygulaması Dersine İlişkin Öğretim Elemanı ve Öğrenci Görüşleri" [Lecturers' and Students' Opinions on Teaching Practice Courses Offered in General, Vocational, and Technical Education Faculties], unpublished MA thesis, Hacettepe University, Ankara, 1997, *passim*.

22. Claire Kramsch, *Content and Culture in Language Teaching* (Oxford: Oxford University Press, 1993), 27.

23. Alan Pulverness, "English as a Foreign Culture: English Language Teaching and British Cultural Studies," in *British Studies: Intercultural Perspectives*, ed. Alan Mountford and Nick Wadham-Smith (Harlow, UK: Pearson Education, 2000), 86.

24. Gideon Toury, *Descriptive Translation Studies and Beyond* (Amsterdam: John Benjamins Publishing, 1995), 174.

SEVEN

WRITING THE ADAPTATION

Teaching an Upper-Division College Course for the Screenwriter

Diane Lake

Screenwriters bring to life on screen the novels, fairy tales, and comic books that we all enjoy. We take material from another medium and adapt it for the medium of film. Being an adapter necessitates getting inside a work and discovering what is cinematic about that work. As a screenwriter, in addition to being commissioned to write several original screenplays for studios/producers, I've adapted a fairy tale for Disney, a biography for Miramax, as well as novels for independent producers. For today's screenwriter, having the ability to work on adaptations is absolutely essential.

ADAPTED VERSUS ORIGINAL SCREENPLAYS

Every year in the world of film, studios—large and small—produce more adapted films than original films. Why is that, one might ask? Why would studios support adaptations over original material? It's an easy answer: studios take less of a risk in producing an adaptation. If they fund the adaptation of a novel, for example, they do so with the knowledge that a publishing company thought the material worthy of being put out as a book. When that's the case, the studio feels as if they're not taking as much of a risk—after all, the publisher believed in the novel, right? People bought the book, right? So there must be something to the story being told.

On the other hand, if a screenwriter pitches an original idea to a studio, that idea hasn't been validated by anyone else. To fund that original concept, the studio has to see what the screenwriter is seeing and trust the screenwriter to translate his or her vision into a workable story for the screen. Imagine yourself to be a studio executive, and ask which script you'd rather fund—the unproven idea that originated in a screenwriter's head or the idea that's already got a following? Because studios produce adaptations at a higher rate than original films, it's of paramount importance that a screenwriter be adept in adapting material from another source for the screen.

THE SCREENWRITER'S FIRST PAYING GIG: ADAPTATION OR ORIGINAL?

Most screenwriting students believe they will break into the business with an original or "spec" script. "Spec" simply means that the script is written on speculation—no one is paying the writer to write the script. The dream of most screenwriters is that they'll write that amazing spec screenplay from their fertile imagination, and it will bring them a six-figure paycheck. Alas, this rarely happens. A much more likely scenario is that the screenwriter will write that spec script—say, a thriller—and if they're lucky, the script will get seen by someone at a studio or production company. If that studio likes the script, will they buy it? Probably not—remember, they really don't want to take the risk. However, the studio may have just bought a novel in the thriller genre, and seeing the screenwriter can write a thriller, they might get him or her a meeting with the studio about adapting that novel. And what happens in that meeting will determine whether or not the screenwriter will get the job to write the adaptation of that novel. Prior to that meeting, the screenwriter will have been given the book and during the meeting will lay out the film he or she will write. In less than twenty minutes, the screenwriter will have to wow the studio executives with the kind of adaptation he or she proposes to write. Basically, the screenwriter auditions for the job. Consequently, if writers have experience writing *only* original material, they will be at an extreme disadvantage in the real world of screenwriting. If you don't know how to take material from another source and adapt it into a screenplay, you can lose your shot at breaking into the business.

CREATING A COURSE IN WRITING THE ADAPTATION: THE CHALLENGE AND THE RESULT

On campuses in the United States, nearly all the screenwriting classes focus on teaching students to create original screenplays. And yet, as mentioned, more than half of films made each year are from adapted—not original—screenplays. In addition to people not realizing this fact, teaching a course in writing the adaptation requires a great deal more from the professor than does teaching any other kind of screenwriting course.

The average screenwriting course—no matter what level—requires the professor to impart wisdom on the art and craft of screenwriting. The students will then write screenplays, or portions of screenplays, which the professor will read and evaluate. In a course on writing the adaptation, the professor does all of that but must also read all of the source material for each student's adaptation. So, if the professor has a class of twelve students and each of them chooses to adapt a novel, the professor must read all the novels, in addition to reading all the students' creative work during the course of the semester. The amount of time required for such a class is demanding, to say the least. Of course, not every student will choose a novel—some might choose a short story or a fairy tale or even a poem to adapt. But whatever the student chooses becomes material the professor must read carefully in order to be able to judge how effectively the student has adapted that material for the screen.

In my own teaching at Emerson College, I had to bear all these ideas in mind: after much mulling over the goals of a course in writing adaptations, this is the course description I created:

> This course focuses on the process of analyzing material from another medium (novels, plays, biographies, comic books, fairy tales, etc.) and translating that material into a screenplay. Through lecture, exercises, viewing films, and discussion with peers, students work to understand the process of adaptation. Students produce two large projects in the course of the semester, one analytical paper and one original first act of a public domain property.

RESTRICTING STUDENTS TO PROPERTIES IN THE PUBLIC DOMAIN: IS THIS NECESSARY?

The easy answer is "no." A property is in the public domain if there are no laws regarding a creative piece of work that restrict the general public from using that work, that is, royalties no longer need to be paid to author or (if the author is deceased) to their estate. Works created and published before 1923 in the United States are generally in the public domain; the same applies to pre-1964 work, if their copyrights were not renewed. The copyright laws have changed over the years, so the student must carefully investigate whether or not a property they're interested in is in the public domain and therefore free to be adapted. If so, then the student can write a screenplay based upon that property and sell it; the original writer of that property and/or the writer's heirs will have no right to the profits from the sale of that screenplay.

Students may choose to adapt a property that is *not* in the public domain if they're aware of what they're doing. If they are fans of a novel that's at the top of the best-seller list, that novel won't be in the public domain for decades. But if students want to adapt it as a classroom exercise or as a writing sample—and understand that they can never sell that adaptation—I have no problem with the idea. I tell them to include, on the cover page of the screenplay, a disclaimer like this: "This screenplay is an adaptation of the novel [title of novel] by [author of novel] published in [year novel was published] by [name of publishing house], and the rights to that novel have *not* been obtained." It's important to realize, though, that if students are using the adaptation simply as a kind of calling card to show what they can do as writers, this kind of sample script with the disclaimer is perfectly justified.

But unless students are absolutely passionate about adapting a certain property not in the public domain, I encourage them to find a public domain property to adapt. After all, writing a script is a great deal of work— why shouldn't they be able to sell the screenplay once they have finished it?

CHOOSING THE TYPE OF PROPERTY TO ADAPT

Properties to adapt include novels, plays, short stories, fables, fairy tales, biographies, nonfiction books, poems, graphic novels, comic books, films and television shows [i.e., remakes], and even video games. The list is growing all the time. I ask students, what do they really want—to take a large property like a four-hundred-page novel and pare it down into just over a hundred pages? That's certainly a challenge. Or would they prefer to take a 4-page fairy tale and expand it into a 100–115-page screenplay? That's another type of challenge. Whichever direction they choose to go in, I encourage students to adapt a property that's in a genre they absolutely love. The fact is, as a writer, you live with that property day and night—you end up *dreaming* about it, it gets so deep into your psyche! So you'd better choose a genre that's close to your heart.

PREPARING THE STUDENT TO ADAPT MATERIAL

The first day of the semester I have students watch the film *Ever After*. Is this my favorite adaptation? Not at all. It is, however, a good adaptation of the Cinderella story that's quite easy to dissect. When *Ever After* came out in 1998, I refused to see it. I remember railing against the prospect of yet another Cinderella story. I never liked the kind of values it seemed to preach to girls—particularly the idea that the ultimate goal in life for a girl is to marry a prince. I not only had ideological problems with the story, but also I found the story so trite, so full of stereotypes, and so hackneyed I really couldn't stand it. Eventually, someone dragged me to the movie, assuring me I'd like it. And he was right. I was enchanted by *Ever After*. It was smart and endearing, transforming the Cinderella character into a real woman with an intellectual inclination—imagine that! It was a clever, fresh take on a familiar story—every adapter's dream. Beginning a class in writing adaptations by showing films like this, and talking about fairy tales, gets the students thinking about how some of the stories they've known since childhood can be the subject of adaptation.

On the second day of the semester, I put students in small groups and have them brainstorm ideas for adapting fairy tales like *Little Red Riding Hood* and *The Three Little Pigs*. I make sure to have multiple groups working on a single fairy tale. The students are told they can set the fairy tale in any time period, they can change it around as they like, they can make it animated or live action, and they can make it literal or metaphorical. After a half hour, during which time they have created a rough three-act structure, each group pitches their idea to the rest of the class. It's absolutely fascinating to see the sheer variety of ideas created; I've had "Red Riding Hood in Space" and "Red Riding Hood in the Wild West." I've had the Three Little Pigs on Wall Street and in Vietnam. Sometimes, students use these ideas as a basis for their writing project at the end of the whole semester.

After the fairy tale exercise, we view clips of films based on familiar tales and discuss the process of taking that source material and adapting it for the screen. One way to understand, in a more organic fashion, how to adapt a property is to study the process in more detail. This constitutes the next stage of the course.

STUDYING "FAITHFUL" AND "NONFAITHFUL" ADAPTATIONS

If you're a film buff, you read a book and very much look forward to the film adaptation of that book. But, more often than not, as you exit the theater you might find yourself saying to your companion, "The book was so much better." Nine times out of ten, those who loved the book will find the film a poor substitute. It's understandable—a 500-page book reduced into a 115-page screenplay is never going to incorporate everything that was in the book. All screenwriters can do is to try to capture the *spirit*, the *essence*, of that work, but how might this be achieved?

In preparing students for this task in their own writing, I find that focusing on a "faithful" and a "nonfaithful" adaptation can prove useful. And when I use the word "faithful" I mean being faithful to the spirit of the book, which doesn't necessarily mean being literally faithful to its plot and characters. Two films I've used for this kind of study are *Practical Magic* and *The Hours*.

Practical Magic was a novel written by Alice Hoffman in 1995 and subsequently written for the screen by Robin Swicord, Akiva Goldsman, and Adam Brooks in 1998.[1] I have students read the book, then watch the film. After the film is over, I ask them, "Is that the book you read?" and they invariably shout "No!" en masse. The film version is so different in terms of tone, location, character, and plot; only two scenes from the novel are actually re-created in it. So, by anyone's estimation, *Practical Magic* is not a faithful adaptation of the novel. Was it a successful film? Yes. Was it a film of the book Alice Hoffman wrote? Not really. And by examining a couple of versions of the screenplay, we can then see the journey that was taken by various screenwriters to create the movie version. We can see that the studio was not particularly concerned with being faithful to the spirit of the book; their interest focused much more on how to alter the plot and the characterization in order to bring more people into the theater and thereby increase the return on their investment.

The Hours is a different story. The novel, written in 2000 by Michael Cunningham was adapted for the screen in 2002 by the British dramatist and screenwriter David Hare.[2] It is what I would term a faithful adaptation in the sense that much of the feel of the novel has been re-created for the screen. Hare took a very difficult book and managed to interweave the stories of the three women in a structure resembling that of the novel. Students read the novel and the screenplay, and subsequently watch the film—in that order, to understand the creative journey Hare undertook. This helps prepare them for a more thorough analysis of a film in their first major assignment of the semester.

THE ANALYTICAL PAPER ASSIGNMENT

Although this class is taught as a screenwriting class, it's my opinion that by analyzing how a film is created from source material through various screenplay adaptations into the finished product, the aspiring screenwriter learns a great deal about the writing process. After choosing from a list of fifty adaptations, each student writes an analytical paper and prepares an oral presentation on the evolution of the screenplay source material to screen. For example, if students choose *Sin City* for this assignment, they will read: (1) the three graphic novels on which the film was based; (2) as many drafts of the screenplay that are available; and (3) the final shooting script for the film. In addition, of course, students will carefully study the film. The aim of this assignment is to look at what part of the source material was left out, changed, or added for the screenplay by the screenwriter(s). Students also concentrate on what they might have done differently in adapting the material and how such choices might have resulted in a different film. By studying the journey the screenwriter took to adapt the source material, students will be in a better position to embark on the same journey in the second major assignment of the semester.

WRITING THE ADAPTED SCREENPLAY

The culmination of the student's work in this class is to produce an outline for a feature film and to write the first act of between twenty-five and thirty pages. I put together what I call *The Studio List*, a list of about one hundred public domain properties that I feel might be interesting to adapt. Sometimes I merely list the source material, and sometimes I give examples of what the "studio" is looking for—the idea being that a studio will have certain criteria in deciding whether to fund the adaptation of a property that the writer needs to fulfill. Here are some examples from my *Studio List*:

Hans Christian Andersen (the studio likes these stories as potential properties for developing as animated children's films or modern-day adult fare: *The Emperor's New Clothes, The Snow Queen,* or *The Ugly Duckling*);
Anton Chekhov (*The Seagull* or *The Cherry Orchard*);
Alexandre Dumas (*The Three Musketeers,* rewritten as an urban dramedy of two men and one woman who unite to do something of import in their city);
Robert Frost (poetry);
Henrik Ibsen (*A Doll's House*: the studio is interested in setting this in 1960s America);
Henry James (*Daisy Miller*: the studio is not interested in doing another embarrassing period piece of this novel but rather prefers a modern-day take of an American girl visiting a Muslim country in the present day—and yes, we're talking about a drama, *not* a romantic comedy).

This semester (spring 2008–2009) students are adapting a wide variety of material—from *Little Red Riding Hood* to *Crime and Punishment,* to stories by H. G. Wells and Edgar Allan Poe and poetry by Carl Sandburg. Such a broad range of subjects makes for an interesting mix of scripts.

Since the students taking this course in adaptation have already taken elementary courses in screenwriting, it's not necessary to spend time on the fundamentals of creating a screenplay. Instead, our time is spent on discussing how one goes about adapting the works they have chosen. Thus, the crux of what we discuss becomes relevant to what the students are adapting.

THE END-OF-SEMESTER ACTIVITY

The semester ends with each student bringing multiple copies of their completed scripts, and the class as a whole reads them aloud. The screenwriters are then able to sit back and listen to how their work sounds. After the reading, each member of the class writes comments on the scripts and hands them back. We also spend time discussing the scripts in class, so the writers get the chance to see whether their adaptations worked. As the material chosen is usually in the public domain, each student is encouraged to finish their adaptation after the course ends. Should they opt to pursue screenwriting as a profession, having a completed example of their work is a good beginning—it shows producers and studios that they possess the ability to adapt material that is not their own. In addition, as the source material is in the public domain, the student might be able to offer the script for sale to any interested producers/studios.

CONCLUSION

One student observed in the evaluation for this course that they were "not sure what I was actually expecting out of the class. I always wanted to write my own thing, or write for an existing show, but I definitely learned the value of—and how hard it can be to write successful—adaptations." From my perspective, that student hit the nail on the head: screenwriters come into programs at college level and have all sorts of ideas about what they'd like to write, the worlds they'd like to create, and the people they'd like to bring to life on the page. But since the majority of films made are adaptations, it's of paramount importance for the screenwriter to know what adapting a film involves. My hope is that, when they're offered that job to adapt a book or play, they'll be able to dig into the work, uncover its spirit or essence, and bring that to life in their adaptation.

NOTES

1. Alice Hoffman, *Practical Magic* (New York: Berkley Trade Books, 2003); *Practical Magic* [1998], Dir. Griffin Dunne, Perf. Sandra Bullock, Nicole Kidman, Stockard Channing (DVD 0790740060: Warner Home Video, 1998).

2. Michael Cunningham, *The Hours* (London: Picador, 2002); *The Hours* [2002], Dir. Stephen Daldry, Perf. Nicole Kidman, Julianne Moore, Meryl Streep (DVD B00005JKTI: Paramount Home Video, 2003).

EIGHT

WHOSE LIFE *IS* IT, ANYWAY?

Adaptation, Collective Memory, and (Auto)Biographical Processes

Suzanne Diamond

> A man is always a teller of tales; he lives surrounded by his stories and
> the stories of others; he sees everything that happens to him through
> them, and he tries to live his life as if he were recounting it.
>
> —Jean Paul Sartre, *Nausea*[1]

Sometimes the approaches that facilitate energizing instruction in a given
field collide head-on with those geared toward producing a more sophisticated critical discourse. In the arena of film adaptation study, I wish to
argue for two pedagogical tenets that could be construed as out-and-out
heresy within adaptation scholarship. First, I propose that we do not *know*
what adaptation *is*, in any satisfactory sense; second, I argue that "fidelity studies"—roundly discredited among adaptation theorists—represent
not only a defensible but also a highly *productive* mode of inquiry for
students from a range of disciplinary backgrounds, those who are just
beginning to think about adaptation, its procedures, and its implications.
The best way to recruit student interest in this fascinating field is to resist
both facile definitions of our subject matter and restrictive rules regarding
our engagement with it. Because these approaches put me at loggerheads
with current critical wisdom, I will digress briefly by way of anchoring
the pedagogy I recommend as part of a conversation with recent adaptation scholarship.

   The final chapter of Linda Hutcheon's book *A Theory of Adaptation*
poses—ultimately to preempt in certain ways—a richly provocative question: "What is *not* an adaptation?"[2] This question, when read rhetorically,

implies a more fundamental one: What *is* adaptation? I mean to argue that
it is critically important—as well as intellectually candid—for instructors to resist potentially reductive answers to this fundamental question
because the question itself has the potential to incite multidisciplinary
speculation from the varied student populations that introductory film
courses currently attract. Why recast an available story for a new age or
within a new medium? Arguably, students with career interests in fields
such as psychology, political science, religious studies, art, economics,
along with those in film studies, literature, and language studies are
likely to have widely varied answers to this question when it functions
as the course's speculative backdrop. In fact, ruminating on what we talk
about when we talk about adaptation opens students' minds to the ex-
plosion of contemporary theorizing about how and why individuals and
cultures invoke the past at all. As Sidonie Smith and Julia Watson argue,
"Memory, the project for the millennium, has now come to preoccupy
scholars from all areas of the academy—from philosophers to neurosci-
entists, from cultural critics to psychologists, from quantum theorists
to poets. Increasingly, scholars are studying the making and unmaking
of memory—personal, collective, biochemical."[3] Various contemporary
psychological and epistemological findings establish that our notions of
the world we inhabit—indeed, our most basic ideas about who we *are*—
come to us by way of the story lines our cultures make possible and the
work we do with these story lines. We are, in other words, constant and
inveterate adapters.

Unfortunately, "what is *not* adaptation?" does not function as a rhetorical or philosophical question for Hutcheon but rather as a practical one;
as she readily acknowledges, the coherence of her theory of adaptation
depends upon a literalistic definition of its object. In her nomenclature,
only works that openly announce and sustain their connection to a designated prior work "qualify" as "adaptations" proper. Resolution trumps
uncertainty here, the resultant hierarchy required in scholarship, perhaps,
but the kiss of death in a classroom. Accordingly, while she grants some
credence to claims such as that of Daniel Fischlin and Mark Fortier (that
"adaptation includes almost any act of alteration performed upon specific
cultural works of the past"), Hutcheon ultimately elects to whitewash
this messy phenomenon with a tidy theory. "From a pragmatic point of
view," she argues, "such a vast definition would clearly make adaptation rather difficult to theorize."[4] Rationalized as "closer to the common
usage of the word," Hutcheon's "more restricted definition" facilitates
generalization, permitting the theorist "to draw distinctions; for instance,
allusions to and brief echoes of other works *would not qualify* as extended
engagements, nor do [sic] most examples of musical sampling, because
they recontextualize only short fragments of music (emphasis mine)."[5]

Defining adaptation this rigidly necessitates other exclusions, too: paro-
dies, plagiarisms (unauthorized and unacknowledged borrowings, by
definition), along with prequels, sequels, and fan fiction—all must be removed from the picture because apparently "there is a difference between
never wanting a story to end . . . and wanting to retell the same story
over and over in different ways."[6] But the most provocative and generative questions that one might pose in a film course are matters Hutcheon
leaves untheorized: whether a differently told story is, in fact, "the same"
story; where "difference" and "sameness" inhere among stories; and who
is authorized to establish these distinctions.[7] Here, theoretical coherence
is purchased at a great pedagogical cost. Resisting the ultimately always
dishonest position of "the one who knows," I propose that encouraging
students' comparisons of oft-retold stories has the potential to instigate a
broader range of future interdisciplinary scholarship and thus to situate
adaptation—highly engaging even when construed literally but richly
productive when released from a literalistic framework—within a larger
and more generative analysis of the interconnections between memory
and identity.

Moving to a second basic tenet of adaptation theory—the often implicit
but sometimes explicit critique of "fidelity studies"—I wish to interrogate
this taboo in the interest of constructive pedagogy as well. As the legacy of
a once dismissive literature-oriented culture, fidelity-oriented approaches
to adaptation tend to trigger defensive responses among contemporary
theorists. This now discredited approach lurks when Hutcheon insists
that the experience of adaptation is a bidirectional "oscillation"—and not
a "hierarchy"—between a former story iteration and a subsequent one.
The precaution is well taken, but, I suggest, it is superfluous—and possibly even pernicious—when applied to contemporary students' experiences, since they frequently enter film courses without the literary prejudices defensively anticipated by such a formulation. Clearly, Hutcheon's
subtext makes sense to readers familiar with the history of adaptation
study; the "oscillation" model counters the knee-jerk dismissal of literary
adaptations—along with other cultural forms once dismissed as "popular
culture"—that at one time too often characterized film analysis.

A judgmental, if largely unidentified, auditor haunts the critical in-
junction against "fidelity" analysis. Hutcheon infers that assessments
of faithfulness betray a kind of class bias when aimed at contemporary
media, reminding readers that adaptation is a practice dating back well
beyond Shakespeare. When an adaptation is viewed as "lowering" a be-
loved text, she cautions, negative assessments are sure to follow, and it is
this unquestioned hierarchy between films and their source texts that she
rightly challenges. My point is simply that students do not tend to express
such prejudices.

Thomas Leitch shares with Hutcheon this emphatic dismissal of critical assessments focused strictly on the issue of how well an adaptation adheres to its putative "source" text.[8] Concurring with Hutcheon's distaste for fidelity-based critiques, though with different reasoning, Leitch similarly urges those engaged in adaptation studies to move beyond reductive notions of what film adaptations ought to accomplish. Citing Dudley Andrew, Leitch wonders,

> In the twenty years since . . . Andrew complained that "the most frequent and most tiresome discussion of adaptation . . . concerns fidelity and transformation," why has the field continued to organize itself so largely around a single one of these positions, the position that novels are texts, movies are intertexts, and in any competition between the two, the book is better?[9]

However justified these recommendations might be, I suggest that in rejecting the critical commonplace that "the book was better" we need not impose an equally categorical prohibition against analyses based on "fidelity and transformation." Of course, measuring a film's "faithfulness" to specified sources for moralistic or righteous purposes is an inherently bankrupt activity, but I would insist that the comparative impulse itself promises to broaden the kinds of analysis adaptation studies could otherwise promote. What if it's occasionally accurate that "the book is better"? Procedural babies, in other words, needn't be cast out with the bathwater of outmoded prejudices.

As those of us who teach courses on film and adaptation can attest, students with concentrations in many academic fields are attracted to these subjects; finding ways to address the preconceptions they bring to our classrooms whets their intellectual appetite for future film analysis. Why forbid readers and viewers from venturing to say that the book—or the movie—"was better" when declarations like this—as I hope to demonstrate—can easily launch productive discussions?

One solution is to situate film adaptation within a broader understanding of social memory work. What if an instructor begins a class by addressing the question of what adaptation is and then applying it to specific texts: a media event, play, novel, or film. By looking at how a text is transformed from one medium into another, film instructors can tether a "fidelity analysis" to a more complicated exploration of culture, psychology, history, politics, and the function of remembering within all of these. This exploration, in turn, can encourage students to draw on developing expertise in these other disciplines in order to speculate on the forces that shape the story's reformulation. What psychological shifts does the "new" story impose on the former one? Which aspects of the former story does the adaptation change, amplify, or forget altogether, and how might these adjustments be explained? How do these questions help to address the prevailing issue of "what is adaptation?" What correlations can be discovered between how we adapt old stories, on the one hand, and how we use our memories, on the other?[10]

In my own teaching, I broaden the notion of adaptation by exploring a specific case study that has occasioned sustained and intensive cultural reworking. No doubt, readers can imagine their own oft-adapted stories to teach, but I find an excellent focus in the 1906 Chester Gillette murder trial, a historic event in New York that caused frenzied attention in the media. As many readers will already know, this event and the proliferated journalistic story building that surrounded it inspired Theodore Dreiser's novel *An American Tragedy*, in 1925, a novel that, in turn, was first adapted by Paramount into a film of the same title in 1931, then into the retitled and better-known film, *A Place in the Sun*, in 1951. In the meantime, this story has seen various adaptations on Broadway and television, most recently in a 2005 opera by Tobias Smith. Something about the tale keeps attracting creative adaptation.

As I demonstrate in the classroom, readers have made sense of this story's continuing attractiveness in different ways. For instance, simultaneously historicizing and dehistoricizing the continued attraction of this plot, F. Paul Driscoll has remarked that this is "a timeless story of the American Dream gone wrong."[11] But, of course, "the American Dream" is culturally and historically *quite* specific—it is anything but "timeless" or value neutral—and such a varied series of retellings as this story involves requires explanation. What is the impact, I ask students, of homogenizing this series of adaptations as Driscoll does? What politics underwrite the impulse to describe this tragedy—or "the American Dream"—as something "timeless"?

Likewise, attending to differences in the story's iterations involves critical politics that can be interrogated in the classroom. Other readers and viewers, for instance, have been more attentive than Driscoll to discrepancies among iterations as this compelling plot has undergone multiple reformulations. Joseph W. Brownell and Patricia W. Enos provide a useful, even if moralistically motivated, guide through the court case, its contemporaneous media representation, and its subsequent reformulations in novel and films.[12] Primary among their purposes is an attempt to recover the basic historical truths of this case in the hope of separating "source" facts from subsequent mythologizing; rather than excluding a study entailing such a presumably reductive or naive purpose, I elect to make this investigation and its authors' interest in "facts" alone the subject of constructive classroom analysis. Why are these historians unnerved by the various fictionalizations of the Chester Gillette case? How and why does their approach to these adaptations compare or contrast with Driscoll's?

Sure enough, the tone of righteousness associated with traditional "fidelity discourse" creeps into Brownell and Enos's account: Dreiser's novel not only "adapts, but takes liberties with, original documentation."[13] They observe that "like a modern screenwriter who creates a motion picture script from an earlier novel, Dreiser carefully sculptured a novel out of an earlier event, the Gillette case."[14] Implicitly, one might say, their book charges that (to adjust Andrew's phrase) "the facts were better," but this purpose does not nullify or disqualify their findings; it helps us to understand their methodology and priorities. For them, Dreiser's novel has transgressed indelibly upon the history that inspired it. Waxing downright peevish, for instance, they marvel at how a story's subsequent retelling could so alter the perceptions of what the original story was that "they [the authors] give falsehood a robust and lasting constitution. Misinformation about the Gillette case continues to abound and it often has its roots in Dreiser."[15]

I contend that, with guidance, students are well up to the challenge of identifying this fidelity obsession—with its "irritations" over "faults," "falsehoods," and "misinformation"—and subsequently distinguishing it from their own purposes in trying to understand the story adjustments implied by an adaptation. Brownell and Enos's ideas might form the basis of a useful classroom discussion: under what circumstances might it be appropriate—or at least understandable—to become "irritated" by the fictional adaptation of a historic event? Which features of the adaptation most upset these authors, and are there trends among the changes that bother them the most? When and why might it be important to keep source "facts" straight?

It is a truism to observe that, once you tell a story, it is no longer yours to control. Who, one might ask, owns the story played out in the courts and popular press by Chester Gillette and Grace Brown, and subsequently by a host of characters with altered names and circumstances? Dreiser's adaptation, as historians readily acknowledge, represents just one in a frenzied succession of reworkings that first surfaced in the media, while the novel itself became a focus of cultural memory, reviving interest in a trial that might otherwise have been consigned to oblivion. As to whether Dreiser adapted too liberally or adhered too slavishly to historical truth, perhaps this is not particularly significant. Brownell and Enos claim "the cast was ready made. Dreiser needed to disguise the principals and alter places and events, but only when necessary to achieve the smooth flow of a fictional story."[16] For this reason, Dreiser was able to "adhere so closely to the truth that in the final scenes, he merely paraphrased parts of the actual courtroom testimony."[17] Throwing up their metaphorical hands, the authors accept that readers can "argue for either unconscious plagiarism or literary genius" in Dreiser's novel. A thought-provoking instructor can capitalize on the ideology underlying such binarisms: What is "plagiarism"? What is "genius"? What logic makes opposites of the two, and how does this logic inform our understanding of creative or adaptive processes?

Brownell and Enos not only engage in a fidelity study themselves but also help students discover that the many representations of this trial and its mythology have themselves been characterized by fundamental struggles over issues of "faithfulness," and hence that "fidelity analysis" might be more than just a bugbear within film adaptation studies; it might just be a crucial beginning point in our understanding of the revision process. When Dreiser's novel was first adapted for the 1931 Paramount film,[18] for instance, the novel's author himself became agitated enough about perceived disparities between the new work and his "source" text that he took immediate legal action. Brownell and Enos summarize that "he was outraged and claimed that the movie completely misrepresented the novel."[19] Ironically, fidelity was the grounds on which he lost this case, as "Supreme Court Justice Gragam Witschief of White Plains, New York, ruled that the film was a *faithful representation* of the book" (emphasis mine).[20] Principals in the legal case, too, carefully guarded the boundaries between representations of the trial and their own involvement in it. For example, when a local theater in Norwich, New York (near Grace Brown's hometown), used newspaper accounts of the Gillette trial to promote the new film, Grace Brown's mother sued both the theater and Paramount studios for the infringement of their story upon her privacy.

Perhaps understandably, given this litigious climate (though Brownell and Enos find it "inexplicable"), the screenwriters who adapted *American Tragedy* for the 1951 film changed every character's name and further altered the tale.[21] These successive adaptations have compounded what Brownell and Enos view as the layered folklore that has clouded our understanding of the actual lives and deaths of Grace Brown and Chester Gillette, to the point where recovering "the real story" has become all but impossible. Bearing this in mind, the fidelities chased down by Brownell and Enos might seem tedious, even "tiresome" (to use Andrew's term) in their minuteness. Yet, both criticism and classroom discourse would be impoverished if pursuits such as this one were discouraged or marginalized. Whether or not one believes in the possibility of retrieving "the real" story, it remains legitimate and pedagogically fruitful to examine the politics of revision as this (or any) story becomes serially adapted. And the serial nature of the adaptation process produces far more complex discourses, rather than simply stating that "the book was better," even if that's where the discussion begins.

I want to suggest that revisions themselves tell cultural stories. Using Brownell and Enos's analysis, we might focus on fidelity-based questions such as the following: What should we make of *A Place in the Sun*'s (1951) adjustment of the fatal holiday weekend from Independence Day (as it was in Chester Gillette's case and in Dreiser's adaptation) to Labor Day? What are the implications of this script's alteration of the pregnant girl's name from Robert Alden, as Dreiser crafted it, to the troublingly allegorical-sounding "Alice Tripp"? How is the story changed by its adjustment of Dreiser's incredibly ironic "collar" factory into a women's swimsuit factory in 1951? Might there be reasons beyond legal self-protection for the change in the title? Did contemporaneous history—for example, the McCarthy hearings—play a role in this iteration of the story or in any of its adjustments? And what about the politics of casting: what are we to make of the often abrasive Shelley Winters in the role of "Alice Tripp"? Viewing a current adaptation through the lens of a past story iteration is crucial in the process of formulating answers to questions like these, questions which, in turn, promote speculation about how and why a current story iteration continues, amplifies, or revises the cultural work of its predecessors. What does the process of adaptation tell us about the past, our ways of remembering, and our contemporary selves? What attracts us to some stories over and over again? What is adaptation doing for—or to—*us*?

Students—along with my own present readers—might reasonably ask: what do adaptation and fidelity-based comparative analyses have to do with ourselves? To answer this question requires backtracking to unpack assumptions we bring to key terms such as "self," "narration," and "memory." Even those of us who might be aware of the slippage between language, on the one hand, and the actualities it purports to represent on the other, can be lulled into believing we hold handy definitions of familiar concepts like "self" and "memory." When we focus on the meanings evoked by these terms, however, we might be able to better apprehend their implications.

Many social and life-writing theorists concur in the view that selfhood is strictly a function of memory work. I mean to extend this insight in order to argue that the analysis of adaptation offers a rich metaphorical corollary to the processes (usually construed as individual) involved in remembering and negotiating "who we are." To develop this argument, I first turn to the robust body of contemporary scholarship on identity and memory. James M. Lampinen, Timothy N. Odegard, and Juliana K. Leding propose that "people's naïve theories of the self" must be addressed in any attempt to explore self-construction in a sophisticated manner.[22] They argue that "evidence suggests that many people are essentialists," believing that "there is some unalterable core that defines us."[23] To understand the concept of self-building—and the function of critical memory work within that process—requires a distancing from such essentialism. Sidonie Smith and Julia Watson argue that this can be done through an examination of first-person narration that, in their view, signifies a historically and culturally situated phenomenon: "What we have understood as the autobiographical 'I' has been an 'I' with a historical attitude—a sign of the Enlightenment subject, unified, rational, coherent, autonomous, free, but also white, male, Western. This subject has been variously called 'the individual' or 'the universal human subject' or 'man.'"[24] The self of autobiography turns out, no less than universals such as "woman" or "truth," to be nothing more than an enduring metaphor, one that has facilitated some strategies while suppressing others. The increasing critical tendency, however, is to construe the self as a function—if not a product—of narration itself. In "Self-Making Narratives," Jerome Bruner states the case radically, observing that, "in effect, there is no such thing as an intuitively obvious and essential self to know, one that just sits there to be portrayed in words. Rather, we constantly construct and reconstruct a self to meet the needs of the situations we encounter, and do so with the guidance of our memories of the past and our hopes and fears for the future."[25] Memories, in this formulation, are the modeling clay—not the cold storage—of a coherent identity. Moreover, self-building memory narratives seem to be confined and channeled by master narratives, that is, by cultural imperatives dictating what may or may not be expressed or even acknowledged as known in a given period. And these master narratives are historically subject to continuous examination and cultural adjustment. Bruner observes, for instance, that "narrative acts of self-making are typically guided by unspoken, implicit cultural models of what selfhood should be and what it might be—and, of course, what it should not be."[26] These narratives exert dominance over how we construe and communicate selfhood; he argues that "telling others about oneself is . . . no simple matter; it depends on what we think they think we ought to be like. Nor do such calculations end when we come to telling ourselves about ourselves."[27]

Implicitly, such self-policing entails conceiving of self-sharing and self-negotiation in the limited terms we believe others will "hear" us through. Yet, Bruner implies that autobiography in its literalistic sense is not the only form of self-shaping communication; we convey who we are every time we feel impelled into discourse, every time we experience occasions important enough to argue about. In metonymic fashion, our interventions in specific discourses also convey our stakes in that discourse and thus a glimpse into our identities. We represent ourselves, in other words, even when we are not referencing our "selves" in a prescribed manner. Conjuring past experiences and inferring present circumstances, we construct and propose social identities. Most of us, according to Bruner,

> never get around to composing a full-scale autobiography. Self-telling, rather, is mostly provoked by episodes related to some longer term concern. Although linked to or provoked by particular happenings, it ordinarily [does not overtly reference but only] presupposes those longer term, larger scale concerns—much as history writing where the *annales* record of particular events is already somehow determined or shaped by a more encompassing *chronique*, which itself bears the stamp of an over-arching *historie*. An account of a battle takes for granted the existence of a war which takes for granted the even larger notion of competitive nation-states and a world order.[28]

And just as we complicate our notion of what selves are and how they are negotiated in discourse, we must interrogate easy understandings of what "memory" means. *Regimes of Memory*, a collection edited by Susannah Radstone and Katharine Hodgkin, attempts to defamiliarize and thus expand how we understand the act of recollection as well because the regimes of memory and of subjectivity, as they point out, are deeply intertwined. They try to focus on "the 'work' memory has done . . . in . . . the production of subjectivity and of the public/private relation," by proposing that the "study of regimes of memory might complicate as well as simply deepen our understandings of related regimes—for instance, of subjectivity, of history, or of the mind."[29]

These theorists, obviously, do not focus on story or film adaptations per se, but their ideas about the cultural implications of memory have clear and direct application to the study of adaptation as memory work. For instance, Radstone and Hodgkin observe that certain "'productions' of memory [highlight] what historical or contemporary figurations of memory 'forget,' exclude, render unthinkable or make marginal [since] all productions of memory are also productions of what memory is not, and . . . such inclusions and exclusions constitute a politics of memory discourses."[30] Their analysis also permits a collective understanding of how cultural memory can be employed; in place of individualized and restrictive—some might say bourgeois—ideas, they propose collective and cultural ways of understanding what we do when we look back:

> In contemporary memory studies, the focus falls not only on individual, private memory, but on historical, social, cultural and popular memory, too [along with] the collective or social domains of memory. This contrasts strikingly with the early modern period, in which memory was the refuge of the individual and where the relation between that individual memory and the public sphere appeared fraught.[31]

We understand our past in historically contingent ways, as Radstone and Hodgkin underscore, and the question of how we remember and forget is inherently political.

Extending this idea, I suggest that in positing what had been important in a past story iteration—or what has been gained or lost in a current one—we employ a similar theoretical strategy. Instructors, along with their students, can *learn* the ways in which the past—personal and cultural—is linked to the present simply by asking "why?" Psychologists have recently begun to question the reductive ways we have understood memory's function: Lampinen and colleagues observe that "memory is not just for memorizing."[32] Christina Papoulis shares this impulse to expand the notion of memory beyond individual assumptions, asserting that memory must be understood in its manifestations as a "material social practice rather than as mental faculty, and as inhering in inter-mental, rather than intra-mental processes: in intersubjective relations, in talk."[33] Applying these notions to adaptation studies enables us to see that, in determining how a given adaptation sustains or departs from *any* remembered "source text," we are doing nothing less than negotiating who we collectively *are*, how we recall, and what we continue to find important. In short, we are negotiating a "we." Instructors and students alike must be free to decide for themselves—on a case-by-case basis—whether or how a current cultural artifact references previous works: to proclaim in our own terms what, in other words, adaptation *is*. Thus, "fidelity-based" analyses—speculations about what has been lost, gained, amplified, or stifled in the transition from old to new—are not only *allowable*, but they also constitute important cultural identity work and therefore represent a critical classroom enterprise.

Personality theorists have observed that, even on an individual level, we continuously consult—and when necessary, revise—memories of the past in accordance with the needs of today. Jessica Cameron, Anne E. Wilson, and Michael Ross confirm a statistically significant "hindsight bias" in the personal use of memories, a process of constant self-serving adaptation and revision and an equally systematic erasure of the inconvenient aspects of a superseded past.[34] In fact, adaptation and life-writing processes share this widely observed tendency to supplant outgrown stories. Autobiography theorist Paul John Eakin observes this tendency in Kim Chernin's account of changes wrought on the author's mother, Rose, by the portrayal of herself that she encountered in her daughter's memoirs. He observes Chernin's recollection, for instance, that

at a bookstore promotion the mother is presented as "simultaneously the Rose Chernin she had always been, as well as, now, the central character of a book her daughter was proudly signing." The shift in power relations between the two is completed when Kim overhears Rose telling one of her own

stories *but in Kim's words*: [Kim notes that,] "after that, my mother never, to
my knowledge, told her stories again in her own voice. From that moment in
the bookstore she had taken over, *or been taken over by*, the voice I had created
for her" (emphasis in Eakin).[35]

This phenomenon is observable yet again when we return to the provocative case study involving Chester Gillette's trial. Brownell and Enos note
that Roy C. Higby, the boy who had first discovered Grace Brown's body
in the South Bay, himself later submits to the version of events imposed
by Dreiser's narrative:

> For decades, Higby had told and retold the story of the search to fascinated
> visitors at his retreat on Big Moose Lake. He was prevailed upon to write
> down his rich memoirs of Adirondack life and publish them [which he did
> in 1974]. No one was ever more qualified. Still, in the chapter that deals with
> the tragic death of Grace Brown, something fails. There is no problem with
> the events related to the search. Higby was there and his recall is dependable.
> The problem lies in the rest of the chapter. When Higby came to describe
> who Chester and Grace were, and how they happened to be at Big Moose,
> he drew not from newspaper files, but from memory. Unfortunately, his
> memory was heavily influenced by *An American Tragedy*.[36]

As these historians acknowledge, the newspapers would hardly have provided Higby with a better guide to the past than the boy's own memory,
and their laundry list of the items Higby gets wrong is characteristically
persnickety: the old man mischaracterizes Gillette's city of origin and his
position at the Gillette factory, he adopts the fictional existence of the rich
girlfriend and Dreiser's account of whether the young man's attorney
was hired by the rich uncle, and so on. For Brownell and Enos, these slips
constitute "failures" of historiography, areas where an adaptation's "influence" makes "problems" for the unmediated recall of "facts." By now, "the
Gillette background he related is what most people today think that they
remember—and they do, but what they remember is the novel and the
movies, not fact."[37] But the borders separating stories, films, and facts are inevitably more permeable than Brownell and Enos might wish; this is under-
scored by Patricia Leavy in *Iconic Events*, a book that explores the cultural
impact of events made "iconic" by media saturation. Leavy observes that

> films are complex and ideological texts. Films do not recount the "truth" of
> the past, but rather present a version of truth that is bound to the time and
> place in which it was produced. Furthermore, film not only depicts some
> aspect of social reality, it also produces and shapes that reality. Films can
> also reinforce or challenge general perceptions about an (imagined) past or,
> as Romanshyn writes, they can portray the "mythology of an age." In these
> ways [they] serve as a means for *rescripting collective memory*. Films, therefore,

are also "memory projects" that activate the repository of collective memory built around a given iconic event (emphasis mine).[38]

Historiography, every bit as complicated as Hutcheon suggests, is also a useful lens through which to view our positing of identities, whether individual or collective, and our manipulation of memories in order to bolster the selves we shape. Cameron and colleagues emphasize the inevitability of this process when they recall the memorable metaphor Ulric Neisser used to describe the impact of current knowledge on even the most conscientious reconstructions of the past:

> In a well-known analogy, Neisser (1967) compared the act of remembering to the paleontologist's task of reconstructing a dinosaur from a few pieces of bone. The paleontologist's reconstruction is guided by the fossil remains, as well as by his or her current understanding of biology and dinosaurs. The same remains might have yielded a quite different reconstruction 100 years earlier, because of shifts in scientific knowledge. Similarly, people reconstruct and interpret episodes from their pasts by using the bits and pieces they retrieve from memory together with their current knowledge and understanding of themselves and their social world. When relevant knowledge and understanding changes with time, so too might memory even if the information retrieved remains constant.[39]

"Presentism" is the term Cameron and her coauthors associate with historians' tendency to "recreate and interpret history on the basis of current ideas and values, rather than from the knowledge and values of the period . . . and to produce a story that justifies and glorifies the present."[40] Presentism, as they remind us, infuses autobiographical memory and adaptation politics as well. Given the needs of now, the past is as putty in our hands: people are historians as well as *adapters*. But whose "present" prevails in a current adaptation? In the realm of adaptation, fidelity analysis enables those who dissent from a given version of presentism to articulate their objections. In democratic discourse, this room for dissent is an important safeguard.

In *Frames of Remembrance: The Dynamics of Collective Memory*, Iwona Irwin-Zarecka helps us further shape these insights with the idea that increasing critical self-reflexivity about memory processes alerts us to value-laden and agency-amenable aspects of memory and historiography. She argues that many forms of popular culture can enrich collective memory and thus bolster a more actively steered collective identity. Echoing Hutcheon's and Leitch's cautions against imposing hierarchies among cultural texts, she contends that

> we all make sense of the past with the help of a whole variety of resources, that this making sense is motivated by our personal experience but facilitated

(or impeded) by public offerings, and that such public offerings are a mixture of presences and absences. A "collective memory"—as a set of ideas, images, feelings about the past—is best located not in the minds of individuals, but in the resources they share. There is no reason to privilege one form of resource over another—for example, to see history books as important but popular movies as not.[41]

Locked within any simple declaration that the book or the movie "was better" is an emergent perspective, a nascent and potentially collective self-story. Our task as teachers who wish to foster the study of adaptation is to constrain the reflex that preempts such proclamations and, instead, to employ these occasions to unpack both the judgments they reveal and the reactions they trigger. Deconstructing an understanding of how and why a given iteration might be better—not to mention interrogating what "better" means—is a critical first step in discovering our stakes in the memory project incited by adaptations. An open-minded teacher can model the idea that memory-based discussion is an integral feature of collective self-making even if self-making, like adaptation itself, is inevitably provisional. Construed this way, adaptations, like other recollections, are ultimately just overtures, tentative gestures aimed at connecting now with then. As Lampinen and colleagues observe, "Identity is an attitude taken toward a constant state of flux."[42]

NOTES

1. Jean Paul Sartre, *Nausea*, trans. Lloyd Alexander (New York: New Directions Publishing Corporation, 1964), 67.
2. Linda Hutcheon, *A Theory of Adaptation* (London: Routledge, 2006), 172–74.
3. Sidonie Smith and Julia Watson, "Introduction: Situating Subjectivity in Women's Autobiographical Practices," in *Women, Autobiography, Theory: A Reader*, ed. Sidonie Smith and Julia Watson, 3–52 (Madison: University of Wisconsin Press, 1998), 39.
4. Hutcheon, *A Theory of Adaptation*, 9.
5. Hutcheon, *A Theory of Adaptation*, 9.
6. Hutcheon, *A Theory of Adaptation*, 9.
7. I suggest that the question of where (not to mention whether) one story ends and another begins—just like the question of what "is or is not" adaptation—cannot be answered prescriptively by one theorist for another or by a teacher for her students. Both questions hinge on politically freighted presuppositions about tradition, uniqueness, and creativity.
8. Thomas Leitch, *Film Adaptation and Its Discontents: From Gone with the Wind to The Passion of the Christ* (Baltimore: Johns Hopkins University Press, 2007).
9. Leitch, *Film Adaptation and Its Discontents*, 6.

10. Research on the developmental role of such scaffolding and its capacity to support of others' story-building processes suggests the general effectiveness of this pedagogical strategy. While the studies I consulted evaluated "elaborative" and detail-"extending" strategies employed by caregivers in work with much younger children, it seems plausible that extending elaboration among older students would be just as productive. See Katherine Nelson, "Narrative Self, Myth and Memory: Emergence of the Cultural Self," in *Autobiographical Memory and the Construction of a Narrative Self: Developmental and Cultural Perspectives*, ed. Robyn Fivush and Catherine A. Haden, 3–28 (Mahwah, N.J.: Erlbaum, 2003); and Elaine Reese and Kate Farrant, "Social Origins of Reminiscing," in *Autobiographical Memory and the Construction of a Narrative Self: Developmental and Cultural Perspectives*, ed. Robyn Fivush and Catherine A. Haden, 29–48 (Mahwah, N.J.: Erlbaum, 2003).

11. F. Paul Driscoll, "A Voice from the Past," *Opera News* 70, no. 6 (2005): 8.

12. Joseph W. Brownell and Patricia W. Enos, *Adirondack Tragedy: The Gillette Murder Case of 1906* (Utica, N.Y.: Nicholas K. Burns Publishing, 2003; original ed. 1986).

13. Brownell and Enos, *Adirondack Tragedy*, 154.

14. Brownell and Enos, *Adirondack Tragedy*, 156.

15. Brownell and Enos, *Adirondack Tragedy*, 171.

16. Brownell and Enos, *Adirondack Tragedy*, 150.

17. Brownell and Enos, *Adirondack Tragedy*, 154.

18. *An American Tragedy*, Dir. Josef von Sternberg, Perf. Phillips Holmes, Sylvia Sidney, Frances Dee (Paramount Pictures, 1931).

19. Brownell and Enos, *Adirondack Tragedy*, 166.

20. Brownell and Enos, *Adirondack Tragedy*, 170.

21. *A Place in the Sun* [1951], Dir. George Stevens, Perf. Montgomery Clift, Elizabeth Taylor, Shelley Winters (DVD B00003CXBZ: Paramount Home Video, 2001).

22. James M. Lampinen, Timothy N. Odegard, and Juliana K. Leding, "Diachronic Disunity," in *The Self and Memory*, ed. Denise R. Beike, James M. Lampinen, and Douglas A. Behrend, 227–53 (New York: Psychology Press, 2004), 246.

23. Lampinen, Odegard, and Leding, "Diachronic Disunity," 247.

24. Smith and Watson, "Introduction," 27.

25. Jerome Bruner, "Self-Making Narratives," in *Autobiographical Memory and the Construction of a Narrative Self: Developmental and Cultural Perspectives*, ed. Robyn Fivush and Catherine A. Haden, 209–26 (Mahwah, N.J.: Erlbaum, 2003).

26. Bruner, "Self-Making Narratives," 210–11.

27. Bruner, "Self-Making Narratives," 211.

28. Bruner, "Self-Making Narratives," 215–16.

29. Susannah Radstone and Katharine Hodgkin, "Regimes of Memory: An Introduction," in *Regimes of Memory*, ed. Susannah Radstone and Katharine Hodgkin, 1–23 (London: Routledge, 2003), 1–2.

30. Radstone and Hodgkin, "Regimes of Memory," 2.

31. Radstone and Hodgkin, "Regimes of Memory," 2.

32. Lampinen, Odegard, and Leding, "Diachronic Disunity," 248.

33. Quoted in Smith and Watson, "Introduction," 14.

34. Jessica Cameron, Anne E. Wilson, and Michael Ross, "Autobiographical Memory and Self-Assessment," in *The Self and Memory*, ed. Denise R. Beike, James M. Lampinen, and Douglas A. Behrend, 207–26 (New York: Psychology Press, 2004).

35. Paul John Eakin, "Storied Selves: Identity through Self-Narration," in *Making Selves: How Our Lives Become Stories*, 99–141 (Ithaca, N.Y.: Cornell University Press, 1999), 140.

36. Brownell and Enos, *Adirondack Tragedy*, 172.

37. Brownell and Enos, *Adirondack Tragedy*, 172.

38. Patricia Leavy, *Iconic Events: Media, Politics, and Power in Retelling History* (Lanham, Md.: Lexington Books, 2007), 150.

39. Cameron, Wilson, and Ross, "Autobiographical Memory," 207.

40. Cameron, Wilson, and Ross, "Autobiographical Memory," 208.

41. Iwona Irwin-Zarecka, *Frames of Remembrance: The Dynamics of Collective Memory* (New Brunswick, N.J.: Transaction Publishers, 1994), 4.

42. Lampinen, Odegard, and Leding, "Diachronic Disunity," 245.

NINE

THE NUMBERS GAME

Quantifying the Audience

Alexis Weedon

The discussion of adaptations often takes the form of an exploration of how the source text—typically a novel, play, or myth—has been transformed into a new form, principally the film. Sometimes the process of transformation entails the shifting of genre, the elision of story lines, and the interpolation of addition of text or abridgement. Adaptation studies focuses on postmodernist notions of intertextuality and hybridity resulting from the circulation of multiple versions of a text. However, there has been little discussion of the influence of paratextuality on an audience's choice of adaptation.

The form of production is important to understanding the attraction of the different versions of the text and how each form influences the consumption of the other. Source texts are often (but not always) print publications. Particularly relevant is the debate over the future of the book in the digital age and the role of the publisher in how and why multiple texts are produced and read.

The exercises in this chapter model the market for print adaptations using simple statistical methods and exploring and critiquing the diagrammatic models of cultural production in publishing. The activities allow students to contextualize this market within the output of publishing and more broadly the links with other media industries. Moving from Pierre Bourdieu to Gérard Genette, the chapter includes an exercise that documents evidence of students' own knowledge of—and use of—the paratexts that surround adaptations and opens a debate on how these influence audience choice. Such debates are taught in two different arenas in higher education: publishing studies and book history.

Publishing courses in higher education take a business perspective, teaching the practices of commissioning, editing, production, marketing, and sales according to a business plan. Such courses are underpinned with textbooks written by publishing professionals explaining the processes and giving practical advice on budgeting and developing the business. They have to be specific to the industry within the country, for example, in the United Kingdom booklists for publishing courses include Giles Clark's look inside publishing, Gill Davies's explanation of the commissioning process, and Alison Baverstock on marketing.[1] Joost Kist and Herbert Bailey have written about business practices in publishing and have proposed numerical formulae to model the different markets and sales, while other professionals reflecting upon the industry from Gordon Graham to Jason Epstein have identified past trends to predict future markets.[2]

Book history courses in higher education take a different perspective, teaching the material history of the book, authorship, and reading. Often situated in literature or history departments, they draw on a substantial body of scholarship that has developed rapidly over the last half century from Henri-Jean Martin and Lucien Fébvre's *The Coming of the Book*.[3] The most obvious product of this scholarship is the national histories of the book from Canada, America, and the United Kingdom (others are in preparation). Anthologies such as the Blackwell's *Companion to the History of the Book*, the *Oxford Companion to the Book*, Ashgate's History of the Book in the West series, and *The Book History Reader* cross national frontiers, while Finkelstein and McCleery's *Introduction to Book History* brings such work into the classroom. Many of these histories are underpinned by quantitative studies of the scale of book production using archival sources.[4]

In this chapter, I draw together these two approaches to show how we can gain insights into the market for adaptations using quantitative methods on statistics that are available online or through surveys carried out by students. I have selected a few of the datasets online, but there are many more, some of which I have referenced in the notes. Publishers, booksellers, and librarians collect statistics on a variety of data so they can quantity the number of each title printed and sold; the variety of titles in the bookshop, the library, or online; the size of the readership; and whether readers borrow or buy books as well as the factors that influence that choice. In parallel movie databases collate information on the new film titles released in the year and their cast. Access to these information sources is now much easier through the Internet, and an examination of them can help us understand what influences the market.

The adaptation industry is a specific example of cultural production and is also subject to markets and market forces. Although it is only a subset of the publishing industry, it is at the intersection between filmmaking, broadcasting, the videogame industry, and publishing. These businesses need statistics and use these to understand markets and market change, so we can use our study of these statistics and ones we can generate ourselves to examine why the adaptation industry is so successful.

Publishing is essentially about creating audiences. There is a common fallacy that a good book will always find a readership, but history tells us this is not always true. For example, Edward Fitzgerald's poem "The Rubiayat of Omar Khayyam" was destined for obscurity until Algernon Charles Swinburne picked it up out of a bookseller's box. It was Swinburne rather than the publisher and bookseller who created the audience for Fitzgerald's poem. To be successful publishers need to identify the potential audience and let them know that this is a work they will like. They also have to be right so that the audience will come back to them for the next recommendation.

It is important to make the distinction here between creating audiences and creating markets. The publisher does of course want to create a market in order to sell the books manufactured. But books are not baked beans, and repeat purchase is not common in the industry as the customer is only likely to buy one copy, or perhaps a second as a gift or replacement. Some limited product marketing can be done through common content as varieties can lead to further sales: baked beans with sausages, vegetarian baked beans, organic baked beans, and so forth. The parallel in publishing is with formulaic fiction publishers such as Harlequin, Mills and Boon, and some children's series such as Beast Quest. However, they do not extend the audience much beyond the market and are not frequently the material in the adaptation industries—on television, in the theater, or in any other media.

Traditionally, publishers have developed their audiences through lists of titles published under an imprint. The imprint acts like a brand indicating that the titles have been included because they share a certain set of values. Within these lists there may be a series further defining a specific group of titles around the theme or category. This may be any number of defining qualities: genre, age group, origin of the text (e.g., reprints), language, historical period, and so on. A study of these categories can reveal how publishers view the associative links between readers' buying choices. The broader categories of what we now would call genre fiction (established in the first half of the twentieth century) have been further refined through subdivision and influenced by other media—film, radio, and television.

In the 1920s, the fledgling radio industry in Britain sought to justify its public value by using arguments about radio's role in creating audiences for books. Indeed, while the company publishing the music broadcast on the radio was not identified, publishers were given different treatment and named. To justify this policy the BBC yearbooks from this period quoted library borrowings of works read on the radio. This approach has continued throughout the history of public broadcasting, and in such programs as *The Big Read*,[5] the BBC reflects a cultural belief in the importance of books and reading in education and personal development. Such programs seek to increase the audience for books, but how can we measure this?

EXERCISE 1: COMPARING BOOK SALES
WITH LIBRARY BORROWING

Today, there are many online sources that offer insights into the industry. Statistics in the public domain or easily available on the Internet show both sales and reading patterns. Since the introduction of electronic point of sale (epos) machines it has become much easier to gather and rank data on sales and to use them for analyzing trends—either historically as John Sutherland has in examining the growth of the book-selling charts in the 1970s,[6] or for observing contemporary fashions such as the *Bookseller*'s Hot 100 or Alex Hamilton's annual roundup of the Top Hundred British Fastsellers that ranks the fastest selling books in any genre for that year. Hamilton cites the sales figures of quick selling mass-market books instead of best sellers that have a steadier and longer term sale.[7] He lists books published in the calendar year with their country of origin, genre, retail price, and the quantity of sales divided between home and exports, and does a simple calculation of their monetary value.[8] From 2005 the *Bookseller* created their Hot 100 for the year listing the best-selling paperbacks using Bookscan data. This gives the title, author, recommended retail price, actual price, and units sold (see table 9.1). Other data sets online include the government measures of the loans of books in public libraries under the public lending right (PLR) in Britain, Canada, and Australia. These statistics rank most popularly borrowed books from a selection of public libraries and therefore reflect the public's choice of reading rather than purchase. A comparison of the two might reveal which authors people prefer to borrow and which they prefer to buy, or perhaps which they prefer to display on their shelves and which are more general reading fare. Similarly, the *New York Times* chart of sales of trade fiction romances can be compared with the romance writers of America's own survey of readers' preferences.[9] Other best sellers charts are also published by the

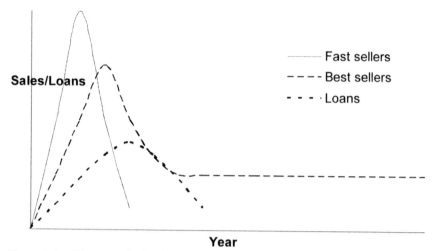

Year

Figure 9.1. Diagram of sales/loans of fast sellers, best sellers, and popular library books over time

trade journals *The Bookseller* and *Publisher's Weekly*, which give sales figures and are often broken down into industry sectors. This allows us to examine trends in sales and loans of different sectors of the book trade.

Let's look at the proposal in figure 9.1, which suggests that for publishers the real *best* sellers remain in print, and in copyright, and bring in a steady income for them. They are the books more likely to show the long tail of sales selling steadily but undramatically over many years. They are what publishers call good backlist books, while the frontlist contains the new books that sell because of their freshness and novelty. It also assumes that fast sellers sell quickly and do not last, while the most popular borrowed books have a longer life through the libraries.

When our students tested this hypothesis against the actual data, we were able to discuss a number of issues that frequently arise when you use real data (see exercise 1 questions at end of chapter). Hamilton's list ranks the titles in order starting with the title with the greatest sales. Fiction and nonfiction, and adult and children's titles, are mixed; the list reflects the year's activity in the high-turnover trade market. The *Bookseller*'s list separates fiction from nonfiction. On the other hand, the PLR publishes statistics on the most borrowed authors from a sample of public libraries in the United Kingdom.[10] On their website they publish the chart toppers, most borrowed titles, most borrowed authors, and loans by categories. The most borrowed titles are divided into most borrowed authors of classics, top children's writers, and other categories. The statistics run from July to June, which makes a direct comparison with Hamilton's list awkward, but it is possible as both Hamilton's and the PLR statistics have

Table 9.1. The Bookseller's Review of 2007: Sales and Price Step Up

Pos	Title	Author	Publisher	RRP	ASP	Units
1	Harry Potter and the Deathly . . . (adult)	Rowling, J. K.	Bloomsbury	£17.99	£9.36	1,268,738
2	Making Money	Pratchett, Terry	Doubleday	£18.99	£11.14	230,246
3	Faces	Cole, Martina	Headline	£18.99	£10.34	200,353
4	Book of the Dead	Cornwell, Patricia	Little, Brown	£18.99	£10.30	195,905
5	This Year It Will Be Different	Binchy, Maeve	Orion	£17.99	£10.84	172,441
6	On Chesil Beach	McEwan, Ian	Cape	£12.99	£10.33	168,481
7	The Quest	Smith, Wilbur	Macmillan	£18.99	£11.99	165,383
8	Crystal	Price, Katie	Century	£9.99	£6.85	156,603
9	Exit Music	Rankin, Ian	Orion	£18.99	£11.88	132,727
10	The Children of Húrin	Tolkien, J. R. R.	HarperCollins	£18.99	£12.30	131,449

Source: Philip Stone, "Review of 2007: Sales and Price Step Up," *The Bookseller*, 10 January 2008, 3.

Table 9.2. Public Lending Right UK statistics from July 2006 to June 2007. Most borrowed fiction titles (adult and children combined)

Pos	Author	Title	Publisher	Year
1	J. K. Rowling	*Harry Potter and the Deathly Hallows*	Bloomsbury	2007
2	Kate Morton	*The House at Riverton*	Pan	2007
3	Kim Edwards	*The Memory Keeper's Daughter*	Viking	2007
4	Simon Kernick	*Relentless*	Corgi	2007
5	Mary Lawson	*The Other Side of the Bridge*	Vintage	2007
6	James Patterson & Michael Ledwidge	*The Quickie*	Headline	2007
7	James Patterson & Maxine Paetro	*The 6th Target*	Headline	2007
8	Mark Mills	*The Savage Garden*	HarperCollins	2007
9	James Patterson	*Cross*	Headline	2006
10	James Patterson & Michael Ledwidge	*Step on a Crack*	Headline	2007

Table 9.3. UK domestic box office yearly chart for 2007

Rank	Movie Title	Studio	Total Gross	Theaters	Opening	Theaters	Open	Close
1	Spider-Man 3	Sony	$336,530,303	4,324	$151,116,516	4,252	5/4	8/19
2	Shrek the Third	P/DW	$322,719,944	4,172	$121,629,270	4,122	5/18	8/9
3	Transformers	P/DW	$319,246,193	4,050	$70,502,384	4,011	7/3	11/8
4	Pirates of the Caribbean: At World's End	BV	$309,420,425	4,362	$114,732,820	4,362	5/25	10/4
5	Harry Potter and the Order of the Phoenix	WB	$292,004,738	4,285	$77,108,414	4,285	7/11	12/13
6	I Am Legend	WB	$256,393,010	3,648	$77,211,321	3,606	12/14	4/10
7	The Bourne Ultimatum	Uni	$227,471,070	3,701	$69,283,690	3,660	8/3	11/29
8	National Treasure: Book of Secrets	BV	$219,964,115	3,832	$44,783,772	3,832	12/21	6/19
9	Alvin and the Chipmunks	Fox	$217,326,974	3,499	$44,307,417	3,475	12/14	6/5
10	300	WB	$210,614,939	3,280	$70,885,301	3,103	3/9	7/12

Source: Box Office Mojo, "Yearly Box Office: 2007 Domestic Grosses," www.boxofficemojo.com/yearly/chart/?yr=2007 (accessed 12 March 2009). There are different views of the highest grossing box office films: see also IMDb, "All-Time Box Office: World-wide," www.imdb.com/boxoffice/alltimegross?region=world-wide (accessed 30 October 2009), and Wikipedia, "List of Highest-Grossing Films," http://en.wikipedia.org/wiki/List_of_highest-grossing_films (accessed 12 March 2009).

been published for more than two decades. They can be further analyzed in terms of the children's and adult markets as both Hamilton and PLR have issued statistics specifically on the children's market.

Unfortunately, the categories used by publishers, film distributors, television schedulers, and librarians are different and continually changing. In our comparison they reflect the difference between a Dewey subject catalog system used by librarians and publisher's genre labels. Illuminatingly, both the *Bookseller* and Hamilton write a commentary in which they reflect on the changing genres and on the year's activity in the high-turnover fiction market, providing some insights into how these categories are perceived. But how academics, librarians, and commercial companies use subject categories for different purposes is a good point to debate because they are not directly comparable. For film theorists the notion of genre is a means of categorizing movies that share common narrative structures—the Western is a typical case. Similarly, literary theorists will group stories according to common structural conventions—the country house whodunit is a well-defined example. But go into a bookshop, or view the marketing information on the nearest film releases, and you will soon see that the industry uses great variety of categories—some of which do not relate to the structural content of the film or book but rather relate it to the audience by other means such as recommendation (e.g., British television presenters Richard Madeley and Judy Finnigan's recommendations), type of author (e.g., celebrities), suitability of different readerships (e.g., age group, book club, etc.). Reflecting on these is good preparation for the second exercise.

With careful qualification the comparison of these two sets of statistics can provide supporting evidence of changing reading—or at least buying—fashions. Of course, a plot of raw data rarely follows a typical graph line, but we did find that the date of publication of the most borrowed titles over a number of years from the PLR fell between the range of one and four years old, although there were a few which continued to be borrowed for longer—the library equivalent of the long tail in lending. We asked two additional questions: are there also differences between the countries that have the PLR scheme? Has its average range changed over the period of the PLR statistics? We wanted to find out if there was evidence for cultural differences and trends in reading choices. Finally, we identified and discussed the many factors that might dramatically increase sale of a book: the author or book hitting the news, fad, fashion and celebrity, a spin-off from a television series, or a film release—and also asked whether the fast sellers were new books or new editions, reprints, or, importantly for us, tie-ins. Careful sifting of the data provided evidence for the influence of other media, particularly of film releases and adaptations on the borrowing and sale of specific titles.

EXERCISE 2: STUDENT SURVEY OF THEIR
OWN CONSUMPTION OF ADAPTATIONS

The form filled out by the students had an additional page for text comments. It can be downloaded from http://madwiki.beds.ac.uk/madwiki/index.php/Report

The coming of digital media has thrown into question this definition of the book. In the Internet bookstores, books, DVDs, CDs, and games are displayed alongside each other. Bookshops also stock DVDs, stationery, games, and other forms of entertainment alongside books. Traditionally, the review trade in newspapers provided guidance to book buyers, but today the group of potential commentators has widened. In Internet bookstores, purchasers' comments are displayed underneath the publisher's blurb. In bookshops, staff members and some readers add small cards of recommendation under selected titles. It's useful to understand these through Gérard Genette's notion of paratextuality.[11] He defines the paratext as the numerous texts—written, verbal, and virtual—that surround the character and its story and that enable the reader to make a choice. In fact, he sees them as the threshold or entrance hall to the story—encouraging the reader to engage with the full text. Genette's definition divides paratexts into two: reviews, interviews with the author, biographies, magazines, the publisher's blurb, and news articles external to the book are the peritext; the mini biography on the cover of the book, the preface, chapter titles, and so forth, that provide guidance inside are the epitext. Some of these internal epitexts—indexes, page numbers, chapters, and the title page—have been used to distinguish the book as a form distinct from a scroll or a website. Many came into use from the twelfth to the fifteenth centuries when it became important to order the written text to aid the reader. From the mid-fifteenth century the technology of the printing press most certainly helped in this process and encouraged standardization.

The more powerful search systems that the personal computer and the Internet have brought enable the reader to locate a phrase of a few words through a string search across a textual database containing thousands of books, images, and paratexts. The book epitexts remain, but they have been augmented by keywords, tags, and other metadata that now provide the means for ordering and accessing the text. Authorial peritexts have also expanded and include engaging with readers through their blogs, fan sites, and other social media. This change, underpinned by new information and communication technologies, has challenged our definition of the book, moving it away from the physical format (i.e., paper or hardback) toward a definition of the form as a specific arrangement of the text (often electronic) that includes the title page, chapters, and length and excludes the surrounding paratexts. For fiction writers this is problematic when the story lines they work on multiply and diversify across these media. We have all come across stories that have been so far removed from their "origin" that they are felt by the audience to be "inauthentic."[12] While sequels and spin-offs are often viewed as derivative, there is also a strong tendency today for innovative, cross-media spin-offs that invest in and expand the story character by developing a side plot, background, or other characters or scenarios alluded to in the original.[13] Writers are actively experimenting with these forms.[14]

To explore the role of these paratexts in influencing readers and viewer selections, Julia Knight, Samantha Lay, and I have recently carried out a pilot study of audience's film viewing and how the choice of film is related to other media.[15] Even on our small sample (ten participants, fifty viewings) we found that half our participants bought a book because of watching the film (these were *His Dark Materials* trilogy by Philip Pullman, *Midnight in the Garden of Good and Evil* by John Berendt, *Atonement* by Ian McEwan, the *Northern Lights* Audio CD by Philip Pullman, and *Sense and Sensibility* by Jane Austen), and four bought a game because of the film tie-in (these were the *Ratatouille* PC and *PS2*, *Revenge of the Sith* PS2, *Star Wars Battlefront II* first-person shooter, and *Rocky: Legends*). Not surprisingly, the "brand" was a very influential factor in children's media consumption. To cite the obvious case: the Harry Potter books have a very successful film series and equally high sale video games with titles that follow the series. Disney has built a business from this, and the litany of their "characters" listed on Amazon reveals the extent of cross-media storytelling. All have the full complement of games, films/television series, books, and toys. In our pilot we observed that children sought out media by character and activity, not by genre or style. Knowing the Pokémon characters was a way into Pokémon games and the Pokémon film. It was quite clear that where there wasn't a shared character this connection was harder to make. In children and adults we found that there was a higher proportion of repeat viewing of films and rereadings because of the adaptation.

Using this method as a basis, I constructed a diary sheet for students to record their viewing and reading of adaptations. Initially, we recorded a single experience that could be reflected upon immediately in class. This led to a discussion of the adaptation of Stanley Kubrick's *Lolita* (1962), which was viewed after one student had read the book; *The Da Vinci Code* (2006), rented because the viewer saw the theatrical trailer; *Babel* (2006), selected on DVD because it was one of the "best movies of 2006"; Jon Krakauer's *Into the Wild* (1996), read because it was a tie-in with a film; and *Bridget Jones' Diary* (2001), a re-viewing because the viewer had read the book and purchased the Céline Dion song "All by Myself."[16] The time between reading the book and viewing the film varied between two months and five years (read for schoolwork), though typically it was a year or two. The most frequent repeat viewer was one student who was cyclically rereading and reviewing *The Lord of the Rings: The Fellowship of the Ring*.[17]

This was followed up by a diary kept for two weeks recording all events; this diary allowed the students to make a free text commentary on their experiences of the adaptation. Following the collation of results and analysis, the class discussion focused on the differences between the games, screen and book adaptations, and the music tie-ins. Radio broadcasts of music used in the films, or the film music itself, extended the enjoyment of the film but was seen as a discrete experience. A significant proportion of students did not play games at all and had no experience of game adaptations, but all had either seen films or watched television adaptations. Students also gained considerable enjoyment from the peritextual sources they used to help them choose. Reading magazine reviews, looking up recommendations, and agreeing or disagreeing with the ratings and opinions given by others were all part of the pleasure of reading the book or viewing the film. About two-thirds of the group also contributed their own opinions either through reviews on websites, on blogs, by word of mouth, or through creating and updating their own lists. A similar proportion said they were either rewatching or rereading the adaptation for enjoyment and to prolong the experience. Most readers had borrowed, bought, or been given the book from a friend or parent, a few used the public library, and only one had read a download. Inevitably, detailed discussions of the comparison between the adaptation and source emerged. Noticing, exploring, and explaining the differences between the film and the book proved a source of great pleasure. In terms of games, most were bought (often preowned) or received as gifts and swapped. However, those who played games showed a different appreciation of the game text. These adaptations were restricted to science fiction, horror films, thrillers, and children's films that fitted into the game genres, and only a third were selected by association with the film or book. For most students, the attraction was the game genre rather than the adaptation, although they did say knowing the protagonists and setting was an advantage.

EXERCISE 3: MAPPING THE CYCLE OF AN ADAPTATION

The questions often put to students of publishing and book history have been framed by the paradigm of the communications circuit articulated in the work of Robert Darnton.[18] Darnton's study on eighteenth-century publishing narrated a history of textual production from the author function, through the editorial and design functions, to production and distribution, finally ending with reading and reception. This paradigm

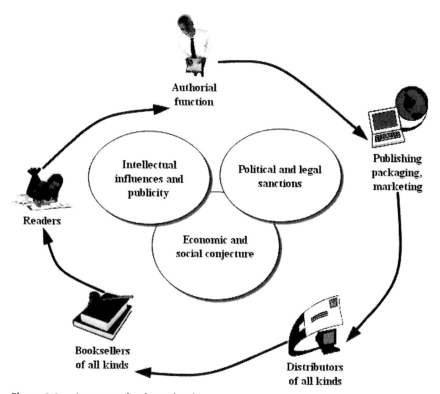

Figure 9.2.   A communications circuit

puts emphasis on the importance of the changes in the cycle of publication throughout history as publishing practices, technologies, and social and political regulatory frameworks changed. While it recognizes that authorship is a collaborative process, and that the "source text" is a problematic concept, the iterative nature of storytelling and retelling that is at the heart of adaptation sits outside this model, and we can critique and redraw this cycle to include the adaptation industries.

Book publication crosses the fields of economic endeavor and cultural production. Publishing is a business, and the economic rewards of a best seller often make headline news. Of course, many authors seek literary acclaim that may—or may not—go hand in hand with financial income. The same headline news stories often quote the quantity of books that have been sold by the author, how many have been translated, the number of adaptations, and sometimes their popularity in libraries. Why should a publisher leave a good story as a one-off when a sequel, a series, or an adaptation can extend its longevity in the market and increase its financial rewards?

The publisher who simply buys the copyright of the story in one form may well miss out on the revenue from other forms of publication. The practice started as early as the nineteenth century when book publishers traditionally bought the rights to publish in volume form, while the author dealt with the magazine or newspaper editor for first serial publication. The common practice was for the novel to be issued as a book toward the completion of publication within the magazine or newspaper—in the belief that serialization created a market for the book. In the early twentieth century, short stories appearing first in magazines were the source of many radio adaptations and silent films, and this is how Sir Arthur Conan Doyle's detective Sherlock Holmes was first introduced to readers, and then went on to be adapted for cinema, radio, and television. Naturally, there are variations to this practice—for example, Baroness Orczy could not find a publisher for her novel *The Scarlet Pimpernel*, and so it was first performed as a theatrical adaptation, and a book publisher was subsequently found. This caused a problem because the owner of the play would not allow it to be made into a film.

The scenario fever of the early years of Hollywood filmmaking gave way in the 1920s and 1930s to a more selective process of seeking suitable subjects for adaptation from literary agents and publishers. In my study of ten British authors alive and flourishing in 1931, I found that the original stories had been published between two and twelve years before the film adaptation appeared.[19] While I can't draw too many conclusions from this—the sample number of adaptations was too small—the fact that we now have access to online movie databases, online bookstores, and library catalogs renders it much easier to do a similar exercise on today's authors. Using this data we can estimate the extent of the subset of "adaptations"—works with movie adaptations—and we can also ask how making an adaptation affects the "long tail" of sales/loans. Perhaps more significantly we can look at how the adaptation and tie-in are linked to the original through the texts and iconography that surround them and reflect on how the diagram of the traditional publishing circuit of communication (see figure 9.2) should be altered to incorporate the movie adaptation.

For this exercise, students used *Box Office Mojo* for the highest grossing films in cinemas that year, and the *Internet Movie Database* (open access) and *Film International* (university library subscription) to search for the keywords "adaptation" or movies "based on" a book or short story, narrowing the search down to a specific year and including only films or television adaptations. They selected between five and ten books or short stories and found the date of first publication using the British Library catalog and Amazon.com to search for movie and TV tie-ins. By collating this data our students calculated the average number of years between the story being published and the film adaptation. They also found out if a new edition of the book was issued when the film adaptation was released and whether the new edition had a tie-in cover that differed from the original publication.

Selecting new books and short stories meant discarding other kinds of adaptation. This provoked a discussion of the range of source material scriptwriters used. By searching for the original editions and tie-ins on Amazon, our students analyzed the shared iconography of the DVD of the film, CD music tie-in, audio book, and film tie-in book cover. A semiotic analysis of a British book cover tie-in and a American book cover tie-in compared to film advertising is also a good way of judging cultural difference: compare the covers and movie poster for Ian McEwan's *Atonement*, for example (you can bring up both through opening a window in amazon.co.uk and amazon.com) with its nuancing of images of loss in war (the image of the war-torn beach with its incongruous fun fair carousel taken from the film forms the background to James McAvoy on the American cover, while the red flowers in corn fields reminiscent of poppies, which are the symbol of the fallen in World War 1, is the background on the British cover), and personal distance.[20] In addition, I used a case study of Tracy Chevalier's book *The Girl with a Pearl Earring*[21] and Peter Webber's 2003 film as a basis for comparing the DVD, book, and CD images (just search for "girl, pearl" on Amazon.co.uk). The images used on the covers are Vermeer's synonymous painting and a film still. The cultural connotations of these images separate the book from the film. The painting has instantly recognizable cultural value and appears on nearly all the book editions. The high art of an old master painting is associated with the book, while the mass-produced photographic image is associated with the film. The 1999 edition has an illustration that includes a miniature of the Vermeer painting. This image also appears on the front cover of the audio cassette, audio CD, and large print edition. However, the DVD cover uses a film still (but not an actual image from the film) that unequivocally states the film's genre, a historical romance. It projects a simplified and not wholly accurate interpretation of the relationship between the protagonists at a key moment of the film. However, the DVD + book combination (a set packaged and sold together) uses the film still with additional stickers of approval in terms of awards and nominations, and the cover makes overt links between the book and the film, with simple graphics on the front and back cover representing an open book and a piece of film. In fact, the DVD + book combination has been marketed to both film viewers and readers, and graphically the book is signaled as the DVD add-on.[22]

A comparison of the dates of publication and adaptation compared with the fast-sellers or best-sellers lists can tell us if popularity of the book has been heightened, or renewed if it is on the backlist, by the publicity

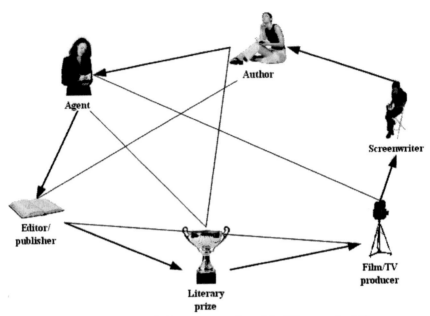

Figure 9.3. **Simone Murray's industry-centered model of literary adaptation**
Source: Redrawn from Simone Murray, "Books as Media: The Adaptation Industry," *International Journal of the Book* 4, no. 2 (2007): 25.

and production of a screen adaptation. For some authors the effect is very clear, as David Lister reported in the *Independent*:

> A screenplay-friendly novel leads to film rights, which in turn spur more sales of the book. The mutual trade-off between book and film has reached its apogee in the nineties with John Grisham. All his books become films. Some 400,000 copies of a special paperback version of *The Pelican Brief* were published simply to tie in with the film release. The most celebrated British case until this week was that of first-time novelist Nicholas Evans, given a pounds 375,000 advance for *The Horse Whisperer*. Before the tale of a man who could talk to horses was even in the shops the film rights were sold to Robert Redford's production company, Hollywood Pictures, for £1.9m.[23]

Another "screenplay-friendly novel," Dan Brown's *Da Vinci Code* (2003) also topped the fast-sellers list showing the phenomenon continues in the twenty-first century. It gives us a different perspective on Clive Anderson's long tail[24] as in publishing a best seller on the backlist may rise and fall in sales through repeated movie and television adaptations.

Inevitably, this brings up the issue of publishers' use of the terms "blockbuster," "classic," or "the no. 1 international best seller." While these are marketing terms, there is useful distinction to be drawn between the literary canonical work (as defined by critics and academics), the popular best seller (defined by sales alone), and the "classic," which is often defined by readers. Adaptations come from all three groups, though literature departments may concentrate on the first. However, a list of the United Kingdom's "top books we cannot live without" in 2007, issued in conjunction with the celebration of UNESCO's World Book and Copyright Day, shows that the popular and the literary are mixed. It looked back to the winners of the national broadcasters (the BBC's *Big Read* series of programs in 2003) through which the viewing public voted for their favorite books and showed that these favorites endured as there had been little change over the intervening period.[25] The three finalists in 2003 included two classic novels that had been recently adapted for the screen: J. R. Tolkien's *The Lord of the Rings* and Jane Austen's *Pride and Prejudice*. The third, Philip Pullman's *His Dark Materials* series, has since been made into a film. The fourth place went to Douglas Adams's *Hitchhiker's Guide to the Galaxy*, and this work more than any other points to the problems of taking a linear view of textual production when studying adaptation. The *Hitchhiker's Guide to the Galaxy* famously began life as a radio drama in 1978, before appearing in book form (1979–), as a television series (1981), as a computer game (1984), as an adaptation in three comic books (1993–), and as a film in 2005.[26] The period between the publication of the original and the adaptation in different categories of work (classic, canonical, and best seller) was a good point for a discussion of the comparison between the communications circuit and Murray's industry model of adaptation (see figure 9.3). This led to a revised model emphasizing the circuits within the adaptation industries and how they converged on the audience. The problem, students noted, was how to convey the role of the paratexts in a diagrammatic way (see figure 9.4)

In this chapter we have looked at how we should remodel the circuit of communication specifically for adaptation studies, moving from a linear production to a cyclic one. Each cycle is interlinked with the others, as one adaptation affects the sales and consumption of the other. Our diagram put audiences in the center, and it is their choice guided by the paratexts that surround each version that determines the level of interaction. A simple analysis of the statistical data published online in the form of sales charts, box office receipts, and library borrowing shows the extent of the overlap and influence of one market on the other. More information can be gained from student's own records of their own choice of adaptations and the texts that lead them to that choice.

These exercises extend the range of approaches that can be used in adaptation studies and remind students that the adaptation industries are

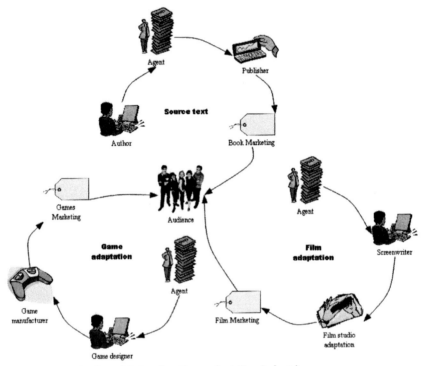

Figure 9.4.   Revised model showing three adaptation industries

businesses with separate and distinct driving factors beyond the desire to build sales and markets. The cultural status of the product from the high culture of the book, to the popular culture, sometime cult status, of video games plays an important role, and this can be seen through an analysis of the iconography of the product packaging. Similarly, the origin of the source text often distinguishes between the gaming, film, and book industries, as, for example, games feature genre more strongly and are more likely to adapt graphic/comic book heroes.

ACKNOWLEDGMENTS

My thanks to the staff and students, both undergraduate and postgraduate, of the class of 2009, and to my publishing students from 1995 to 1999 who did earlier versions of these exercises. The film diaries pilot was a joint venture with Samantha Lay and Julia Knight, and I am grateful to them for allowing me to use this work. The research into cross-media adaptation arises from my Arts and Humanities Research Council (AHRC)–funded research project ("Cross-Media Cooperation in Britain in the 1920s and 1930s"; grant number AR112216). Vincent L. Barnett, Steven Conway, Rebecca Delaney, and my coinvestigator Simon Eliot all contributed to the published outcomes. In this chapter, I have sought to show relevance of the project to contemporary adaptation studies.

APPENDIXES

Exercise 1

1. What is the public lending right?
2. Analyzing the PLR most borrowed titles, do a simple bar graph of the number of loans of each genre of adult fiction.
3. Do a simple bar graph of the number of fast sellers of each genre in Hamilton's list. What are the problems of genre definition that you face?
4. What proportion of fast sellers have (a) a film tie-in? (b) a television series or celebrity tie-in? (c) a brand tie-in? Does this differ when compared to the PLR most borrowed titles?
5. Are there any common characteristics of the authors and publishers who have tie-ins?
6. Can you speculate on some of the influences that have affected both fast sellers and library borrowing?

Going back over your findings and reading both the PLR summaries and Hamilton's interpretation of the best sellers lists, prepare, in groups, a short presentation on your findings.

Sources: See www.plr.uk.com/; for Hamilton's fast sellers, see www .thebookseller.com/ or *The Guardian* each December or January.

Exercise 2

Record your viewing of adaptations over a period of two weeks at the time you watched, read, or played the work. The form filled out by the students had an additional page for text comments.

Exercise 3

Using the *Internet Movie Database* or *Film International* search for (keywords) movie "adaptations" or movies "based on" a book or short story by year, and narrow the search to films or TV adaptations. Identify the book or short story, and find the date of first publication for the adaptations made that year. You can search Amazon for the first edition and any tie-ins.

1. How long on average between the book being published and the film adaptation?
2. Was a new edition of the book issued when the film adaptation was released, and did the new edition have a tie-in cover?
3. If there is a new cover, compare the two.
4. What terms can be used to describe the book (e.g., fast seller, best seller, or classic). Explain and justify their use.

NOTES

1. Giles N. Clark, *Inside Book Publishing*, 3rd ed. (London: Routledge, 2000); Gill Davies, *Book Commissioning and Acquisition* (London: Routledge, 2004); Alison Baverstock, *How to Market Books: The Essential Guide to Maximizing Profit and Exploiting All Channels to Market*, 4th ed. (London: Kogan Page, 2008).

2. Joost Kist, *New Thinking for 21st Century Publishers* (Oxford, UK: Chandos, 2009); Herbert S. Bailey Jr., *The Art and Science of Book Publishing* (Athens: Ohio University Press, 1970); Gordon Graham (former editor of *Logos: The Professional Journal for the Book World*), interview with Alexis Weedon, 22 March 2009; Jason Epstein, *Book Business: Publishing Past, Present and Future* (New York: W. W. Norton, 2002); John Dessauer, *Book Publishing: The Basic Introduction* (London: Continuum, 1998).

3. Lucien Fébvre and Henri-Jean Martin, *L'Apparition du Livre* [*The Coming of the Book*] (Paris: Éditions Albin Michel, 1958).

4. Simon Eliot and Jonathan Rose (eds.), *A Companion to the History of the Book* (Oxford, UK: Wiley-Blackwell, 2009); Michael F. Suarez S.J. and H. R. Woudhuysen, *The Oxford Companion to the Book* (Oxford: Oxford University Press, 2010); David Finkelstein and Alistair McCleery (eds.), *The Book History Reader*, 2nd ed. (New York: Routledge, 2006); David Finkelstein and Alistair McCleery, *An Introduction to Book History* (New York: Routledge, 2005); Ranald Nicholson, *The Edinburgh History of the Book in Scotland Vol. 2: The Later Middle Ages* (Edinburgh: Edinburgh University Press 2007); *The Cambridge History of the Book in Britain*, 8 vols. (Cambridge: Cambridge University Press, 2005–); Patricia Lockhart Fleming, Gilles Gallichan, Yvan Lamonde (eds.), *Histoire du Livre et de l'imprimé au Canada* (Montreal: Presses de l'Université de Montréal, 2004).

5. BBC, *The Big Read*, 2005, www.bbc.co.uk/arts/bigread (accessed 16 May 2009).

6. For example, John Sutherland, *Reading the Decades: Fifty Years of History through the Nation's Bestsellers* (London: BBC Books, 2002).

7. Stephen Evans calls them the "evergreens" in "The Evergreens: 12 Books that Sell and Sell," *Daily Telegraph*, 9 August 2008, 16. The market research firm Nielsen's "BookScan research of 1.8 million titles found that only 12 have appeared in the top 5,000 selling books every week for the past decade, making them the most consistent sellers. These books have what is termed in retail a 'long tail,' in other words they sell for a long time after the initial peak." They include *Birdsong* by Sebastian Faulks, *The Very Hungry Caterpillar* by Eric Carle, and *The Hobbit* by J. R. R. Tolkien.

8. You should all ways check the source and reliability of any Web statistics. I wrote to Alex Hamilton to check before drawing any conclusions, and grumpy old bookman phoned him, http://grumpyoldbookman.blogspot.com/2007/01/uk-fastbestsellers-of-2006.html. John Feather and Hazel Woodbridge got there with their analysis before I did. See Feather and Woodbridge, "Bestsellers in the British Book Industry 1998–2005," *Publishing Research Quarterly* 23, no. 3 (September 2007): 210–23, www.springerlink.com/content/22j2070t41827h52 (accessed 12 May 2009).

9. Readership statistics for romance readers can be found at www.rwanational .org/cs/the_romance_genre/romance_literature_statistics (accessed 12 May 2009).

10. See www.plr.uk.com/mediaCentre/mostBorrowedTitles/top20Titles/ 2007-2008Top20Titles.pdf (accessed 13 May 2009).

11. Gérard Genette, *Paratexts: Thresholds of Interpretation*, trans. Jane E. Lewin (Cambridge: Cambridge University Press, 1997).

12. My personal bête noirs are the Disney versions of *Winnie the Pooh* that contain a North American gopher, an animal that is not in the original and is also not British, has no lines from the original A. A. Milne work, and lacks the wit and humor of Milne's piece.

13. See grumpyoldbookman.blogspot.com/2005/07/copyright-in-characters .html.

14. Kate Pullinger's "Inanimate Alice." Her experiences of being a reader and a contributor in this project, can be accessed at www.inanimatealice.com/ (accessed 13 May 2009). For a discussion, see her paper given at the Playful Paradox conference at the University of Bedfordshire, 23 May 2009, at http://cwparadox .wikidot.com/keynote (accessed 27 May 2009).

15. Julia Knight, Samantha Lay, and Alexis Weedon, "Digital Film and Cross-Media Influences: Pilot Study Report." http://madwiki.beds.ac.uk/madwiki/ index.php/Report (accessed 26 May 2009).

16. *Lolita* [1962], Dir. Stanley Kubrick, Perf. Sue Lyon, James Mason, Peter Sellers (DVD B000UJ48VI: Warner Home Video, 2007); *The Da Vinci Code* [2006], Dir. Ron Howard, Perf. Tom Hanks, Audrey Tautou, Ian McKellen, Widescreen Two-Disc Special ed. (DVD B00005JOC9: Sony Pictures, 2006); *Babel* [2006], Dir. Alejandro González Iñárritu, Perf. Brad Pitt, Cate Blanchett (DVD B000PC86DG: Ufa/DVD, 2007); *Into the Wild* [2007], Dir. Sean Penn, Perf. Emile Hirsch, Marcia Gay Harden, William Hurt (DVD B00194WZJA: Paramount Home Entertainment, 2008); *Bridget Jones' Diary* [2001], Dir. Sharon Maguire, Perf. Renee Zellweger, Hugh Grant, Colin Firth (DVD B00031V22G: Alliance [Universal], 2004).

17. *The Lord of the Rings: The Fellowship of the Ring* [2001], Dir. Peter Jackson, Perf. Elijah Wood, Ian McKellen (DVD B000067DNF: New Line Home Entertainment, Platinum Series Special Extended Edition, 2002).

18. Robert Darnton, "What Is the History of Books?" *Daedalus* 111, no. 3 (Summer 1982): 65–83.

19. Alexis Weedon, "Textual Production and Dissemination in Book History: A Case Study of Cross-Media Practice between the Wars," in *English Today*, ed. Marianne Thormahlen, 266–82 (Lund, Sweden: University of Lund, 2008).

20. I am indebted to Juliet Gardiner's talk at the Cross-Media Colloquium, held at the University of Bedfordshire and Institute for English Studies, University of London, 12 April 2008, for this example.

21. Alexis Weedon, "In Real Life: Book Covers in the Internet Bookstore," in *Judging a Book by Its Cover: Fans, Publishers, Designers, and the Marketing of Fiction*, ed. Nicole Matthews and Nickianne Moody, 117–25 (Farnham, UK: Ashgate Publishers, 2007).

22. *Girl with a Pearl Earring* [2003], Dir. Peter Webber, Perf. Colin Firth, Scarlett Johansson, Tom Wilkinson, DVD + Book ed. (DVD B0001US81O: Lions Gate Video, 2004).

23. David Lister, "Forget Novels, Just Write the Movie," *The Independent* (London), 18 July 1997, 3. See also Joel Rickett, "On the Latest News from the Publishing Industry," *The Guardian*, 8 December 2007, 23.

24. Clive Anderson, *The Long Tail: How Endless Choice Is Creating Unlimited Demand* (London: Random House, 2007). Anderson argues that digitization has given consumers access to works for which previously it may not have been viable to keep in print for the low number of sales they generate (the long tail of sales).

25. See the comparison four years later on World Book Day: "*Pride and Prejudice* Tops List of Books We Cannot Live Without," *Daily Telegraph* (London), 1 March 2007, 14.

26. *The Golden Compass* [2007], Dir. Chris Weitz, Perf. Nicole Kidman, Daniel Craig, New Line Platinum Series Two-Disc Widescreen ed. (DVD B0013IJ2LQ: New Line Home Video, 2008); *The Hitchhiker's Guide to the Galaxy* [2005], Dir. Garth Jennings, Perf. Mos Def, Warwick Davis, Martin Freeman (DVD B0009H-BEGI: Touchstone Video, 2005).

TEN

ENGAGING THE EAR
Teaching Radio Drama Adaptations
Elke Huwiler

RADIO DRAMA

When teaching radio drama in general in a European context, there are two main, initial questions to be asked: firstly, do students even have a notion about what radio drama is; do they have any sort of accessibility to the aural medium? And, secondly, how do they define radio drama as such? It turns out that students of different European countries have very divergent notions on the concept of the art form. Personal experience has shown that students in English-speaking countries in Europe see the art form as a literary one—they define it as literary drama for the ears. Mostly, they do have some experience in listening to radio drama, since the BBC is still striving to maintain this tradition in radio (the longest running radio drama soap, *The Archers*, is known by every student, for example). In German-speaking countries, however, experimental forms of radio drama or *Hörspiel* are much more common. Here, a lot of students have very varied notions about radio drama, since they know the traditional, literary forms of the 1950s very well but are also familiar with more experimental, general acoustic art, which is called Hörspiel as well. Yet here, some students do not have the experience of listening to radio drama at all, since radio drama is only aired by very few radio stations and at unusual time slots. In the Netherlands, finally, radio drama has never achieved the status of an art form at all. Here, students not only think of radio drama or *hoorspel* as an exclusively literary genre but also see it as an old-fashioned, out-of-date medium, which was popular only when there was no television yet. Whereas in German-speaking countries some of the students do have experience in listening to radio drama, in the Netherlands students usually have never listened to one in their lives. Therefore, it is often important to accustom the students to the aural medium in the first place by listening to different types of radio drama productions.

Moreover, the mentioned varying notions on the definition of the art form have to be taken into consideration when talking about radio drama in an academic context. The reasons for these divergent views on the art form are to be found in the history and development of radio drama in different countries but also in the extent to which radio drama figures as an issue in academic research in those countries. Whereas in English- and German-speaking countries, radio drama is, although a marginal, yet still an existing topic in research, in the Netherlands there are almost no major academic publications on the topic to be found.

A closer look at the history of radio drama shows that definitions of how radio drama should be defined as an art form have changed dramatically and repeatedly through the almost ninety years of its existence, especially in German-speaking countries. This does not have a lot to do with the simple question of naming the art form: in English-speaking countries, the art form was called radio drama from the beginning, thereby emphasizing the assumed strong connection between radio art and literary drama. In German-speaking countries, however, one named the art form Hörspiel, which means *listening play* or *listening game*. The double meaning of the word *Spiel* is very important here, since it makes it possible to remove the focus from the connection to the literary tradition (which the first meaning—*Spiel* as *play*—still entails) and to shift it toward a work of art that playfully works with the audio features the medium has to offer. In the course of the history of German radio drama, the strong focus on this playfulness in the 1960s and 1970s was responsible for a major shift in the production and perception of Hörspiel toward being an art form in its own right.[1]

In English-speaking radio drama production, the closeness of the art form to literary drama is still very strong today.[2]

When talking about the importance and arbitrariness of naming a new art form, it can prove very useful to make a link to semiotics and post-structuralist concepts: the *name* we give to the objects shape and determine our view of the world. This approach helps to sharpen the view on the study of the historical development of radio drama as an art form. It is astonishing how arbitrary and sometimes artificial views managed to define radio drama as an art form throughout its history.

In the 1920s, the medium radio was introduced as a public device, and as a consequence, people found themselves in the position of inventing a new art form along with it. In most radio stations throughout Europe and also the United States, adaptations of existing literary works—drama or prose—were the obvious choice, since there was no "poetics" of radio drama yet. But soon demands of a specific radiophonic art form arose, and different radio stations came up with different answers to that demand. The BBC broadcast what today is widely known as the first radio drama written especially for the medium, Richard Hughes's *A Comedy of Danger*, produced by the BBC and first broadcast there on 15 January 1924. As Andrew Crisell mentions, this radio drama "perhaps showed an excessive concern for radio's limitation,"[3] since it is set in a coal mine where the lights go out. Indeed, it has always been quite common to define radio drama through its limitations rather than its intrinsic features, the most famous notion being that radio is a medium for the blind. Tim Crook elaborates on the incorrectness of this concept: "Notions of radio's 'blindness' . . . need to be abandoned as a gesture of intellectual and philosophical insecurity. Radio's imaginative spectacle presents a powerful dynamic which is rarely prioritized by alternative electronic media. By giving the listener the opportunity to create an individual filmic narrative and experience through the imaginative spectacle the listener becomes an active participant and 'dramaturgist' in the process of communication and listening. This participation is physical, intellectual, and emotional."[4]

The notion of radio as a limited medium has in fact accompanied the historical development of the art form radio drama in varied ways and has influenced choices of setting or story lines for radio drama pieces. The German Hörspiel of the 1950s, for example, in an embittered struggle to differentiate itself from theater, was expected to have specific contents impossible to be played in a theater: voices of souls, trees, or other non-human figures; of allegorical figures; or of nonphysical concepts were to be heard. One believed that only such contents, which could not be conveyed through another medium in the same way, made radio drama an art form of its own. Mostly, these demands came from powerful directors at radio drama departments who decided what a radio drama should be like. They had the power to accept or refuse incoming manuscripts and produce only the ones they thought were meeting the (or their) standards of the art form. This was, and still is, especially the case in national broadcast concepts without free competition. In Germany, it was only in the 1980s, when "the monopoly of the public radio stations was broken [and] private broadcasters were allowed on the air,"[5] and in Great Britain, the BBC still owns the monopoly of the public radio.

Only in the 1960s and 1970s, a sort of "revolution" of the writers themselves was able to change German radio drama, at least for a while. At that time, radio drama writers themselves protested against the rigid definition of their art form and postulated a different definition: Hörspiel should not tell a literary shaped story in dialogues and monologues with voices of persons and their consciousnesses, but it should present its most important feature, language, as an acoustic feature with which one can play. Here, as already mentioned, Hörspiel as *listening game* foregrounds the playful experiment with everything that belongs to the realm of the acoustic, of what one can listen to. Mostly, these radio plays did not tell or show any stories but rather experimented with audio and technical features. Soon, the *Neues Hörspiel* as a concept was widely rejected for being elitist and too difficult for a mass audience to follow, yet it did impose a major change on the development of German radio drama production and the shaping of the art form as such. The main factor in this changing process was the insight that radio drama did not have to be primarily focused on a realistically represented, acoustical story with depersonalized voices.

After a period in which the Neues Hörspiel dominated the radio landscape, stations again began to broadcast plays that "told a story." But the impact of the so-called experimental phase was, and still is, strongly felt. Radio plays in the style of the literary radio drama of the 1950s are still being produced, but they are only one form among others. More important nowadays are radio plays that integrate numerous styles and acoustical elements, like the radio plays of Andreas Ammer and F. M. Einheit. These work with different musical styles like pop, opera, jingles, chorals, and hip hop, and use recitals, dialogues, monologues, citations, reports, and commentary as rhetorical features, while using electroacoustical manipulation and stereophony as technical ones.[6] They put these elements together and thereby allow a story to unfold indirectly instead of telling it in a baldly linguistic manner. In general, the influence of the Neues Hörspiel, and also of experimental music and digital techniques, is immense in contemporary radio drama production in German-speaking countries. A large diversity of styles exists within the acoustic play: apart from the genre-mixing style described above, there are also dialogue and monologue plays (although mostly integrating a large range of acoustical features), "experiments" with language and music, documentary features, radio comics, epic adaptations of literature, interactive radio plays, and so on. So-called experimental, nonnarrative sound plays that find their roots not only in the Neues Hörspiel but also in the avant-garde sound experiments of the 1920s that have been rediscovered in recent decades[7] are still produced today, but there is a general tendency within radio drama production in German-speaking countries toward *telling stories.* However, these now integrate a variety of acoustical features, thus making use of the whole range of possibilities the medium can offer.

At this point in the historical development of German radio drama, it seems that the Hörspiel of the twenty-first century is the only "real" Hörspiel that finally found its only true and intrinsic shape. There is indeed a tendency toward openness that allows a variety of different formats to figure as radio drama. The attempts to formulate rigid dramaturgy for radio plays (as in the 1950s and the 1970s) were not successful, and so an open dramaturgy seems to be best fitted for this art form. Yet, that does not mean the development of the art form has come to an end. Nowadays, it is especially the exploring of new media channels that pushes the boundaries of the art form: performances of audio art, computer-based audio plays via Internet, audio drama on CDs, and so forth, challenge the original form of radio drama. The media channel of *radio* is indeed not an intrinsic feature of the audio drama per se anymore.

ADAPTATION

Whilst notions of the concept of radio drama differ from student to student depending on their national background, notions of the concept of adaptation are no more identical between students, although for different reasons. One prejudice surrounding the concept, however, still seems to be very consistent, namely, that adaptations are inferior to the original. Most students know adaptations mainly from film adaptations of famous books. Therefore, in a teaching situation, it proves useful to look at a wider scale of adaptations—in terms of media as well as in terms of history. As Linda Hutcheon points out, adaptations have always been a part of Western culture:

> Adaptations are obviously not new to our time . . . ; Shakespeare transferred his culture's stories from page to stage and made them available to a whole new audience. Aeschylus and Racine and Goethe and da Ponte also retold familiar studies in new forms. . . . The critical pronouncements of T.S. Eliot or Northrop Frye were certainly not needed to convince avid adapters across the centuries of what, for them, has always been a truism: art is derived from other art; stories are born of other stories.[8]

A close look at some of the most famous literary pieces, operas, or films— that are at the same time adaptations—always sharpens students' judgments of the concept of adaptation. In opera, for example, it has long been customary to take an already existent story from literature or oral culture, and nobody would actually claim that, for example, the opera *Carmen* is inferior to the literary text it derived from. It is a genuine opera, working with its intrinsic features and musical possibilities, only based on a story that is already known. Once students realize that, they may look at radio drama adaptations differently.

A close look at the history and development of radio drama and radio drama adaptations provides a focus for a discussion about the subject on a metalevel. When examining the way radio stations treated adaptations over the years, all the common prejudices Robert Stam mentions in his study about adaptation in film are to be found: "infidelity," "betrayal," "deformation," "violation," "bastardization," "vulgarization," and "desecration."[9]

As already mentioned, in the beginning of radio drama production, almost all radio drama departments drew on adaptations of literary drama when looking for suitable material for artistic expression in the new medium of radio. Usually, Richard Hughes's *A Comedy of Danger* is seen as the first radio drama in history. Yet, there were other radio drama productions before that—only they were adaptations and as such not counted as "real" radio drama pieces. In the United States on 3 August 1922, a radio drama based on a theater play by Eugene Walter was aired—*The Wolf*, broadcast on WGY, Schenectady, New York. In winter and spring 1922 and 1923, a total of forty-three plays were adapted for radio and aired on WGY.

Also in Germany, there existed numerous radio drama adaptations before the radio play now known as the first German Hörspiel was broadcast—*Zauberei auf dem Sender* by Hans Flesch, produced by the Berlin Vox-House and first aired on 24 October 1924. On 26 June 1924, Studio Frankfurt had already broadcast the radio drama adaptation *Lancelot und Sandarain*, and the Stuttgarter Sender aired *Erster Klasse*, a radio drama adaptation by Ludwig Thoma, two months later.[10] The distinction between so-called original Hörspiele and adaptations has accompanied German radio drama production from the very beginning, and astonishingly, it is still an important factor today when radio drama producers draw up their schedules. That only the original radio drama is to be seen as the genuine art form of the medium is a claim that existed from the beginning, as seen above, but was strongly consolidated in the 1950s by powerful radio drama producers like Heinz Schwitzke: "In the 1950s an almost ideological argument between Hamburg and Cologne arose. It consisted of the question [of] what a real Hörspiel should be like. Schwitzke and Hymnen [Hamburg] won with their concept of the 'original' radio play. From there on, only 'original' radio plays were real radio plays."[11] The concept of the "original" Hörspiel once again was perceived in negative terms: a radio play should not be an adaptation of an already existing (literary) piece. In a strange confusion of content and form, in this definition every Hörspiel had to be an original piece written for radio.

What is most astonishing when looking at the development of German Hörspiel is that, even though adaptations of literary texts were not accepted, everybody assumed that literary writers were the exclusive creators of radio drama. This "rule" was never really challenged until the 1990s and helped create the literary association that radio drama had and still has today. At the same time, the closeness of radio drama to literature was not appreciated, since radio drama producers wanted to emphasize that radio art was different to literature. This created a paradoxical situation in which radio drama was influenced by literary genres and styles, as literary writers were the producers of the manuscripts, while at the same time directors at radio stations looked for ways to distinguish their work from literature as an art form. The main way to do that was to ban or demolish adaptations of literary works.

Hence, what was fought against was not literary style but rather literary content; it was forbidden to take a story already told in a literary genre and adapt it for radio. But what is literary content? In fact, literary content does not exist. As adaptation studies show, stories exist independent of their form of expression. In narrative terms, stories do not depend on a specific discourse or a specific media channel. Although this is a long and widely known truism, the whole development of German radio drama is built on the assumption that "literary content" was to be banned from radio drama production.

It was only in the 1990s that this view began to change, although only partly: when radio drama production began to widen the scope of media channels, artists other than literary writers began to be interested in the art form. Two of the most famous were Andreas Ammer and Heiner Goebbels. Andreas Ammer began to perform audio drama in front of a live audience, in coproduction with a radio station that broadcast the live event on radio at the same time. Heiner Goebbels produced his audio art at studios independent from radio studios and distributed it on CDs and cassettes. They both worked with the intrinsic features audio art has to offer and thereby emancipated themselves from the literary-inspired radio drama. Yet, when we look at their pieces, it is astonishing how many adaptations of literary texts we find: Heiner Goebbels has adapted many literary pieces of the famous German writer Heiner Müller, while Andreas Ammer drew on literary texts as the basis for his audio plays: the German epos of the *Nibelungen*, the Greek epos of *Ulysses*, the Bible, or Dante's *Divine Comedia*. Only here, nobody would speak of "deformation" or "violation," since it is clear that these media artists take the literary works as inspiration and source but work mainly with the intrinsic features of the audio medium.

Throughout the history of radio drama, there have been two different types of adaptations: first, the above-described type of taking the literary text as source material to create a new work of art; and second, the type of adaptation that takes the literary text as the main basis for storytelling. In the latter, the primary concern is to transport the story of the literary text into another medium. Of course, the production of this second type can also result in an original work of art, when radio's intrinsic features are used to retell the story. It is first of all the expectations producers and listeners bring to a radio play adaptation that differentiates the first type from the second: a radio drama adaptation that should "only" tell the story of the literary piece is in fact literature in audio form. An adaptation that takes the literary text as source material for a new work of art, however, is mainly seen as a radio drama piece, based on a literary work.

The difference is mainly a result of a medial strategy: to produce literature in audio form is a way to attract the audience and to make radio drama popular again. Moreover, these radio drama pieces are often distributed as CDs or audiocassettes and are no longer radio drama pieces in the strict sense. But since the name for the art form is simply *listening play* in German (Hörspiel), all these formats of audio stories are called the same.

In radio drama departments of German Hörspiel production, directors depend on these "popular" literature adaptations, since their cooperation with publishing houses that distribute the audio plays on CDs and cassettes can be very lucrative. On the other hand, they try to sustain the integrity of radio drama by asking the question, what are the unique features of the genre? Some of them come up with the "old" answer: only an "original radio drama" (as opposed to an adaptation) is a real radio drama. Yet, it should be clear that there is no simple answer to that question. In fact, the question is a wrong one to be posed. There is not *one* form of radio drama and certainly not *one* type of content. There is not even *one* single medium for radio drama distribution anymore. And it should also have become clear that directors of radio drama departments have never succeeded in defining the genre. It is the openness of the art form that is to be seen as the most important factor today. Therefore, a lot of radio stations have adapted to the situation and are ready to integrate numerous styles of radio drama into their programs. Also, they cooperate with other media for the broadcasting of the art form, for example, when broadcasting live from a performance where an audio play is performed or when interacting live with the audience by allowing them to place telephone calls and change the course of the radio play they are listening to.

ANALYZING RADIO DRAMA ADAPTATIONS

All of these different forms of radio play production should be taken into consideration when looking at concrete radio drama adaptations in a seminar environment. Students should be taught to listen closely to the radio drama adaptations. When looking at the story that is adapted in the radio play, a narratological and semiotic approach proves most useful. Students will identify the various semiotic features a radio drama contains to let a story unfold. There is not only the language but also music and sound. Voices can convey meaning only through tonal differences. Even silences can "tell a story." Also, technical features like cutting, fading, electroacoustical manipulation, or the positioning of the signals in the acoustic space contribute to a specific narrative understanding of the story that unfolds acoustically.[12] When looking at recent adaptations, the specific medium also has to be taken into account: what does the act of performing an audio play do to the story that is being told acoustically? How do telephone calls of the audience at home interfere with the story line?

Such points can be best understood through a close analysis of a radio drama adaptation, for example, the adaptation of a short story by the German writer and media artist Dieter Kühn, called "Das Lullische Spiel" ("The Lullic Game"; 1977). The story is about the life of Raimundus Lullus or Ramon Lull, a Catalan monk who lived in the thirteenth century and who invented a number of eccentric logical techniques, among others the "lullic system," the so-called *Ars magna combinatoria*, in which he took words from different fields of knowledge and combined them in a systematic way. To start the analysis, it is possible to just look at the story and the radio drama adaptation, and examine the narrative told in both works of art through a semiotic approach. Yet, in the case of radio drama, it proves useful to place the adaptation in a historical context as well and look at the possibilities media artists had at the time, at the status quo the art form as such had at that particular time, and at the circumstances of the production. In 1975, the legacy of the Neues Hörspiel was still very much evident in radio stations, and Dieter Kühn was famous for his experimental style. In this particular radio piece, it is astonishing how he manages to use a varied range of audio features to express a story that is, in the literary piece, told in a quite simple and straightforward manner. In the original story, the life of the historic figure is told as if someone is reading "aloud" about Ramon Lull.[13] The heterodiegetic narrator tells the reader what she or he reads in the present tense:

> Reading about Ramon Lull or Raimundus Lullus, born in 1235, died in 1315, as is written in any encyclopaedia. . . . Reading that the young Ramon lives at the court of Mallorca, as page of the king's son. . . . Reading further, that Ramon becomes officer of the crown at that court, that he learns the courtly manners and engages in courtly entertainments.[14]

Only at one point in the story there is a sort of flashback, recounted from the point of view of Ramon who is looking back at different stages of his life: "At this time a review of Ramon, who in the meantime is well into his 70s: Ramon as page, Ramon as officer of the crown, Ramon as lover of the courtly ladies, Ramon as father, Ramon as agricultural worker, Ramon as hermit."[15] This flashback from the point of view of the old Ramon is the starting point and the main structural principle of the adapted radio piece, in which the same story of Ramon Lull's life with the same events are told.[16]

The old Ramon Lull recounts his life story in this binaurally recorded piece. His voice is always located at the center of the acoustic space. When recalling an episode from his early life, Ramon is suddenly accompanied by a voice uttering (almost) the same words but coming from another position within the acoustic space. While in his account the old man uses verbs in the past tense, the other voice gives the same account using verbs in the present tense. This other voice grows louder, while the old man's voice grows softer, eventually fading out completely. It becomes clear that the second voice is that of the young Ramon, describing his life in the present tense. After a while, old Ramon's voice takes up the account again, starting to talk about another event in his life, until another voice, located at a position different from those of the first two voices, comes in to take over the story, this time representing Ramon at yet another stage of his life. In the course of the play, four different voices, located at four different positions in the acoustic space, are heard, representing Ramon at four separate stages of his life. Moreover, the accounts of the different stages are accompanied by specific musical pieces: medieval dance music for the episode when Ramon was very young and Gregorian chant for the time that he worked as a missionary. Thus, various sign systems are used to perform a specific narrative function: fading-in and fading-out, music, voice, and, above all, the positioning of the signals in the acoustic space indicate the different episodes within the story being told, the life of Ramon Lull.[17]

After listening to the play for some time, the audience has no problem in locating the different episodes of Ramon's life—mostly just by realizing which acoustic positions the accounts come from. At the end of the play, the storytelling itself draws on our ability to differentiate between temporal levels: old Ramon Lull becomes ill and develops a fever. At this point, the audience realizes that the positions of the signals do not stay static anymore but seem to wander around in the acoustic space: the voices and music, until then assigned to one specific position and therefore one story time, begin to get jumbled up with voices and music that belong to other episodes in the story. Also, words get cut off in the middle or put together with other words or fragments of words. All these processes indicate the increasing fever of old Ramon and his decreasing ability to recall the events of his life correctly. At the end of the play, a multitude of nonverbal sign systems tells the final events of the story: while the audience first hears the diegetic noises of waves and birds (the old man is lying on the deck of a ship), a nondiegetic "white noise," used purely as a storytelling device at the level of discourse, takes over and soon smothers the whole scene, representing the loosening of the sick man's grip on reality. At the end, the white noise cuts off, leaving total silence—another sign system that is used here to indicate the final event of the story: the old man's death.

The use of a wide range of audio features in this radio drama adaptation is astonishing. This was historically only possible after the rise of the Neues Hörspiel in the 1960s, when a change occurred regarding the dramaturgy of radio drama, which had been quite fixed and inflexible before. In this manner, every radio piece should be put in its historical context to understand its originality. As for the question of adaptation, the fact that the author of the radio piece and of the literary piece were the same, contributed to the accepting of the radio piece as artistically "valuable" at the time of its first broadcast. Adaptations by people different from the authors of the radio piece were usually very much exposed to the mentality that "the original" was always better, baldly put. This has to be taken into consideration when looking at the adaptation. Also, as already mentioned, with modern radio drama adaptations, the medial factor becomes very important and opens up another very interesting range of questions to work within an academic context.

CONCLUSION

Concepts like *radio drama* or *adaptation* can, as shown, not be defined easily. Their meaning changes throughout history; therefore, looking at this history is indispensable when teaching radio drama adaptations. It is the openness of the concepts that makes analyzing radio drama adaptations so interesting. Although they can all be analyzed by the described narratological and semiotic approach on a structural level, many historical factors have to be taken into account in order to come to a thorough understanding of the adaptation. Only then is it possible to compare radio drama adaptations from different times in history as well as different countries. Such a comparison can prove useful precisely in order to examine the different notions of different times and countries. It will certainly become clear that artists, media producers, and also audiences do have a lot of power when it comes to defining an art form like radio drama as well as accepting or rejecting a concept like adaptation.

As for the notion of radio drama adaptation, examples as the one in this article show very clearly that this aural art form is not just "theatre (or literature) for the blind." Crook's statement about the involvement of the listener—"By giving the listener the opportunity to create an individual filmic narrative and experience through the imaginative spectacle the listener becomes an active participant and 'dramaturgist' in the process of communication and listening"[18]—proves very true here: the listener or the student has to engage actively with the aurally told story. As this engagement is to a certain extent very individual, and certainly totally different from the engagement involved when reading a novel or watching a movie, the adapted story is by definition a changed product. Therefore, categories like "infidelity" or "deformation" are a priori not applicable. An adapted radio play is a work of art different from the literary piece used as source material. Therefore, it proves much more useful to look at the piece of art as such—especially at the way the story is told aurally— instead of only comparing the story of the literary work with the one in the adapted radio piece. The way the story is told is the basis for the listeners (or the students in the classroom) upon which they build their own "imaginative spectacle." This imaginative spectacle will not be more convincing the closer the radio drama sticks to the exact words or order of storytelling of the original literary piece. Rather, it will be a successful adaptation when the radio piece is able to use the own intrinsic medial features in order to let the story unfold. Only then it is truly a radio piece and not just aurally told literature.

NOTES

1. See Mark Ensign Cory, *The Emergence of an Acoustical Art Form: An Analysis of the German Experimental Hörspiel of the 1960s* (Lincoln: University of Nebraska Press, 1974), passim.

2. In recent works about English-speaking radio drama, the art form is still being called a literary genre: for Tim Crook, it is "one of the most unappreciated and understated literary forms of the twentieth century" (Tim Crook, *Radio Drama: Theory and Practice* [London: Routledge, 1999], 3); and Dermot Rattigan calls it "an aural literature" (Dermot Rattigan, *Theatre of Sound: Radio and the Dramatic Imagination* [Dublin: Carysfort Press, 2002], 3).

3. Andrew Crisell, *An Introductory History of British Broadcasting*, 2nd ed. (London: Routledge, 2002), 21.

4. Crook, *Radio Drama*, 66.

5. Andreas Hepp, "Radio and Popular Culture in Germany: Radio Culture between Comedy and 'Event-isation,'" in *More than a Music Box: Radio Cultures and Communities in a Multi-Media World*, ed. Andrew Crisell, 189–212 (New York: Berghahn Books, 2004), 191.

6. Ammer and F. M. Einheit are the most influential and successful German radio drama artists of the last decade and have won numerous national and international prizes, including first prize at the International Radio Festival of New York, the Prix Futura, and the Prix Italia Special Prize.

7. For example, the first German soundscape, *Weekend* by Walter Ruttmann. Walter Ruttmann, *Weekend Remix* (Munich: Intermedium records, 2000; Interme-

dium rec. 003, Indigo CD 93172). The soundscape was first broadcast on 13 June 1930 by the *Berliner Rundfunk* and directed by Walter Ruttmann himself.

8. Linda Hutcheon, *A Theory of Adaptation* (London: Routledge, 2006), 2.

9. Robert Stam and Alessandra Raengo (eds.), *Literature and Film: A Guide to the Theory and Practice of Film Adaptation* (Malden, Mass.: Blackwell, 2005), 3.

10. For more information about these radio drama adaptations, see Stefan Bodo Würffel, *Das deutsche Hörspiel* (Stuttgart, Germany: Metzler, 1978), 12–13.

11. Ulrich Gerhardt, "Materialkunst" ["Take It or Leave It"], in *HörWelten. 50 Jahre Hörspielpreis der Kriegsblinden 1952–2001*, ed. Bund der Kriegsblinden Deutschlands/Filmstiftung Nordrhein-Westfalen, 272–73 (Berlin: Aufbau-Verlag, 2001), 272 (translated by the author).

12. For a detailed study of the semiotics and narratology of radio drama see Elke Huwiler, *Erzählströme im Hörspiel. Zur Narratologie der elektroakustischen Kunst* (Paderborn, Germany: Mentis, 2005), passim.

13. Dieter Kühn, "Das Lullische Spiel" ["The Lullic Game"], in *Ludwigslust* [Stories], 33–57 (Frankfurt-am-Main, Germany: Suhrkamp, 1977).

14. Kühn, "Das Lullische Spiel," 33–38 (translation by the author).

15. Kühn, "Das Lullische Spiel," 55.

16. Dieter Kühn, *Das Lullische Spiel*, dir. Heinz Hostnig (Hamburg: North German Broadcasting Company [NDR], first broadcast 13 December 1975).

17. This illustrates that the positioning of signals within the acoustic space is not a feature with a fixed narrative function, either. Although throughout the history of radio drama production it has been used primarily to indicate the *spatial* positions of characters in a realistically represented setting, this example shows that it can be used in a much more varied way.

18. Crook, *Radio Drama*, 66.

ELEVEN

THE PLEASURES OF "THEATER FILM"

Stage to Film Adaptation

Milan Pribisic

"Adaptation studies are hot!" I came to this conclusion after talking on the phone the other day with my friend Paris Hilton. She was asking me what am I up to these days, and I told her that the new academic year has just started and that beyond that I have been working on an article about "theater film" to be included in an anthology on teaching adaptation studies. "What's theater film, and what has it to do with adaptation?" asked the always curious Paris. I responded by saying that theater film is a film based on an existing live theater show, a film recording of a performance that goes beyond mere record of what was put on the stage. "That's hot!" exclaimed Ms. Hilton.

All right, maybe I just adapted my dream a little to fit this introduction, or maybe this is how in my dream our conversation unfolded for real; in any case, there is something to be said about adaptation, intermedia, and hotness, and that is exactly what I will be doing in this chapter, which has been structured around a series of questions and answers to be explored by students and instructors in the classrooms all over the world immersed in the issues of media dialogism, convergence, and multimedia participatory culture.

WHY ADAPTATION STUDIES?

Adaptation is everywhere; we may even start by saying that the adaptation could serve as one of the central metaphors for the development of human civilization as a whole, as well as for our contemporary moment in culture, economy, and media development. One approach to human species' development and change is the theory of evolution, understood primarily as the phenomenon of natural selection and the species adaptation to the changing environmental, genetic, social, and historical circumstances. To adapt to the outside world is to learn to balance the assimilation of it to one's needs and wishes with the accommodation to the world's rules and regulations. The phenomenon of globalization on the other hand, pervasive in current world economy and politics, is addressed as an issue of adaptation, understood as a process of negotiation between local, regional, national, and international interests and trends. The media studies buzz word of the moment, media convergence, refers to the vast array of media relations, remediations, and adaptations of the "original" text across the media that have become standard in our culture of post- and media literacy.[1]

If adaptation is then taken as a paradigm in multiple academic and theoretical disciplines, the adaptation studies that frame the discussion here narrow down the concept to the fields of art and literature, as practiced in American performing arts departments curricula in particular, within which "adaptation" focuses on the interrelation between different kinds of text, whose meaning stems from the emerging relationship between them. Teaching and studying adaptation studies opens the way to better understanding of the interconnectedness between artistic disciplines, media, and genres, helping us along the way to find meaning and, perhaps, discover stability within the complexities of postmodern culture.

WHAT IS ADAPTATION STUDIES?

Adaptation studies refer to a network of textual relations established in the culture of postliteracy among multiple media, texts, producers, and consumers. If traditional adaptation studies within the arts and humanities implied a transfer of a literary work into a film medium, the current moment of adaptation studies expands this narrow notion to include new models of adaptation, including nonliterary sources as well as all other sources beyond the source text (e.g., social sources, history, genre, performance, marketing, media, and media literacy). These new models and trends in adaptation studies are part of the effort to make adaptation studies a place of negotiation, a hybrid space of cultural recycling. Adaptation studies explore the dynamics and intertextual strategies of adaptation in an effort to illuminate, explain, and understand adaptations as richly layered texts full of haunting textual ghosts, whose meaning depends on the context of production and reception of cultures.[2]

To initiate a discussion on the subject of adaptation, especially amongst students, we might concentrate on the following questions. This might constitute part of class discussion or be formulated as an individual research project conducted outside of class time. This list is not exhaustive and might be further developed by students and instructors.

1. *What's in a name* (adaptation studies)? What are the consequences of favoring the term adaptation studies rather than literary or film studies?
2. What lines of historical development (its phases) can we detect in adaptation studies?
3. What are the most popular literary sources and genres to be adapted? Why? How often?
4. Compile an annotated bibliography of major critical contributions to the discipline of adaptation studies.

"THEATER FILM"?

One of the major topics for discussion in the adaptation studies discipline is the relationship of theater to film. I suggest that we should look at this in a different way; rather than favoring a traditional approach, wherein film adaptation always implied a transfer of a literary work (novel, short story, or play) to the medium of film, I suggest we look at "theater film": a model that expands the field of adaptation studies to fit the postmodern intermediality and allows for discussion of all the nonliterary sources now at play within adaptations and among adapters. This is a forward-looking model designed to include a variety of options, intertexts, and intermedia. Discussion of this model in class might begin with the following questions: what's in a name (theater film), and what are the consequences of including theater film within the field of adaptation studies? Béatrice Picon-Vallin describes theater film, understood as film adaptation of existing live theater shows, as an encounter between two media—theater and film—wherein the emphasis is on the tense and complicated, multifaceted nature of this meeting, not on the fusion and blending between them that would hide their differences. Picon-Vallin departs from previous terms such as "theater (drama/literature) on film" and "filmed theater" in order to move away from the rather hackneyed idea that theater film is simply a mechanical, static recording of a live performance ready to be shelved in a theater archive or a library's special collection. Rather, Picon-Vallin hopes to shed light on film adaptations of theater productions such as Peter Brook's *Marat-Sade* (1966) or Louis Malle's *Vanya on 42nd Street* (1994) that preserve the stage performance both on the margins and at its center.

Theater film moves away from the question of faithfulness (does the film "preserve" the "qualities" of the stage production) and, instead, openly exploits its site of origin, the stage, as well as offering new possibilities for research into the productive, relational dialectics between the two media (stage and screen).[3]

Once these questions have been posed, they can be discussed in class with students, focusing in particular on how the linguistic choice of the term "theater film" differs from the previously used "filmed theater." What are the theoretical and pragmatic consequences of this new term? The following is an example of how teachers might put this theoretical discussion into practice. The order of proceeding may vary—one may want to start with the final product, the film itself, and then go backward to the theater source and the text from which the theater production originated; or one might start with the work of literature, move to the theatrical adaptation, and conclude with the film adaptation. The third approach, combining the previous two approaches in a zigzag procedural movement of analysis, is also an option.

The example of adaptation analysis that follows starts with the class watching Guy Maddin's *Dracula: Pages from a Virgin's Diary*, a film adaptation of a stage ballet, and proceeds with the discussion of the layers and meanings traceable in the film; returns to the primary source, Bram Stoker's nineteenth-century novel; and only after this detour comes back to Maddin's original source, the stage ballet. This journey devotes most discussion time to the present (2002, the year of the made-for-TV film, and the year in which I began teaching the course/topic), then goes back to the past (1897) of the novel source, and returns to the stage ballet performance source (1998). This movement should serve as a diachronic survey of the dialogic nature of film theater as adaptation and as a methodology for achieving the principal goal of adaptation studies—the unraveling of the palimpsestic intertextuality of this particular adaptation and of adaptation in general.

The class should be divided into as many groups as there are media sources that participate in this "transmedia storytelling."[4] In the case of *Dracula*, the three obvious groups include one that will explore Maddin's film adaptation in the context of film history, with special attention paid to early silent film aesthetics as a source of inspiration, as well as the early Soviet film avant-garde. The second group should research Stoker's *Dracula* and the Gothic literary tradition, while the third group's focus should be on dramatic, ballet, and musical adaptations inspired by Stoker's novel. Each group then shares their findings with the rest of the class and thereby provides an in-depth analysis of the adaptation process in contemporary culture as cumulative, complex, and multilayered.

The remainder of this chapter will offer certain suggestions on how this process of research might be constructed. I begin by focusing on the original novel *Dracula*. Stoker published *Dracula* (1897) as part of the Gothic novel revival of the 1880s and 1890s, with the focus of its narrative deriving from vampire legends, interwoven with a medieval atmosphere of mystery and terror (represented by all things foreign), plus a scientific, analytical frame (embodied by things and enterprises rooted in Victorian England) as a way of seeking solutions to such problems. Having looked at the novel's epistolary structure, students could then focus on how these elements—the vampire legends and the Victorian science—have been combined in the novel and whether Stoker has successfully fused the two elements. This forms a basis for the next stage of discussion, which should concentrate on Mark Godden's adaptation for the Royal Winnipeg Ballet. First adapted in 1998, it was remounted in 2004/2005 so there was a slight possibility that some of my students might have seen it live; some of its video-recorded fragments are available on youtube.com, but for most students, the only access to the original stage production will be through the documentation available on the Web, such as the production archive of the Royal Winnipeg Ballet at www.rwb.org.[5] Godden's narrative ballet, set to symphonic music by Gustav Mahler, tells the Count Dracula narrative in large, detailed strokes. He uses devices perceived impure within the traditional ballet, such as a projected text used as a backdrop to provide plot summaries and a voice-over delivering a combination of spoken and written words used to tell the story. The ballet is just over two hours long and divided into two acts. Act 1 depicts Lucy's response to Dracula's advances, her willing submission to the vampiric seduction, her suitor's efforts to save her through blood transfusion, her death and reappearance as a vampire, and her second death. This is the dance of a sexually awakened female, in which sexual desire merges with a death wish, only to be salvaged by the honorable and selfless work of a few good men. Act 2 starts with a merger of dance and "program notes" combining dance, pantomime, and voice-over in order to include Stoker's introduction about Jonathan Harker's journey to Transylvania and the legend of the undead as a classical and folk archetype. The action then returns to the seduction of another female victim, Mina. A darker-hair version of Lucy, she is the archetypal Englishwoman but with a difference: she overcomes her status as victim to become one of the vampire hunters. She is a victor and virtue embodied.[6]

In Godden's rendering, female innocence and the vampire's threat to it are the center of the narrative. The males are grouped together, functioning as a chorus of masculinity that is both destabilized and restored by the foreign threat to their females and their homeland. Harker becomes just one of the endangered young males, thus losing the prominence given to his character in Stoker's original. Native manhood in its prime is disrupted by the infiltration of the foreign undead's sexual prowess. While Stoker depicts this evil force of darkness as an old, pale, unappealing, but curiously strong and virile figure, Godden shows the Count as a racial Other—a young, attractive, and seductive presence. The only old male in this adaptation is Van Helsing, a wise man standing at the gates of the empire's regime of power-knowledge-pleasure, initiating and perpetuating the discourse on sex in which roles for domestic and foreign men and women are strictly prescribed, so that any deviation from them is promptly pursued and punished. The pleasure of the hunt and punishment of this "pornography of the morbid" hides behind the severity of national security under a foreign threat and "justifies the racisms of the state."[7]

Godden's choice of Mahler's dramatic, symbolic tonality inspired by Romanticism keeps fear and horror as points of departure but also lets the dancers' body movements and gesticulation follow the sound world of the music, transforming the narrative into a story of pure love under attack by impure, morbid impulses. Mahler's late music is often dominated by dualities, contrasts, conflicts, and a variety of moods (life/death, passion/resignation, progression/arrest, terror, irony, peaceful bliss, and brazen calmness).[8] His symphonic work is also characterized by a transfiguration of different genre conventions and a play upon genre that gradually refutes the audience's horizon of expectations.[9] In 2002, Maddin was hired by Vonnie Von Helmolt to make a cinematic adaptation of Godden's ballet for the Canadian Broadcasting Corporation's *Opening Night* TV program.[10] This was Maddin's first for-hire job, and he felt somewhat reluctant about doing it. What seemed particularly troublesome was the whole ballet "thing"—a form he was neither very familiar with nor much interested in. He knew about Dracula, of course, and once he had embarked on the project, he decided "to make the most faithful adaptation of the novel ever made, with a strange exception that it is all being danced."[11] Von Helmolt loved the ballet so much that she wanted as many people as possible to see it, and preserving it on the made-for-TV film seemed the way to go. To do this Maddin turned away from Godden's stage ballet and turned back instead to Bram Stoker's 1897 novel. Most critics who discuss vampiric seduction in Stoker see the novel as primarily about a symbolic seduction of women (Mina and Lucy) and their "vampiric affinities," perceiving English solicitor Harker's function in the narrative as a preface to this central theme.[12] The film follows this approach and begins with the first of Dracula's female victims, Lucy, and her vampiric betrothal by a scream. Gone are Harker's travels to Transylvania and the building of suspense about the count's identity.

Contemporary film audiences are well aware of the Dracula myth and do not require introduction or explication. Following Lucy's seduction and rescue from the eternal damnation of the undead, the film's narrative swiftly moves to Mina, Dracula's second female victim and the future Mrs. Jonathan Harker, and her initiation into uncleanliness. Maddin's seventy-two-minute film closes with the final duel between the devil and the vampire hunters.

From Stoker's *Dracula* Maddin selected his favorite themes, such as male jealousy and xenophobia in the face of liberated female sexuality, as well as his favorite episodes looking forward to cinematically reworking and retelling them.[13] "Episode" seems to be the key word here, since Stoker's novel is a long, multivoiced narrative from a multiplicity of perspectives about the invasion of a foreign entity threatening the foundations of Victorian England: domestic bliss built upon female purity and male dominance, and a bourgeois order dependant on the individual initiative of courageous, knowledgeable, bread-winning men. Stoker delivers this epistolary narrative through a compilation of different characters' diary entries, newspaper clippings, police reports, and other documents—a sort of collage of voices and perspectives "placed in sequence,"[14] trying to illuminate the mysterious and dangerous force infiltrating sacred English soil. Class discussion of the novel can focus on these thematic episodes and the various formal/genre categories employed in the construction of the novel's overall plot.

Maddin explores popular images of Dracula—he is perceived as a threat coming from foreign, uncharted territory in order to terrorize a fundamentally conservative society. Meanwhile, Van Helsing is constructed as a native, righteous person asserting his identity by protecting, by any means necessary, the homeland's sacred property (its women) and territoriality. The conflict between the two main characters necessarily leads to the mandatory "duel until sunrise" between the good guy and the bad guy, with the good guy winning and taking as a reward the restored purity of his society's female population. Maddin never really finished reading Stoker's novel and was more interested in reworking the principal archetypes associated with the myth of Dracula in his film adaptation and thereby enabling, in Umberto Eco's memorable phrase, "the archetypes [to] hold a reunion" and celebrate their coming together.[15]

This topic could be pursued further in class, by asking students to read the novel *Dracula* and subsequently compare it with popular images of the character, as represented in other adaptations or in popular culture. Once they have engaged in this comparison, they are then in a position to look at Maddin's film. One of the most interesting aspects of Maddin's work is his use of other intertextual frames, drawn from other cinematic traditions, which in this case help students to understand what the term "theater film" might mean. Maddin uses techniques drawn from silent film: the dancers tell the story only through body movements and facial expressions. As Maddin states, they dance with every fiber of their bodies.[16] While the focus of the audience watching the stage production is on the whole body, silent cinema's big discovery was close-ups of movie stars' "big faces" that spoke more than a thousand words. In his film adaptation, Maddin draws on the conventions of silent film. We now have medium- and long-shot dance scenes of passion, fear, and madness, combined with dancers' close-ups to underline emotion, dramatic moments, or shifts in the characters' relationships. If this strategy has cut the amount of dance that was previously visible on stage, it has certainly augmented its suspenseful and dramatic impact on film by providing angles and sights that could not be appreciated in live theater. It also proves a great device for more clearly showcasing not only the dancers' balletic craft but their acting ability as well. David Moroni's iconic performance as the mad scientist Van Helsing, with a clandestine attraction to virgins, is a magical embodiment of what Michel Foucault terms "the image of the imperial prude . . . emblazoned on our restrained, mute, and hypocritical sexuality."[17]

Maddin's debt to silent film is also evident in the predominantly pantomimed interpersonal exchanges between the characters, to the accompaniment of postrecorded sound effects and the music of Mahler. This recalls the familiar mood of the silent era, when playback operators and musical accompanists added sound during the projection. However, Maddin brings the film simultaneously up to date through digital editing and computer-generated effects.[18] This deliberate juxtaposition of disparate styles and technologies emphasizes how a theater film incorporates different traditions, foregrounding the text's hybrid quality. To complicate the issue Maddin, like directors of silent films, uses intertitles and subtitles; some are his directorial observations ("Immigrants!!") interspersed with quotes from the novel ("There are bad dreams for those who sleep unwisely"). Introducing direct quotes from Stoker's book also serves as a reminder of the original source, for both ballet adapter Godden and film adapter Maddin. Reading these phrases on the screen parallels the reader's activity when reading Stoker's novel. The subtitles belong to the culture of literacy and print, intruding into the domain of the media dominated by the theater's "showing" mode and by Maddin's use of digital technology. In thematic terms, the use of subtitles resembles Stoker's narrative, which shows the undead's trying to infiltrate and pollute a world by means of seduction.[19]

Once students have looked at Maddin's film in detail, they might be able to reflect on the nature of theater film. To understand this, I suggest they draw upon Sergei Eisenstein's theory of the "montage of attractions," in which the screen is filled with myriad images designed to attract our attention and leaving us hungry for more. The film can also be used as a basis for discussion on the transcoding, across media, of a stage ballet into a kinetic dance of stage and cinematic images, bodies, and music. The discussion on theater film might culminate with the following questions, which can be approached as research issues or classroom discussion topics:

1. What are the main tenets of the Soviet avant-garde film as envisioned by Eisenstein;
2. What other sources of inspirations from the early cinema are visible in Maddin's film adaptation?
3. What are the main aesthetic differences between silent and sound films?
4. What is the relation between ballet film and dance film? How does the film musical, with its numerous dance numbers, fit into this classification?
5. In what way does a theater film such as Maddin's version of *Dracula* differ from a straight musical adaptation?

PALIMPSESTIC INTERTEXTUALITY

Guy Maddin's bringing together of three media (film, novel, and stage) requires different modes of audience engagement through which each operates: the novel tells the story, while stage and film show and tell. Since Western theater's appearance in its dramatic form in ancient Greece, the text (or telling of the drama) has often been perceived as its dominant element—from which the new medium of film, in a search for its own language, needed to detach itself. As Picon-Vallin shows in her discussion of theater film, this historical theater/film split, seen primarily as a text/image split, is slowly being abandoned in favor of a theoretical debate about theater and film as different types of images and showing—that is, the theater audiovisual image versus the cinematic audiovisual image. Each of these contains a fundamental contradiction: a live, three-dimensional audiovisual theater image is framed by the codes and conventions of the medium that stands as a representation of the real; and a two-dimensional, "flattened" audiovisual cinematic image seduces by its recorded, technology-mediated, realistic simulation of reality.[20] Teaching a film like Maddin's *Dracula*, and looking at the ways in which it creates a theater film, enables students to understand the close proximity of these different media and their languages, histories, and interrelations. Maddin builds upon all these different genre sources and transmutations; his *Dracula* is a Gothic horror story set in Victorian England, re-created

meticulously in the studio by his (not Godden's) set designer Deanne
Rhode, using ballet dancers as "perfect melodramatists [sic],"[21] and
showing high drama of the human heart and blood in need of the con-
tainment and balance provided by reason and spiritual peace. Maddin's
use of Mahler is further complicated by his use of digital sounds—
mixing and layering, not unlike a DJ, the different movements of Mahler's
music.[22] This strategy produces new qualities and sounds, emphasizing
the decisiveness of the "color of the tone" and "physicality of instrumental sound"[23] in Mahler's music—thus balancing well with the silent
movie's black-and-white images and the hybridity of genre conventions
and expectations. In the end, the tale of horror and melodrama of mind
and body is situated within the frames and codes of silent film, which
Maddin uses as "the perfect stepping stone between literal-minded movies of today and all other art forms, plastic or otherwise."[24] It is the silent
film's openness to different influences and varieties of interpretations that
makes it so fascinating for Maddin and so multipurposeful for contemporary audiences.

Maddin's *Dracula* finds Godden's ballet, returns to Stoker's novel,
and revisits music videos alongside the history of early cinema; it was
also shot on Super-8 and Bolex cameras like an amateur home movie,
and eventually spa treated on the computer to edit its image and sound,
generating digital effects by adding colors and filters to the "primitive"
primary material. The traces of all these previous influences are visible in
the finished, new product, making Maddin's *Dracula* a postmodern pas-
tiche and collage *par excellence*. His theater film of Godden's ballet based
on Stoker's nineteenth-century novel *Dracula* was already "palimpsestuous,"[25] for in Maddin's adaptation we see all things he saw and remembered; we are taken on a ride, with his camera as a time machine; and we
discover layers, resonances, and repetitions with subtle differences. Maddin's intertextual competence becomes our own, and through this sharing
we become aware of our time, the passing of it, and the remembrances
that remain.

The film becomes a perfect site for the discussion of new approaches
to adaptation studies in class, focusing on the ways an adaptation not
only incorporates different texts but also can create new genres (in this
case the theater film), which have nothing to do with issues of fidelity but
rather try to unify elements from different genres in a satisfying whole.
The film could serve as a basis for discussing further questions such as
the following: What are the differences between the audiovisual images
delivered by theater and film? How are they unified in Maddin's work?
How does Maddin employ other modes of representation, such as music
video aesthetics or home movies?

All of this is good and useful stuff for students to know. The lesson taught by teaching adaptation studies in relation to this film, focusing in particular on the layers and interstices of cultures and cultural productions, is that every text is always already an adaptation of the previous adaptation adapted from a text or texts that preceded it. There are, to be sure, many pleasures to be had in tracing back and teasing out adaptation's intertextual relations and palimpsestic layers. On the other hand, however, what is to be made out of the connoted systems, of the myths in the Barthesian sense of the word,[26] produced by this perpetual process of adapting adaptations out of adaptations? This is particularly appropriate to the theater film in which different genres are consciously unified. This can form another segment of an adaptation studies course, prompting a fresh cycle of reflections and debates about the function and signification of adaptation studies. Issues to be explored could include the following: Is adaptation the main (only?) human way of survival, perception, reflection, and creation? Is adaptation our prison? Is adaptation an enemy of innovation and revolutionary change? What is the relation between adaptation, appropriation, and invention?

TO BE CONTINUED . . . IN THE CLASSROOM!

NOTES

1. The literature is too vast to document here; consult, for example, Jean Piaget, *Six Psychological Studies* (New York: Random House, 1968); Manfred Steger, *Globalization: A Very Short Introduction* (Oxford: Oxford University Press, 2000); Henry Jenkins, *Convergence Culture: Where Old and New Media Collide* (New York: New York University Press, 2006); and the first issue of *Adaptation: The Journal of Literature on Screen Studies* (2008) published by Oxford University Press as the long overdue journal that establishes the autonomy of adaptation studies from both literary and film studies.

2. The latest crop of titles that deals with adaptations includes, among others, Thomas Leitch, "Adaptation Studies at a Crossroads," *Adaptation* 1, no. 1 (2008): 63–77; Christine Geraghty, *Now a Major Motion Picture: Film Adaptations of Literature and Drama* (Lanham, Md.: Rowman & Littlefield, 2008); Deborah Cartmell and Imelda Whelehan (eds.), *The Cambridge Companion to Literature on Screen* (Cambridge: Cambridge University Press, 2007); James M. Welsh and Peter Lev (eds.), *The Literature/Film Reader: Issues of Adaptation* (Lanham, Md.: Scarecrow Press, 2007); Linda Hutcheon, *A Theory of Adaptation* (London: Routledge, 2006); Julie Sanders, *Adaptation and Appropriation* (New York: Routledge, 2006).

3. Béatrice Picon-Vallin's study *Le film de théâtre* was published in Paris by CNRS in 1997; an excerpt from it entitled "Passages, Interférences, Hybridations: Le Film de théâtre" appeared in *Theatre Research International* 26, no. 2 (July 2001): 190–97.

4. Henry Jenkins defines a transmedia story as "a story [that] unfolds across multiple media platforms, with each new text making a distinctive and valuable contribution to the whole" (Jenkins, *Convergence Culture*, 95–96).

5. For background on the ballet, see the review published on the Detroit Opera House website, "Dracula," 6 September 2006, www.michiganopera.org/press/06sep5dracula.html (accessed 6 May 2009).

6. Elizabeth Miller, "Dracula," *Dracula's Homepage*, 2005, www.webliterature.net/literature/Stoker/WL1-dracula (accessed 6 May 2009); and Royal Winnipeg Ballet, "*Dracula* Study Guide," www.rwb.org/ (accessed 6 May 2009).

7. Michel Foucault, *The History of Sexuality Vol. 1: An Introduction*, trans. Robert Hurley (New York: Vintage Books, 1980), 54.

8. See, for example, Vera Micznik, "The Farewell Story of Mahler's Ninth Symphony," *Nineteenth-Century Music* 20, no. 2 (1996): 144–66; James Buhler, "'Breakthrough' as Critique of Form: The Finale of Mahler's First Symphony," *Nineteenth-Century Music* 20, no. 2 (1996): 125–43.

9. Vera Micznik, "Mahler and 'The Power of Genre,'" *Journal of Musicology* 12, no. 2 (1994): 117–51.

10. *Dracula: Pages from a Virgin's Diary* [2003], Dir. Guy Maddin, Perf. Zhang Wei-Qiang, David Moroni, Tara Birtwhistle (DVD B0001US800: Zeitgeist Films, 2004).

11. Guy Maddin, "Count of the Dance: Guy Maddin on *Dracula: Pages from a Virgin's Diary*," interviewed by Mark Peranson, *Cinema Scope*, March 2002, 9. It is curious, to say the least, that Maddin is after the most faithful adaptation of the novel that he, according to different sources, either "read pretty carefully and picked up my favorite episodes" (according to Maddin's audio commentary on the Zeitgeist Films DVD of *Dracula*) or "hated . . . it's boring and I only read the first half of it" (Guy Maddin, "Conversations with Guy Maddin," interviewed by William Beard [Edmonton, Canada: Metro Cinema Society, 2007], 8). There seems to be a sort of self-projection and resonance with the figure of Dracula himself at work here, as exemplified in a 2004 interview with Maddin: "I do feel a bit like Dracula in Winnipeg. I'm safe, but can travel abroad and suck up all sorts of ideas from other filmmakers—both dead and undead. Then I can come back here and hoard these tropes and cinematic devices. . . . And I sit here in almost eternal darkness all winter long and try to make these dead things live" (Marie Losier and Richard Porton, "The Pleasures of Melancholy: An Interview with Guy Maddin," *Cineaste* [Summer 2004]: 25).

12. For a recent summary of criticism on Stoker's *Dracula*, consult Dejan Kuzmanovic, "Vampiric Seduction and Vicissitudes of Masculine Identity in Bram Stoker's *Dracula*," *Victorian Literature and Culture* 37, no. 2 (2009): 411–25.

13. Guy Maddin, audio commentary on *Dracula: Pages from a Virgin's Diary* DVD.

14. Bram Stoker, *Dracula*, ed. Brooke Allen (New York: Barnes and Noble Classics, 2003), 4.

15. Umberto Eco, "*Casablanca*: Cult Movies and Intertextual Collage," in *Travels in Hyperreality: Essays*, trans. William Weaver, 197–211 (San Diego: Harcourt Brace Jovanovich, 1986), 208–9.

16. Maddin, audio commentary on *Dracula: Pages from a Virgin's Diary* DVD.

17. Foucault, *The History of Sexuality Vol. 1*, 3.

18. For example, approximately 80 percent of the shots were digitally reframed, making it perhaps "the most digitally driven movie ever made in Canada," according to Maddin, "Count of the Dance," 11.

19. For seduction as mastery over the symbolic universe, see Jean Baudrillard, *Seduction*, trans. Brian Singer (New York: St. Martin's Press, 1990), 8.

20. Picon-Vallin, "Passages, Interférences, Hybridations," 193.

21. Guy Maddin, CBC Radio One interview on *Dracula: Pages from a Virgin's Diary* DVD.

22. Maddin, CBC Radio One Interview.

23. Karen Painter, "The Sensuality of Timbre: Responses to Mahler and Modernity at the 'Fin de siècle.'" *Nineteenth-Century Music* 18, no. 3 (1995): 236–56.

24. Maddin, "Count of the Dance," 6.

25. Michael Alexander, quoted in Hutcheon, *A Theory of Adaptation*, 6.

26. For Roland Barthes a connoted system is a staggered system of two systems of significations that are out of joint with each other: the signifiers of the second system consist of the familiar signs from the first system of signification, but the new context attaches the new signifieds to them. Or, in other words, the old rhetorics produce new, hidden ideologies that need to be uncovered by the critical activity of semiological research. See, for example, Roland Barthes, *Elements of Semiology*, trans. Annette Lavers and Colin Smith (New York: Hill and Wang, 1991), 89–98.

FILMOGRAPHY

An American Tragedy, Dir. Josef von Sternberg, Perf. Phillips Holmes, Sylvia Sidney, Frances Dee (Paramount Pictures, 1931).

Babel [2006], Dir. Alejandro González Iñárritu, Perf. Brad Pitt, Cate Blanchett (DVD B000PC86DG: Ufa/DVD, 2007).

Bonfire of the Vanities [1990], Dir. Brian De Palma, Perf. Tom Hanks, Bruce Willis, Melanie Griffith (DVD B00004VYLV: Warner Home Video, 2000).

The Borgias [1981], Dir. Brian Farnham, Perf. Oliver Cotton, Adolfo Celi, Louis Selwyn (BBC Television, 1981).

Boy A [2007], Dir. John Crowley, Perf. Andrew Garfield, Alfie Owen (DVD B001CDFY6Y: Miriam Collection, 2008).

Bridget Jones' Diary [2001], Dir. Sharon Maguire, Perf. Renee Zellweger, Hugh Grant, Colin Firth (DVD B00031V22G: Alliance [Universal], 2004).

The Da Vinci Code [2006], Dir. Ron Howard, Perf. Tom Hanks, Audrey Tautou, Ian McKellen, Widescreen Two-Disc Special ed. (DVD B00005JOC9: Sony Pictures, 2006).

Dracula: Pages from a Virgin's Diary [2003], Dir. Guy Maddin, Perf. Zhang Wei-Qiang, David Moroni, Tara Birtwhistle (DVD B0001US800: Zeitgeist Films, 2004).

Esmeralda [1905], Dir. Alice Guy, Victorin-Hippolyte Jasset, Perf. Denise Becker, Henry Vorins (Societé des Établissements L. Gaumont, 1905).

Girl with a Pearl Earring [2003], Dir. Peter Webber, Perf. Colin Firth, Scarlett Johansson, Tom Wilkinson, DVD + Book ed. (DVD B0001US81O: Lions Gate Video, 2004).

The Golden Compass [2007], Dir. Chris Weitz, Perf. Nicole Kidman, Daniel Craig, New Line Platinum Series Two-Disc Widescreen ed. (DVD B0013IJ2LQ: New Line Home Video, 2008).

A Good Woman [2005], Dir. Mike Barker, Perf. Helen Hunt, Scarlet Johansson, Stephen Campbell Moore (DVD B0003UAFC: Lionsgate Video, 2006).

The Hitchhiker's Guide to the Galaxy [2005], Dir. Garth Jennings, Perf. Mos Def, Warwick Davis, Martin Freeman (DVD B0009HBEGI: Touchstone Video, 2005).

The Hours [2002], Dir. Stephen Daldry, Perf. Nicole Kidman, Julianne Moore, Meryl Streep (DVD B00005JKTI: Paramount Home Video, 2003).

The Hunchback of Notre Dame [1923], Dir. Wallace Worsley, Perf. Lon Chaney, Patsy Ruth Miller (DVD B000TEUS16: Image Entertainment, Ultimate Edition, 2007).

The Hunchback of Notre Dame [1939], Dir. William Dieterle, Perf. Charles Laughton, Cedric Hardwicke (DVD B000B8V9FE: Warner Home Video, Warner Classics Mega Collection, 2005).

The Hunchback of Notre Dame [1996], Dir. Gary Trousdale, Kirk Wise, Voices Jason Alexander, Tom Hulce (DVD B00005NYXO: Buena Vista Home Entertainment, 2001).

Into the Wild [2007], Dir. Sean Penn, Perf. Emile Hirsch, Marcia Gay Harden, William Hurt (DVD B00194WZJA: Paramount Home Entertainment, 2008).

Lady Windermere's Fan [1916], Dir. Fred Paul, Perf. Milton Rosmer, Netta Westcott, Nigel Playfair (VHS, London: British Film Institute).

Lady Windermere's Fan [1985], Dir. Tony Smith, Perf. Helena Little, Tim Woodward, Stephanie Turner (DVD B000062XE1: BBC Video, 2002).

Lolita [1962], Dir. Stanley Kubrick, Perf. Sue Lyon, James Mason, Peter Sellers (DVD B000UJ48VI: Warner Home Video, 2007).

The Lord of the Rings: The Fellowship of the Ring [2001], Dir. Peter Jackson, Perf. Elijah Wood, Ian McKellen (DVD B000067DNF: New Line Home Entertainment, Platinum Series Special Extended Edition, 2002).

Lucrèce Borgia [1953], Dir. Christian-Jaque, Perf. Martine Carol, Pedro Armendáriz (DVD B000NTPB9S: LCJ, 2007).

A Place in the Sun [1951], Dir. George Stevens, Perf. Montgomery Clift, Elizabeth Taylor, Shelley Winters (DVD B00003CXBZ: Paramount Home Video, 2001).

Practical Magic [1998], Dir. Griffin Dunne, Perf. Sandra Bullock, Nicole Kidman, Stockard Channing (DVD 0790740060: Warner Home Video, 1998).

Sunset Boulevard [1950], Dir. Billy Wilder, Perf. Gloria Swanson, William Holden, Erich von Stroheim (DVD B001EXE2ZG: Paramount Video, Sunset Boulevard Centennial Collection, 2008).

Terminator: The Sarah Connor Chronicles [2008–2009], Dir. Various, Perf. Lena Headey, Thomas Dekker, Summer Glau (DVD B000T9OP7G: Warner Home Video, the Complete First Season, 2008).

The Third Man [1949], Dir. Carol Reed, Perf. Joseph Cotten, Orson Welles, Trevor Howard (DVD B000NOK0GM: Criterion Collection, Two-Disc ed., 2007).

Žižek! [2005], Dir. Astra Taylor, Perf. Slavoj Žižek (DVD B000FII32Y: Zeitgeist Films, 2006).

BIBLIOGRAPHY

Akünal, Zuhal. "English Medium Education in Turkey: A Myth or an Achievable Goal? An Evaluation of Content-Based Second Language Education at Middle East Technical University." Unpublished PhD diss., University of Kent, 1993.

Anderson, Clive. *The Long Tail: How Endless Choice Is Creating Unlimited Demand.* London: Random House, 2007.

Andrew, Dudley. *Concepts in Film Theory.* Oxford: Oxford University Press, 1984.

The Arts Council of England's National Policy for Theatre in England. 2000. www.artscouncil.org.uk/media/uploads/documents/publications/300.pdf (accessed 8 June 2009).

Arts, Enterprise and Excellence: Strategy for Higher Education [in the United Kingdom]. 2006.www.artscouncil.org.uk/media/uploads/documents/publications/artsenterpriseexcellence_phpT0mNbm.pdf (accessed 8 June 2009).

Atwill, Janet M. "Introduction: Finding a Home or Making a Path." In *Perspectives on Rhetorical Invention,* edited by Janet M. Atwill and Janice M. Lauer, xi–xxi. Knoxville: University of Tennessee Press, 2002.

Atwill, Janet M., and Janice M. Lauer (eds.). *Perspectives on Rhetorical Invention.* Tennessee Studies in Literature, vol. 39. Knoxville: University of Tennessee Press, 2002.

Babbage, Frances, Robert Neumark Jones, Lauren Williams, and Oscar Wilde. "No Small Parts." Unpublished play script, 2007.

Bağıoğlu, Gülşen. "Genel, Mesleki, ve Teknik Eğitim Fakülterindeki Öğretmenlik Uygulaması Dersine İlişkin Öğretim Elemanı ve Öğrenci Görüşleri" [Lecturers' and Students' Opinions on Teaching Practice Courses Offered in General, Vocational, and Technical Education Faculties]. Unpublished MA thesis, Hacettepe University, Ankara, 1997.

Bailey, Herbert S., Jr. *The Art and Science of Book Publishing.* Athens: Ohio University Press, 1970.

Barnett, Ronald, Gareth Parry, and Kelly Coate. "Conceptualising Curriculum Change." *Teaching in Higher Education* 6, no. 4 (2001): 435–49.

Barthes, Roland. "The Death of the Author," translated by Stephen Heath. In *Image, Music, Text,* 142–48. New York: Hill and Wang, 1977.

———. *Elements of Semiology,* translated by Annette Lavers and Colin Smith. New York: Hill and Wang, 1991.

———. *S/Z,* translated by Richard Miller. Oxford, UK: Blackwell, 1974.

Bartlett, Steve, Diana M. Burton, and Nick Peim. *Introduction to Education Studies.* London: Sage, 2001.

Baudrillard, Jean. *Seduction,* translated by Brian Singer. New York: St. Martin's Press, 1990.

Baverstock, Alison. *How to Market Books: The Essential Guide to Maximizing Profit and Exploiting All Channels to Market,* 4th ed. London: Kogan Page, 2008.

BBC. *The Big Read.* 2005. www.bbc.co.uk/arts/bigread (accessed 16 May 2009).

Bellonci, Maria. *Lucrezia Borgia.* London: Phoenix, 2000.

Benjamin, Walter. *Illuminations,* translated by Harry Zohn. London: Pimlico, 1999.

———. "The Work of Art in the Age of Mechanical Reproduction," translated by Edmund Jephcott and Harry Zohn, second version (1935–1936). In *Selected Writings,* vol. 3, edited by Howard Eiland and Michael W. Jennings, 101–33. Cambridge, Mass.: Harvard University Press, 2002.

Berk, Özlem. *Translation and Westernisation in Turkey: From the 1840s to the 1980s.* Istanbul: Ege Yayınları, 2004.

Blake, William. *Selected Poems.* London: Wordsworth, 2000.

Bluestone, George. *Novels into Film.* Berkeley: University of California Press, 1957.

Bolton, Gillian. *Reflective Practice: Writing and Professional Development.* London: Paul Chapman, 2001.

Bowie, A. M. *Aristophanes: Myth, Ritual and Comedy.* Cambridge: Cambridge University Press, 1993.

Boyum, Joy Gould. *Double Exposure: Fiction into Film.* New York: Plume Books, 1985.

"Brokeback Mountain on the London Underground." Master's project, University of East London, 2007–2008. www.uel.ac.uk/writing/projects/underground.htm (accessed 12 January 2009).

Brownell, Joseph W., and Patricia W. Enos. *Adirondack Tragedy: The Gillette Murder Case of 1906.* Utica, N.Y.: Nicholas K. Burns Publishing, 2003 (original ed. 1986).

Bruner, Jerome. "Self-Making Narratives." In *Autobiographical Memory and the Construction of a Narrative Self: Developmental and Cultural Perspectives,* edited by Robyn Fivush and Catherine A. Haden, 209–26. Mahwah, N.J.: Erlbaum, 2003.

Buhler, James. "'Breakthrough' as Critique of Form: The Finale of Mahler's First Symphony." *Nineteenth-Century Music* 20, no. 2 (1996): 125–43.

The Cambridge History of the Book in Britain. 8 vols. Cambridge: Cambridge University Press, 2005–.

Cameron, Jessica, Anne E. Wilson, and Michael Ross. "Autobiographical Memory and Self-Assessment." In *The Self and Memory,* edited by Denise R. Beike, James M. Lampinen, and Douglas A. Behrend, 207–26. New York: Psychology Press, 2004.

Cardwell, Sarah. *Adaptation Revisited: Television and the Classic Novel.* Manchester, N.Y.: Manchester University Press, 2002.

Cartmell, Deborah. "Screen to Text." In *Adaptations: From Text to Screen, Screen to Text,* edited by Deborah Cartmell and Imelda Whelehan, 143–45. London: Routledge, 1999.

Cartmell, Deborah, and Imelda Whelehan (eds.). *The Cambridge Companion to Literature on Screen.* Cambridge: Cambridge University Press, 2007.

Chang, Eileen. *Lust, Caution.* London: Penguin, 2007.

Chapple, Freda, and Chiel Kattenbelt. "Key Issues in Intermediality in Theatre and Performance." In *Intermediality in Theatre and Performance,* edited by Freda Chapple and Chiel Kattenbelt, 11–25. Amsterdam: Rodopi, 2006.

Clark, Giles N. and Angus Phillips. *Inside Book Publishing,* 3rd ed. London: Routledge, 2000.

Cloud, Dana L. "The Materiality of Discourse as Oxymoron: A Challenge to Classical Rhetoric." *Western Journal of Communication* 58 (1994): 141–63.

Cook, Jon. "Creative Writing as a Research Method." In *Research Methods for English Studies,* edited by Gabriele Griffin, 179–97. Edinburgh: Edinburgh University Press, 2005.

Corrigan, Timothy. *Film and Literature: An Introduction and Reader.* Boston: Prentice Hall, 1999.

Cory, Mark Ensign. *The Emergence of an Acoustical Art Form: An Analysis of the German Experimental Hörspiel of the 1960s.* Lincoln: University of Nebraska Press, 1974.

Coxe, Louis O., and Robert Chapman. *Billy Budd.* New York: Hill and Wang, 1965 (original ed. 1951).

Crisell, Andrew. *An Introductory History of British Broadcasting.* 2nd ed. London: Routledge, 2002.

Crook, Tim. *Radio Drama: Theory and Practice.* London: Routledge, 1999.

Cunningham, Michael. *The Hours.* London: Picador, 2002.

Darnton, Robert. "What Is the History of Books?" *Daedalus* 111, no. 3 (Summer 1982): 65–83.

Davies, Gill. *Book Commissioning and Acquisition.* London: Routledge, 2004.

DeBona, Guerric. "Dickens, the Depression and MGM's *David Copperfield.*" In *Film Adaptation,* edited by James Naremore, 106–28. London: Athlone Press, 2000.

Dessauer, John. *Book Publishing: The Basic Introduction.* London: Continuum, 1998.

Detroit Opera House. "Dracula," 6 September 2006. www.michiganopera.org/press/06sep5dracula.html (accessed 6 May 2009).

Dickinson, Emily. "A Bird Came Down the Walk." http://quotations.about.com/cs/poemlyrics/a/Bird_Came_Down.htm (accessed 6 November 2009).

Driscoll, F. Paul. "A Voice from the Past." *Opera News* 70, no. 6 (2005): 8.

Eakin, Paul John. "Storied Selves: Identity through Self-Narration." In *Making Selves: How Our Lives Become Stories,* 99–141. Ithaca, N.Y.: Cornell University Press, 1999.

Eco, Umberto. "*Casablanca*: Cult Movies and Intertextual Collage." In *Travels in Hyperreality: Essays,* translated by William Weaver, 197–211. San Diego: Harcourt Brace Jovanovich, 1986.

Eliot, Simon, and Jonathan Rose (eds.). *A Companion to the History of the Book.* Oxford, UK: Wiley-Blackwell, 2009.

Epstein, Jason. *Book Business: Publishing Past, Present and Future.* New York: W. W. Norton, 2002.

Evans, Stephen. "The Evergreens: 12 Books that Sell and Sell." *Daily Telegraph*, 9 August 2008, 16.

Feather, John, and Hazel Woodbridge. "Bestsellers in the British Book Industry 1998–2005." *Publishing Research Quarterly* 23, no. 3 (September 2007): 203–23. www.springerlink.com/content/22j2070t41827h52 (accessed 12 May 2009).

Fébvre, Lucien, and Henri-Jean Martin. *L'Apparition du Livre* [*The Coming of the Book*]. Paris: Éditions Albin Michel, 1958.

Finkelstein, David, and Alistair McCleery (eds.). *The Book History Reader*, 2nd ed. New York: Routledge, 2006.

———. *An Introduction to Book History.* New York: Routledge, 2005.

Fleming, Patricia Lockhart, Gilles Gallichan, and Yvan Lamonde (eds.). *Histoire du Livre et de l'Imprimé au Canada.* Montreal: Presses de l'Université de Montréal, 2004.

Foucault, Michel. *The History of Sexuality Vol. 1: An Introduction*, translated by Robert Hurley. New York: Vintage Books, 1980.

———. "What Is an Author?" In *Reading Architectural History: An Annotated Anthology*, edited by Dana Arnold, 71–81. London: Routledge, 2002.

Freund, Elizabeth. *Return of the Reader: Reader Response Criticism.* London: Methuen, 1987.

Genette, Gérard. *Palimpsests* (1982), translated by Channa Newman and Claude Doubinsky. Lincoln: University of Nebraska Press, 1997.

———. *Paratexts: Thresholds of Interpretation*, translated by Jane E. Lewin. Cambridge: Cambridge University Press, 1997.

Geraghty, Christine. *Now a Major Motion Picture: Film Adaptations of Literature and Drama.* Lanham, Md.: Rowman & Littlefield, 2008.

Gerhardt, Ulrich. "Materialkunst" ["Take It or Leave It"]. In *HörWelten. 50 Jahre Hörspielpreis der Kriegsblinden 1952–2001*, edited by Bund der Kriegsblinden Deutschlands/Filmstiftung Nordrhein-Westfalen, 272–73. Berlin: Aufbau-Verlag, 2001.

Giroux, Henry A. "Schooling as a Form of Cultural Politics: Towards a Pedagogy of and for Difference." In *Critical Pedagogy: The State and Cultural Struggle*, edited by Henry A. Giroux and Peter McLaren, 142–67. Albany: State University of New York Press, 1989.

Graham, Gordon (former editor of *Logos: The Professional Journal for the Book World*). Interview with Alexis Weedon, 22 March 2009.

Gürçağlar, Şehnaz Tahir. *The Politics and Poetics of Translation in Turkey 1923–1960.* Amsterdam: Editions Rodopi, 2008.

Hand, Richard J. *The Theatre of Joseph Conrad: Reconstructed Fictions.* London: Palgrave, 2005.

Hepp, Andreas. "Radio and Popular Culture in Germany: Radio Culture between Comedy and 'Event-isation.'" In *More than a Music Box: Radio Cultures and Communities in a Multi-Media World*, edited by Andrew Crisell, 189–212. New York: Berghahn Books, 2004.

The Higher Education Act [in the United Kingdom]. 2004. http://en.wikipedia.org/wiki/Higher_Education_Act_2004 (accessed 8 June 2009).

Hodson, Daren. Letter to Laurence Raw, 10 April 2000.

Hoffman, Alice. *Practical Magic.* New York: Berkley Trade Books, 2003.

Hugo, Victor. *Oeuvres Complètes: Théâtre I.* Paris: Robert Laffont, 1985.

———. *Victor Hugo: Four Plays,* edited by Claude Schumacher. London: Methuen, 2004.

Hutcheon, Linda. *A Theory of Adaptation.* London: Routledge, 2006.

Huwiler, Elke. *Erzählströme im Hörspiel. Zur Narratologie der elektroakustischen Kunst.* Paderborn, Germany: Mentis, 2005.

Irwin-Zarecka, Iwona. *Frames of Remembrance: The Dynamics of Collective Memory.* New Brunswick, N.J.: Transaction Publishers, 1994.

Iser, Wolfgang. *The Act of Reading: A Theory of Aesthetic Response.* Baltimore: Johns Hopkins University Press, 1978.

Jenkins, Henry. *Convergence Culture: Where Old and New Media Collide.* New York: New York University Press, 2006.

Jewitt, Carey. *Technology, Literacy and Learning: A Multimodal Approach.* London: Routledge, 2006.

Kist, Joost. *New Thinking for 21st Century Publishers.* Oxford, UK: Chandos, 2009.

Knight, Julia, Samantha Lay, and Alexis Weedon. "Digital Film and Cross-Media Influences: Pilot Study Report." http://madwiki.beds.ac.uk/madwiki/index .php/Report (accessed 26 May 2009).

Kramsch, Claire. *Content and Culture in Language Teaching.* Oxford: Oxford University Press, 1993.

Kranz, David L., and Nancy C. Mellerski (eds.). *In/Fidelity: Essays on Film Adaptation.* Newcastle, UK: Cambridge Scholars Publishing, 2008.

Kühn, Dieter. "Das Lullische Spiel" ["The Lullic Game"]. In *Ludwigslust [Stories]*, 33–57. Frankfurt-am-Main, Germany: Suhrkamp, 1977.

———. *Das Lullische Spiel,* dir. Heinz Hostnig. Radio drama. Hamburg: North German Broadcasting Company (NDR), first broadcast 13 December 1975.

Kuzmanovic, Dejan. "Vampiric Seduction and Vicissitudes of Masculine Identity in Bram Stoker's *Dracula.*" *Victorian Literature and Culture* 37, no. 2 (2009): 411–25.

Lacan, Jacques. "Seminar on 'The Purloined Letter,'" translated by Jeffrey Mehlman. *Yale French Studies* 48 (1973): 39–72 (originally published in Lacan's *Écrits*).

Lampinen, James M., Timothy N. Odegard, and Juliana K. Leding. "Diachronic Disunity." In *The Self and Memory,* edited by Denise R. Beike, James M. Lampinen, and Douglas A. Behrend, 227–53. New York: Psychology Press, 2004.

———. "Rhetorical Invention: The Diaspora." In *Perspectives on Rhetorical Invention,* edited by Janet M. Atwill and Janice M. Lauer, 1–15. Knoxville: University of Tennessee Press, 2002.

Leavy, Patricia. *Iconic Events: Media, Politics, and Power in Retelling History.* Lanham, Md.: Lexington Books, 2007.

Leitch, Thomas. "Adaptation Studies at a Crossroads." *Adaptation* 1, no. 1 (2008): 63–77.

———. *Film Adaptation and Its Discontents: From Gone with the Wind to The Passion of the Christ.* Baltimore: Johns Hopkins University Press, 2007.

———. "How to Teach Film Adaptations, and Why." Unpublished paper given at the 33rd American Studies Association of Turkey Conference, Istanbul, 8–10 October 2008.

———. "Twelve Fallacies in Contemporary Adaptation Theory." *Criticism* 45, no. 2 (2005): 149–71.

Lévi-Strauss, Claude. *Structural Anthropology,* translated by Claire Jacobson and Brooke Grundfest Schoepf. Harmondsworth, UK: Penguin, 1972.

Lister, David. "Forget Novels, Just Write the Movie." *The Independent* (London), 18 July 1997, 3.

Losier, Marie, and Richard Porton. "The Pleasures of Melancholy: An Interview with Guy Maddin." *Cineaste* (Summer 2004): 25.

Macedo, Donaldo. "Preface." In *Politics of Liberation: Paths from Friere,* edited by Peter MacLaren and Colin Lankshear, iv–xxii. London: Routledge, 1994.

McFarlane, Brian. *Novel to Film: An Introduction to the Theory of Adaptation.* Oxford, UK: Clarendon Press, 1996.

McGough, Roger. "The Leader." www.poemhunter.com/poem/the-leader/ (accessed 5 November 2009).

Maddin, Guy. "Conversations with Guy Maddin." Interviewed by William Beard. Edmonton, Canada: Metro Cinema Society, 2007.

———. "Count of the Dance: Guy Maddin on *Dracula: Pages from a Virgin's Diary.*" Interviewed by Mark Peranson. *Cinema Scope,* March 2002, 9.

Meyer, Stephanie. *Twilight.* London: Atom Books, 2007.

Micznik, Vera. "The Farewell Story of Mahler's Ninth Symphony." *Nineteenth-Century Music* 20, no. 2 (1996): 144–66.

———. "Mahler and 'The Power of Genre.'" *Journal of Musicology* 12, no. 2 (1994): 117–51.

Miller, Elizabeth. "Dracula." *Dracula's Homepage.* 2005. www.webliterature.net/literature/Stoker/WL1-dracula (accessed 6 May 2009)

Mills, Sara. *Michel Foucault.* London: Routledge, 2002.

Murray, Charles. *Real Education: Four Simple Truths for Bringing America's Schools Back to Reality.* New York: Crown Forum, 2008.

Murray, Simone. "Books as Media: The Adaptation Industry." *International Journal of the Book* 4, no. 2 (2007): 23–30.

Nelson, Katherine. "Narrative Self, Myth and Memory: Emergence of the Cultural Self." In *Autobiographical Memory and the Construction of a Narrative Self: Developmental and Cultural Perspectives,* edited by Robyn Fivush and Catherine A. Haden, 3–28. Mahwah, N.J.: Erlbaum, 2003.

Nicholson, Ranald. *The Edinburgh History of the Book in Scotland Vol. 2: The Later Middle Ages.* Edinburgh: Edinburgh University Press 2007.

Painter, Karen. "The Sensuality of Timbre: Responses to Mahler and Modernity at the 'Fin de siècle.'" *Nineteenth-Century Music* 18, no. 3 (1995): 236–56.

Partridge, Burgo. *A History of Orgies.* London: Anthony Blond, 1958.

Piaget, Jean. *Six Psychological Studies.* New York: Random House, 1968.

Picart, Caroline Joan ("Kay"), S. Picart, Frank Smoot, and Jayne Blodgett (eds.). *The Frankenstein Film Sourcebook.* Westport, Conn.: Greenwood, 2001.

Picon-Vallin, Béatrice. "Passages, Interférences, Hybridations: Le Film de Théâtre." *Theatre Research International* 26, no. 2 (July 2001): 190–97.

"Pride and Prejudice Tops List of Books We Cannot Live Without." *Daily Telegraph* (London), 1 March 2007, 14.

Proulx, Annie. "Getting Movied." In *Brokeback Mountain: Story to Screenplay*, edited by Annie Proulx, Larry McMurtry, and Diana Ossana, 129–38. New York: Scribners, 2005.

Proulx, Annie, Larry McMurtry, and Diana Ossana (eds.). *Brokeback Mountain: Story to Screenplay*. New York: Scribner's, 2005.

Pullinger, Kate. "The Future for Writers is Digital." Keynote talk for Playful Paradox: 2009 Postgraduate Creative Writing Conference, University of Bedfordshire, 23 May 2009. http://cwparadox.wikidot.com/keynote (accessed 27 May 2009).

———. "Inanimate Alice." www.inanimatealice.com/ (accessed 13 May 2009).

Pultar, Gönül, and Ayşe Lahur Kırtunç. "Cultural Studies in Turkey: Education and Practice." *Review of Education, Pedagogy and Cultural Studies* 26, nos. 2/3 (2004): 120–55.

Pulverness, Alan. "English as a Foreign Culture: English Language Teaching and British Cultural Studies." In *British Studies: Intercultural Perspectives*, edited by Alan Mountford and Nick Wadham-Smith, 85–89. Harlow, UK: Pearson Education, 2000.

Radstone, Susannah, and Katharine Hodgkin. "Regimes of Memory: An Introduction." In *Regimes of Memory*, edited by Susannah Radstone and Katharine Hodgkin, 1–23. London: Routledge, 2003.

Rattigan, Dermot. *Theatre of Sound: Radio and the Dramatic Imagination*. Dublin: Carysfort Press, 2002.

Raw, Laurence. *Adapting Henry James to the Screen: Gender, Fiction and Film*. Lanham, Md.: Scarecrow Press, 2006.

———. *Adapting Nathaniel Hawthorne to the Screen: Forging New Worlds*. Lanham, Md.: Scarecrow Press, 2008.

———. "Perspectives on British Studies in Turkish Universities." In *British Studies: Intercultural Perspectives*, edited by Alan Mountford and Nick Wadham-Smith, 21–35. Harlow, UK: Pearson Education, 2000.

———. "Reconstructing 'Englishness.'" Presented to the 6th University of Warwick/British Council Conference on British Cultural Studies, September 1999. www.britishcouncil.org/studies/england/raw.htm (accessed 4 January 2000).

———. "Translating Theatre Texts: *As You Like It*." *Shakespeare Worldwide* 14/15 (1995): 91–102.

Reese, Elaine, and Kate Farrant. "Social Origins of Reminiscing." In *Autobiographical Memory and the Construction of a Narrative Self: Developmental and Cultural Perspectives*, edited by Robyn Fivush and Catherine A. Haden, 29–48. Mahwah, N.J.: Erlbaum, 2003.

Report of the National Committee of Inquiry into Higher Education [in the United Kingdom]. 1997. www.leeds.ac.uk/educol/ncihe (accessed 8 June 2009).

Reynolds, Peter. *Novel Images: Literature in Performance*. London: Routledge, 1993.

Rickett, Joel. "On the Latest News from the Publishing Industry." *The Guardian*, 8 December 2007, 23.

Ridiculusmus. "The Importance of Being Earnest." www.ridiculusmus.com/performance/current-show (accessed 19 January 2009).

Robb, Graham. *Victor Hugo*. London: Picador, 1997.

Royal Winnipeg Ballet. "*Dracula* Study Guide." www.rwb.org/ (accessed 6 May 2009).

Ruttmann, Walter. *Weekend Remix*. Munich: Intermedium records, 2000; Intermedium rec. 003, Indigo CD 93172.

Sabancı University, Department of Cultural Studies. "Welcome." www.sabanci univ.edu/ssbf/cult/eng (accessed 28 October 2008).

Sabancı University, Faculty of Arts and Social Sciences. 2008 course list. http:// suis.sabanciuniv.edu/HbbmInst/SU_DEGREE.p_list_courses?P_TERM= 999999&P_AREA=FC_FASS&P_PROGRAM=&P_FAC=S&P_LANG=EN&P _LEVEL=UG (accessed 28 October 2008).

Sandbach, F. H. *The Comic Theatre of Greece and Rome*. London: Chatto and Windus, 1977.

Sanders, Julie. *Adaptation and Appropriation*. New York: Routledge, 2006.

Sartre, Jean-Paul. *Nausea*. Trans. Lloyd Alexander. New York: New Directions Publishing Corporation, 1964.

Schlueter, June. *Metafictional Characters in Modern Drama*. New York: Columbia University Press, 1979.

Sinyard, Neil. *Filming Literature: The Art of Screen Adaptation*. London: Croom Helm, 1986.

Smith, Sidonie, and Julia Watson. "Introduction: Situating Subjectivity in Women's Autobiographical Practices." In *Women, Autobiography, Theory: A Reader*, edited by Sidonie Smith and Julia Watson, 3–52. Madison: University of Wisconsin Press, 1998.

Stam, Robert. "Introduction: The Theory and Practice of Adaptation." In *Literature and Film: A Guide to the Theory and Practice of Film Adaptation*, edited by Robert Stam and Alessandra Raengo, 1–52. Malden, Mass.: Blackwell, 2005.

———. *Literature through Film: Realism, Magic and the Art of Adaptation*. Malden, Mass.: Blackwell, 2005.

Stam, Robert, and Alessandra Raengo (eds.). *Literature and Film: A Guide to the Theory and Practice of Film Adaptation*. Malden, Mass.: Blackwell, 2005.

Steger, Manfred. *Globalization: A Very Short Introduction*. Oxford: Oxford University Press, 2000.

Stoker, Bram. *Dracula*, edited by Brooke Allen. New York: Barnes and Noble Classics, 2003.

Stone, Philip. "Review of 2007: Sales and Price Step Up." *The Bookseller*, 10 January 2008, 3.

Suarez, Michael F., S. J., and H. R. Woudhuysen. *The Oxford Companion to the Book*. Oxford: Oxford University Press, 2010.

Sutherland, John. *Reading the Decades: Fifty Years of History through the Nation's Bestsellers*. London: BBC Books, 2002.

Toury, Gideon. *Descriptive Translation Studies and Beyond*. Amsterdam: John Benjamins Publishing, 1995.

Tudor, David. Review of Oxford Theatre Guild's *Lady Windermere's Fan* for *Rogues and Vagabonds*. 12 April 2006. www.oxfordtheatreguild.com/ (accessed 19 January 2009).

Vygotsky, L. S. *The Collected Works of L.S. Vygotsky Vol. 1: Problems of General Psychology*. New York: Plenum, 1987.

Weedon, Alexis. "In Real Life: Book Covers in the Internet Bookstore." In *Judging a Book by Its Cover: Fans, Publishers, Designers, and the Marketing of Fiction*, edited by Nicole Matthews and Nickianne Moody, 117–25. Farnham, UK: Ashgate Publishers, 2007.

———. "Textual Production and Dissemination in Book History: A Case Study of Cross-Media Practice between the Wars." In *English Today*, edited by Marianne Thormahlen, 266–82. Lund, Sweden: University of Lund, 2008.

Welsh, James M., and Peter Lev (eds.). *The Literature/Film Reader: Issues of Adaptation*. Lanham, Md.: Scarecrow Press, 2007.

Whitman, Cedric H. *Aristophanes and the Comic Hero*. Cambridge, Mass.: Harvard University Press, 1964.

The Widening Participation Act [in the United Kingdom]. 2006. www.dcsf.gov.uk/hegateway/uploads/6820-DfES-WideningParticipation2.pdf (accessed 8 June 2009).

Wilde, Oscar. *The Importance of Being Earnest*. In *The Plays of Oscar Wilde*. London: Wordsworth, 2002.

———. *Lady Windermere's Fan*. Harmondsworth: Penguin, 1995.

Würffel, Stefan Bodo. *Das deutsche Hörspiel*. Stuttgart, Germany: Metzler, 1978.

INDEX

acoustic space, 141, 142
active literacy, 81
Adams, Douglas, 127
adaptation, 57, 71, 147–50, 157; and
    creativity, 1–3, 5–15; as critical
    essay, 1–2; and fidelity, 31, 32, 37,
    38, 39, 52; industry model of, 127;
    intercultural, 58–61; interlingual, 20;
    intermedial, 20, 55–56, 58–61, 147,
    149; to the stage, 1–16; television,
    27; textual, 20; tie-ins, 124
adaptation pedagogy, 85–93; class
    assignments, 90–92; course
    description, 87; examples of source
    material, 91; student evaluation, 92
adaptation process, 85–93; copyrighted
    material, 87–88; role of fidelity,
    89–90; role of the screenwriter, 85;
    role of studio, 85–86, 90
afterlife, 41. See also Benjamin, Walter
Amazon, 125, 129
Ammer, Andreas, 136, 139
An American Tragedy, 99
Anderson, Clive, The Long Tail, 126
Andrew, Dudley, 46
anteriority, 52

archetype, 151, 153
assessment, 40, 60, 61, 62
Atonement, 121, 125
audiovisual image; cinematic, 155–56;
    theater, 155–56
Austen, Jane, 39, 121, 127
auteur, 34. See also authorship
authorship, 2, 34–35. See also auteur

Babel (2006), 121
Bailey, Herbert, 112
Barthes, Roland, 35, 38, 157
Baverstock, Alison, 112
BBC (British Broadcasting
    Corporation), 36–37, 133, 135
Beast Quest, 113
"Beautiful Soup," 77
Benjamin, Walter, 41. See also afterlife
Berendt, John, 121
best sellers, 114, 115, 116, 125, 126
Bertin, Louise, 19
the Bible, 139
The Big Read, 114, 127
"A Bird Came Down the Walk," 77
Blake, William, 31, 32, 33, 34, 36, 37,
    39, 40

blended learning, 32
blogs/blogging, 32, 37, 39
Bolton, Gillian, 45
Bonfire of the Vanities, 39
book history, 112,
book sales and revenue, 123
Bookscan, 114
Bookseller's Hot 100, 114, 115, 116
Box Office Mojo, 118, 124
Borgia, Lucrezia, 20, 21–22
The Borgias, 21
Bourdieu, Pierre, 111
Bournemouth University, 32, 42
Boy A, 37
Boyum, Joy Gould, 33
Bridget Jones' Diary (2001), 121
Brokeback Mountain (2005), 46, 47, 52
Brook, Peter, 149
Brown, Dan, 126
Brown, Grace, 100–101
Brownell, Joseph W., 99–102, 106
Bruner, Jerome, 103–4

Cameron, Jessica, 105, 107
Cardwell, Sarah, 31, 39, 41, 42
Carroll, Lewis, 77
Cartmell, Deborah, 38
Chaney, Lon, 18
Chavelier, Tracey, 125
Clark, Giles, 112
collaborative writing, 50
A Comedy of Danger, 135
comic books, 32
communications circuit, 123
convergence. *See* media convergence
Cook, John, 45
Corrigan, Timothy, 33, 41
creative writing, 45
Crisell, Andrew, 135
critical theory modules, 63–64
critical thinking abilities, 75
Crook, Tim, 135, 143
cultural dynamics, 75
cutting, 141, 142, 143

The Da Vinci Code (2006), 121, 126
Dante Alighieri, 139

Darnton, Robert, 122
"Das Lullische Spiel," 141
Davies, Gill, 112
DeBona, Guerric, 38
DePalma, Brian, 39
Dewey catalog system, 119
Dickinson, Emily, 77
Divine Comedy, 139
Donizetti, Gaetano, 21
Doyle, Conan Arthur, 124
Dracula: ballet, 150–51; novel, 151, 153, 156
Dracula: Pages from a Virgin's Diary, 150, 155–56
Dreiser, Theodore, 99–102
Driscoll, F. Paul, 99, 109
DVD, 120, 125

Eakin, Paul John, 105–6
Eco, Umberto, 153
Einheit, F. M., 136
Eisenstein, Sergei, 154–55
electroacoustical manipulation, 141
empty verbalism, 72
English language teaching, 73
English Studies and Performing Arts (ESPA), 56, 57
Enos, Patricia W., 99–102, 106
Epstein, Jason, 112
Erster Klasse, 138
Esmeralda (1905), 18
La Esmeralda, 19
Ever After (1998), 88–89

Farnham, Brian, 21
fading (audio), 141, 142
fan fiction (fanfic), 31, 41
Fastsellers, 114, 115, 119, 125, 127
Febvre, Lucien, 112
Film Adaptation and Its Discontents (Leitch), 71
Film International, 124, 125, 127
film: language of, 56, 59–61; sales, 118; studies, 149
Finnigan, Judy, 119
Fitzgerald, Edward, 113

"Five Creative Strategies of
Adaptation," 17, 18, 27, 28, 29
Fivush, Robin, 109
Flesch, Hans, 138
folklore, 87, 89
Foucault, Michel, 35, 154
Freund, Elizabeth, 33, 40

Genette, Gerrard, 111, 120
genre, 119
Gillette, Chester, 99, 101, 106
The Girl with a Pearl Earring, 125
Giroux, Henry, 73
Glaser, Paul Michael, 42
globalization, 148
Godden, Mark, 151–52, 154, 156
Goebbels, Heiner, 139
Gothic literary tradition, 150–51, 155
Graham, Gordon, 112
graphic novel, 88, 91

Hamilton, Alex, 114, 115, 119, 125, 127
Harlequin Publishing, 113
Harry Potter series, 121
hermeneutics, 46
heteroglossia, 39
Higby, Roy C., 106
Hilton, Paris, 147
His Dark Materials, 121
The Hitchhikers Guide to the Galaxy, 127
Hörspiel, 133–43
The Hours, 90
Hughes, Richard, 135, 138
Hugo, Victor, 18, 19, 20, 22, 26, 28, 29
The Hunchback of Notre Dame (1939,
1996) 18
Hutcheon, Linda, 1, 15, 31, 33, 37, 41,
95, 97–98, 107–8, 137

iconography: in CDs, 125; in DVDs,
125
The Importance of Being Earnest, 3, 15,
16
interdisciplinary, 58–61
Internet Movie Database (IMDB), 127
intertextuality, 39, 58–61, 149;
intertextual frames, 153;

intertextual competence, 156–57.
See also palimpsestic intertextuality
intermedial weave, 55, 56
Into the Wild (1996), 121
Irwin-Zarecka, Iwona, 107–8
Iser, Wolfgang, 37, 40

Jacob's Ladder (1990), 37
Jewitt, Carey, 33

King, Stephen, 42
Knight, Julia, 121, 127
knowledge fields, 56, 57, 58
Kühn, Dieter, 141

Lady Windermere's Fan, viii, 3–16
Lampinen, James M., 102, 105, 108
Lancelot und Sandarain, 138
language, 141
Laughton, Charles, 18
Lay, Samantha, 121, 127
"The Leader," 77
Le roi s'amuse, 19
Leding, Juliana, 102, 105, 108
Lee, Ang, 46
Leitch, Thomas, 81, 98, 108
Les Misérables, 18
Levi-Strauss, Claude, 40
library borrowing, 115, 117, 119, 123
literary, 33, 56, 57, 59–61, 71–72, 73, 74,
81, 148, 154
literary studies, 149
"Little Red Riding Hood," 89
Lolita (1962), 121
Lord of the Rings (2001), 121, 127
Lucrèce Borgia (1953), 21
Lucretia Borgia, 19–29
Lucrezia Borgia (1833 stage play), 21
Lust, Caution (2007), 46, 52

Maddin, Guy, 150, 152–56
Madeley, Richard, 119
Mahler, Gustav, 151–52, 154, 156
Malle, Louis, 149
Marat-Sade (1967), 149
Martin, Henri-Jean, 112
McEwan, Ian, 121, 125

McFarlane, Brian, 31
McGough, Roger, 77
media: convergence of, 147–48;
    dialogism in, 147; literacy, 148;
    remediation, 148
medium specificity, 53
Midnight in the Garden of Good and Evil,
    121
model of literary adaptation, 126
montage of attractions. *See* Eisenstein,
    Sergei
Moroni, David, 154
Müller, Heiner, 139
Murray, Simone, 126, 127
music, 141, 142
Myst, 37
myth. *See* Barthes, Roland

narratology, 140–43
Neisser, Ulric, 107
Nelson, Katherine, 109
Neues Hörspiel, 136, 141, 143
Never Seek To Tell Thy Love, 31, 32, 33,
    34, 41. *See also* Blake, William
new media, 32; and education, 64–66;
    and language, 56, 61–62
New York Times, 114
Nibelungen, 139
Northern Lights, 121
*Notre-Dame de Paris/The Hunchback of
    Notre Dame*, 18
novel, 1, 18, 32, 42, 46, 52, 63, 74, 76,
    85–88, 90, 98, 99–101, 111, 124, 126,
    127, 144, 149, 150–51, 153, 155

Odegard, Timothy, 102, 105, 108
Opening Night (CBS), 152
opera, 67–68
Orczy, Emmuska, 124
originality, 34, 38

palimpsestic intertextuality, 150, 155,
    157
palimpsestuous, 156
Papoulis, Christina, 105
parallel texts, 32
paratextuality, 111, 120

participatory culture, 147
pedagogy, 33, 34, 40, 41
pedagogies of intermedial adaptation:
    building blocks, 59–61; knowledge
    modules, 62–64; reflection and
    research, 64–69
The Persecution and Assassination
    of Jean-Paul Marat as Performed
    by the Inmates of the Asylum of
    Charenton Under the Direction of
    the Marquis de Sade. *See Marat-
    Sade.*
perception, 56, 67
Picon-Vallin, Béatrice, 149, 155
The Scarlet Pimpernel, 124
A Place in the Sun, 102, 109
poetry, viii, 32–40, 60, 64, 76, 77, 78,
    80–81, 82, 87, 91, 113
Pokémon, 121
polyphonic, 55
polysemic, 34
post-literacy, 148
postmodern performance, 8–14
Practical Magic (1998), 90
practice-based research, 45
Pride and Prejudice, 127
Proulx, Annie, 47, 52
public domain properties, 87–88
public lending right (PLR), 114, 115,
    117, 119, 129
Publishers' Weekly, 115
publishing studies, 112
Pullman, Phillip, 121

radio, 114
radio drama, 133–43
Radstone, Susannah, 104
Ratatouille (game), 121
reader response, 33, 37, 40
reception, 33
reflection, 33, 34, 40, 41
reflective practice, 45
remediation. *See* media
reorientation, 71
Revenge of the Sith (game), 121
rewriting, 53
Reynolds, Peter, 32

Rhode, Dianne, 156
Ridiculusmus, 3, 15
Rigoletto, 19
Rocky Legends (game), 121
Romanticism, 152
Ross, Michael, 105
Rowling, J. K., 32, 116–17
Royal Winnipeg Ballet, 151
The Running Man, 42
Ruy Blas, 19, 20

Sanders, Julie, 36, 39, 41
The Sarah Connor Chronicles, 37
Sartre, Jean Paul, 95
Schlueter, June, 28
Schumacher, Claude, 19, 20
Schwitzke, Heinz, 138
screen play, 126; adapted, 85–93;
    original, 85–88
seduction, 154
Se, Jie. See Lust, Caution
semiotics, 59–61, 134, 140–43
Sense and Sensibility, 121
Shakespeare, William, 26, 97
Sherlock Holmes, 124
short story, 46, 47, 52, 76, 80, 87, 124,
    129, 141, 149
silence, 141, 143
silent film, 154–56; aesthetics of, 150
Sin City, 90
Sinyard, Neil, 1–2, 15
Smith, Sidonie, 96, 103
sound, 141
source text, 123, 127
Soviet film avant-garde, 150, 155
spec scripts, 86–87
stage play, viii, 2–3, 5, 7, 9, 14–15, 18–24,
    26, 55, 60, 87, 92, 124, 138, 149
Stam, Robert, 33, 38, 138
Star Wars Battlefront II (game), 121
statistical methods, 111, 114
Stoker, Bram, 150–54
Studio Frankfurt, 138

Stuttgarter Sender, 138
Sunset Boulevard (1950), 23
Swanson, Gloria, 23

theater; film, 147, 149–50, 154–57;
    language of, 56, 57, 59–61
The Third Man (1949), 23
Thoma, Ludwig, 138
The Three Little Pigs, 89
transcoding, 155
transmedia storytelling, 150

Ulysses, 139
Underworld (2003), 37
UNESCO World Book and Copyright
    Day, 127
University of East London, 46

Vanya on 42nd Street (1994), 149
Verdi, Giuseppe, 19
Victorian England, 151, 155
videogames, 32, 38
voice, 141, 142
Von Helmolt, Vonnie, 152
Vox-Haus, 138
Vygotsky, 77, 82
Vygotsky's model of collaborative
    learning, 77

Wagner, Geoffrey, 39
Walter, Eugene, 138
Watson, Julie, 96, 103
Welles, Orson, 23
westernization, 73
WGY, 138
Wilde, Oscar, 3, 4, 5, 15, 16
Wilson, Anne E., 105
Winters, Shelley, 102
The Wolf, 138

Zauberei auf dem Sender, 138
Zizek, Slavoj, 39
Zizek!, 39

ABOUT THE EDITORS
AND CONTRIBUTORS

Frances Babbage is senior lecturer in Theatre Studies at the University of Sheffield, United Kingdom. She has published extensively on adaptation and performance, most recently on staging Edgar Allan Poe for *Adaptation in Contemporary Culture: Textual Infidelities* (2009); other articles examine dramatizations of *The Turn of the Screw* (*Comparative Drama* 39, no. 2 [2005]) and Babbage's own adaptation of Charlotte Lennox's novel *The Female Quixote* for solo performance (*Studies in Theatre and Performance* 21, no. 3 [2002]). Other practice and research interests include community arts and theater for development, and she is the author of *Augusto Boal* (2004).

Richard Berger is reader in Media and Education at the Centre for Excellence in Media Practice, Bournemouth University, United Kingdom. He coordinates pedagogic research in the Media School at Bournemouth. His other interests include the adaptation of literature, comic books, and video games to film and television. Berger is also an experienced broadcaster and journalist is editor of *The Media Research Journal*.

Deborah Cartmell is director of the Centre for Adaptations at De Montfort University, United Kingdom, and has published on Shakespeare in film and the history of adaptations. She is editor of *Shakespeare* and *Adaptation* and is general editor of the series Screen Adaptations. She is currently completing a monograph on *Pride and Prejudice* on screen.

Freda Chapple is program director of the Literature and Creative Media program at the University of Sheffield, Institute for Lifelong Learning, United Kingdom. She is coconvener with Chiel Kattenbelt (Utrecht University) of the Intermediality in Theatre and Performance working group for the International Federation for Theatre Research; coeditor with Kattenbelt of *Intermediality in Theatre and Performance* (2006); and guest editor for a special edition on *Intermediality* for the journal *Culture, Language and Representation* (2008). Other recent publications include "Adaptation as Education: A Lady Macbeth of the Mtsensk District," in *Adaptation in Film and Performance* (2007); and "The Intermedial Theatron: A Paradigm Shift in Education and Performance in the Public Sphere," in *Theater und Medien* (2008).

Dennis Cutchins is associate professor of English at Brigham Young University, Utah, where he teaches adaptation studies as well as American and Western literature. He won the 2000 Carl Bode award for an article on Leslie Silko's *Ceremony*, and in 2004, he received the Charles Redd Center's Mollie and Karl Butler Young Scholar Award in Western Studies.

Suzanne Diamond is associate professor of English at Youngstown State University, Ohio, where she teaches courses in film, literature, and writing; her research investigates the rhetorical dynamics of memory, identity, and narration.

Richard J. Hand is professor of theater and media drama at the University of Glamorgan, Cardiff, United Kingdom. Recent publications include *London's Grand Guignol and the Theatre of Horror*, with Michael Wilson (2007); *Monstrous Adaptations: Generic and Thematic Transmutations in Horror Film*, coedited with Jay McRoy (2007); and *Terror on the Air: Horror Radio in America 1931–52* (2006).

Elke Huwiler works as assistant professor at the German Department of the University of Amsterdam. She studied German and Spanish literature and language as well as literary studies at the Universities of Freiburg and Berlin and received her PhD from the University of Freiburg. The subject of her dissertation research was the narratology of radio drama. She then worked in the field of media adaptations and performance studies and is currently doing research on theater plays in the scope of a postdoctoral research grant.

Since completing a MA in theatre and performance studies at Sheffield University, **Robert Neumark Jones** has been teaching in a primary school and has signed with an actors' agent.

Diane Lake's screenwriting credits include *Frida*, nominated for six Academy Awards in 2003. She has written screenplays for Paramount, Miramax, Columbia, and Disney, as well as various independent production companies. She is also a screenwriting professor at Emerson College in Boston.

Mark O'Thomas is director of the Institute for Performing Arts Development (IPAD) at the University of East London, United Kingdom, where he teaches both theater and creative writing. He is a playwright, translator, and adapter. Previous credits include *Almost Nothing* and *At the Table* for the Royal Court Theatre, *Dona Flor and Her Two Husbands* for the Lyric Hammersmith, and *Speedball* (an adaptation based on the life of Chet Baker) for the London Jazz Festival.

Milan Pribisic holds a PhD in Theatre Studies, teaches in the School of Communication at Loyola University Chicago, and freelances as dramaturge in the Chicagoland theater scene. He has published articles in *Theatre Journal, Theatre Survey, Journal of Dramatic Theory and Criticism, Theatre Studies, The Gay and Lesbian Review Worldwide, Biography*, and *Filmske Sveske*, and has contributed to the *LGBTQ America Today* encyclopedia (2009) and to the anthologies *Novi Holivud* [*New Hollywood*] (2002) and *Playing with Memories: Essays on Guy Maddin* (2009). He is working on a monograph currently entitled "Rainer Werner Fassbinder: A Playwright with a Movie Camera."

Laurence Raw teaches in the Department of English at Başkent University, Ankara, Turkey. Prior to this, he spent many years at several state and private universities in Ankara, Izmir, and Istanbul. He also worked for the British Council as a cultural affairs officer in the Eastern European Region. Recent publications include *Adapting Henry James to the Screen: Gender, Fiction and Film* (2006), *Adapting Nathaniel Hawthorne to the Screen: Forging New Worlds* (2008), a collection of theater reviews (*Nights at the Turkish Theatre/Türk Sahnelerinden İzlenimler* [translated by Sevgi Şahin; 2009]), and *The Ridley Scott Encyclopedia* (2009).

Sevgi Şahin graduated from Başkent University, Ankara, Turkey, Department of English Language Teaching, in 2008. She is currently pursuing a master's in the same discipline at Middle East Technical University, Ankara, and is working as a research assistant at the Department of Foreign Language Teaching at Başkent University.

Alexis Weedon is professor of Publishing and Head of the Division of Journalism and Communications at the University of Bedfordshire,

United Kingdom. He is coeditor of *Convergence: The International Journal of Research into New Media Technologies* and is currently working on an Arts and Humanities Research Council–funded project entitled "Cross-Media Co-operation in Britain in the 1920s and 1930s."

James M. Welsh was educated in Bloomington, Indiana, and Lawrence, Kansas. Besides founding the Literature/Film Association and coediting *Literature/Film Quarterly* for thirty-two years, he has authored and edited over sixteen books dealing with drama, literature, and film. In 1973, he hosted a television series, *The Films of the Gatsby Era*, originally broadcast on East Coast Public Broadcasting Stations from Boston to Miami, and for seven years thereafter, he was arts editor for the CBS affiliate in Salisbury, Maryland, where he now resides as professor emeritus of Salisbury University. He served two terms as Fulbright Lector of American Studies at the Universitatea "A. I. Cuza" in Iași, Romania, in 1994 and 1998.

Since completing her master's in theatre and performance studies at Sheffield University, **Lauren Williams** has gained experience in professional theatre working as an assistant stage manager at the Royal Opera House. She currently lives and works in Sheffield.